Performance and Phenomenology

This book offers a timely discussion about the interventions and tensions between two contested and contentious fields, performance and phenomenology, with international case studies that map an emerging twenty-first-century terrain of critical and performance practice. Building on the foundational texts of both fields that established the performativity of perception and cognition, *Performance and Phenomenology* continues a tradition that considers experience to be the foundation of being and meaning. Acknowledging the history and critical polemics against phenomenological methodology and against performance as a field of study and category of artistic production, the volume provides both an introduction to core thinkers and an expansion on their ideas in a wide range of case studies. Whether addressing the use of dead animals in performance, actor training, the legal implications of thinking phenomenologically about how we walk, or the intertwining of digital and analog perception, each chapter explores a world comprised of embodied action and thought. The established and emerging scholars contributing to the volume develop insights central to the phenomenological tradition while expanding on the work of contemporary theorists and performers. In asking why performance and phenomenology belong in conversation together, the book suggests how they can transform each other in the process and what is at stake in this transformation.

Maaike Bleeker is a professor of theatre studies at Utrecht University, The Netherlands.

Jon Foley Sherman is an independent scholar and an award-winning actor and deviser.

Eirini Nedelkopoulou is a lecturer in theatre at York St John University, UK.

Routledge Advances in Theatre and Performance Studies

18 The Unwritten Grotowski
Theory and Practice of
the Encounter
Kris Salata

19 Dramas of the Past on the
Twentieth-Century Stage
In History's Wings
Alex Feldman

20 Performance, Identity and the
Neo-Political Subject
*Edited by Matthew Causey and
Fintan Walsh*

21 Theatre Translation in
Performance
*Edited by Silvia Bigliazzi,
Peter Kofler, and
Paola Ambrosi*

22 Translation and Adaptation in
Theatre and Film
Edited by Katja Krebs

23 Grotowski, Women, and
Contemporary Performance
Meetings with
Remarkable Women
Virginie Magnat

24 Art, Vision, and Nineteenth-
Century Realist Drama
Acts of Seeing
Amy Holzapfel

25 The Politics of Interweaving
Performance Cultures
Beyond Postcolonialism
*Edited by Erika Fischer-Lichte,
Torsten Jost and Saskya
Iris Jain*

26 Theatre and National Identity
Re-Imagining Conceptions
of Nation
Edited by Nadine Holdsworth

27 Nationalism and Youth in
Theatre and Performance
*Edited by Angela Sweigart-
Gallagher and Victoria
Pettersen Lantz*

28 Performing Asian
Transnationalisms
Theatre, Identity and the
Geographies of Performance
Amanda Rogers

29 The Politics and the
Reception of Rabindranath
Tagore's Drama
The Bard on the Stage
*Edited by Arnab Bhattacharya
and Mala Renganathan*

30 Representing China on the
Historical London Stage
From Orientalism to
Intercultural Performance
Dongshin Chang

31 Play, Performance, and Identity
How Institutions Structure
Ludic Spaces
*Edited by Matt Omasta and
Drew Chappell*

32 Performance and
Phenomenology
Traditions and Transformations
*Edited by Maaike Bleeker,
Jon Foley Sherman, and Eirini
Nedelkopoulou*

Performance and Phenomenology
Traditions and Transformations

Edited by
Maaike Bleeker, Jon Foley Sherman,
and Eirini Nedelkopoulou

NEW YORK AND LONDON

First published in paperback 2018

First published 2015
by Routledge
711 Third Avenue, New York, NY 10017

and by Routledge
2 Park Square, Milton Park, Abingdon, Oxon OX14 4RN

Routledge is an imprint of the Taylor & Francis Group, an informa business

© 2015, 2018 Taylor & Francis

The right of Maaike Bleeker, Jon Foley Sherman, and Eirini Nedelkopoulou to be identified as the authors of the editorial material, and of the authors for their individual chapters, has been asserted in accordance with sections 77 and 78 of the Copyright, Designs and Patents Act 1988.

All rights reserved. No part of this book may be reprinted or reproduced or utilised in any form or by any electronic, mechanical, or other means, now known or hereafter invented, including photocopying and recording, or in any information storage or retrieval system, without permission in writing from the publishers.

Trademark notice: Product or corporate names may be trademarks or registered trademarks, and are used only for identification and explanation without intent to infringe.

Library of Congress Cataloging-in-Publication Data

   Performance and phenomenology : traditions and transformations / edited by Maaike Bleeker, Jon Foley Sherman, and Eirini Nedelkopoulou.
     pages cm. — (Routledge advances in theatre and performance studies ; 40)
   Includes bibliographical references and index.
     ISBN 978-1-138-80551-4 (hardback) — ISBN 978-1-315-75236-5 (ebook)
     1. Performing arts—Philosophy. 2. Theater—Philosophy. I. Bleeker, Maaike, editor. II. Sherman, Jon Foley, 1972– editor. III. Nedelkopoulou, Eirini, 1980– editor.
   PN1584.P425 2015
   792.01—dc23   2014038425

ISBN: 978-1-138-80551-4 (hbk)
ISBN: 978-0-8153-7650-7 (pbk)
ISBN: 978-1-315-75236-5 (ebk)

Typeset in Sabon
by codeMantra

Contents

List of Figures — vii

Introduction — 1
MAAIKE BLEEKER, JON FOLEY SHERMAN, AND
EIRINI NEDELKOPOULOU

1 The Stage Struck Out of the World: Theatricality
  and Husserl's Phenomenology of Theatre, 1905–1918 — 20
  PANNILL CAMP

2 Movement as Lived Abstraction: The Logic of the Cut — 35
  MAAIKE BLEEKER

3 Process Phenomenologies — 54
  SUSAN KOZEL

4 The Actor's Work on Attention, Awareness, and
  Active Imagination: Between Phenomenology,
  Cognitive Science, and Practices of Acting — 75
  PHILLIP ZARRILLI

5 Playing the Subject Card, Strategies of the Subjective — 97
  PHILIPA ROTHFIELD

6 Fleshing Dead Animals: Sensory Body Phenomenology
  in Performance — 111
  PETA TAIT

7 Vibrant Materials: The Agency of Things in the Context
  of Scenography — 121
  JOSLIN MCKINNEY

8 Doing Time with the Neo-Futurists 140
JON FOLEY SHERMAN

9 The In-Common of Phenomenology: Performing KMA's
   Congregation 152
EIRINI NEDELKOPOULOU

10 Transracial Intimacy and "Race Performativity":
   Recognition and Destabilizing the Nation's
   Racial Contract 173
SHIRLEY TATE

11 Passing Period: Gender, Aggression, and the
   Phenomenology of Walking 186
GAYLE SALAMON

12 Doing Phenomenology: The Empathetic Implications of
   CREW's Head-Swap Technology in 'W' *(Double U)* 204
SIGRID MERX

13 Performance as Media Affect: The Phenomenology of
   Human Implication in Jordan Crandall's *Gatherings* 222
MARK B.N. HANSEN

List of Contributors 245
Index 249

List of Figures

3.1 Scan of notes taken during Small Acts (2010) on the front side of the map given to the audience members to navigate the performance. 59
3.2 Scan of notes taken during Small Acts (2010) on the back side of the map given to the audience members to navigate the performance. 60
3.3 Drawing reproduced with kind permission from Efva Lilja, 2012. 61
3.4 Drawing reproduced with kind permission from Efva Lilja, 2012. 62
3.5 Crop from Small Acts notes. 65
3.6 Reproduced with kind permission from Efva Lilja, 2012. 65
3.7 Drawing from participants of the heart(h) workshops for the whisper(s) wearable project (2004). 65
3.8 Drawing from participants of the heart(h) workshops for the whisper(s) wearable project (2004). 66
3.9 Drawing from participants of the heart(h) workshops for the whisper(s) wearable project (2004). 66
3.10 Drawing from participants of the heart(h) workshops for the whisper(s) wearable project (2004). 67
7.1 *Beneath the Forest Floor* 2013, photo: David Shearing. 127
7.2 *Beneath the Forest Floor* 2013, photo: David Shearing. 129
7.3 *Beneath the Forest Floor* 2013, photo: David Shearing. 130
7.4 *Beneath the Forest Floor* 2013, photo: David Shearing. 131
7.5 *Beneath the Forest Floor* 2013, photo: David Shearing. 131
7.6 *Beneath the Forest Floor* 2013, photo: David Shearing. 133
8.1 From Maurice Merleau-Ponty, *Phenomenology of Perception* (London: Routledge, 2012) 400. 140
9.1 *Congregation*, Rockbund Art Museum, Shanghai, 2010. Photo: Sun Zhongqin. 153
9.2 *Congregation*, Tapseac Square, Macau, 2012. Photo: Kit Monkman. 154

9.3 *Congregation*, Market Square, Pittsburgh, 2014.
Photo: Kit Monkman. 155
9.4 *Congregation*, Rockbund Art Museum, Shanghai, 2010.
Photo: Tom Wexler. 156
9.5 *Congregation*, 2010, Tate Britain. Photo: Kit Monkman. 161
9.6 *Congregation*, 2010, Tate Britain. Photo: Kit Monkman. 166
12.1 Participant in 'W' *(Double U)* equipped with
technology © Santi Fort, 2009. 205
12.2 Hands of participant in 'W' *(Double U)* touched by
CREW member © Eric Joris, 2009. 213

Introduction
*Maaike Bleeker, Jon Foley Sherman, and
Eirini Nedelkopoulou*

Performance and phenomenology propose that the world is fundamentally mysterious as well as the site of all that we can know. They are modes of thinking and embodied engagement with the world that invite ambiguity instead of identification, and that locate the stakes of grasping that world in our urgent and inconclusive contact with others. Both performance and phenomenology engage with experience, perception, and with making sense as processes that are embodied, situated, and relational. These aspects have become increasingly important with the transformations referred to as the end of the grand narratives (Lyotard), the performative turn and the experiential turn, as well as with the emergence of new, experimental forms of theater, dance, and other performances.

With this book we aim to foster interactions between these mercurial fields through case studies addressing both the phenomenological tradition and a wide variety of performance practices. We have chosen contributions that address concepts and performances from the traditional to the edges of the technologically possible and the morally acceptable, reaffirming the foundations of these fields while also pointing to directions in which they can develop. In chapters covering the act of witnessing corpses from another species, perspective-swapping technologies, acting pedagogy, dance performance, and the performances of gender and race amongst others, our volume demonstrates how performance can be a privileged object of phenomenological investigation as well as a means of developing phenomenological practice.

THE PERFORMATIVITY OF PHENOMENOLOGY

Phenomenology explains how experience and cognition result from interactions with the material and social environment, interactions that determine not only how we experience the world, but also what of it we experience. Phenomenology considers the perception of the world to be an act, or a series of acts, rather than a given state of being. Maurice Merleau-Ponty observes: "We must not, therefore, wonder whether we really perceive a world, we must instead say: the world is what we perceive" (*Phenomenology of Perception* xxx).

His central claim that our perception institutes the world breaks from the intellectualist tradition that held that the world is only what we make of it. Instead, he elaborates on Edmund Husserl in thinking that the world can only be known through the experience of it. Joona Taipale describes the perspectives opened up by this realization:

> everything that has the sense of something 'existing' is now grasped as receiving its experiential characterization (its 'sense') in and through our conscious experiencing. In this sense *appearing* is discovered as constitutively more fundamental than objective existence, which is posited in the process of appearing. In this sense, consciousness has a *constitutive* primacy over the world (7).

In other words, phenomenology posits that the world requires a consciousness to experience it.

Central to the phenomenological approach is the unraveling of the relationship between the world and the experiencing subjectivity. This is the aim of what Husserl calls the phenomenological reduction, or *epoché*, which has served as the starting point—albeit subsequently abandoned by many phenomenologists—for phenomenological reflection. The *epoché* involves bracketing phenomena, removing them from our everyday experiences of and assumptions about them. By taking a critical distance towards one's assumptions concerning the validity and manner of being in the world, the idea goes, one can attempt to become aware of and describe how the world comes to exist for us and how it comes to be taken for granted.

Commenting on Husserl, Jacques Derrida noted that "phenomenological reduction is a scene, a theatre stage" (86). The operative assumption is that, if the Husserlian phenomenological approach invites us to take a distance from direct involvement with the world, this same distance will replicate the purported distance between what happens on stage and audience members. Accordingly, theater presents a staged version of the *epoché* because they both involve perception apart from the quotidian. As Mark Franko observes, "The very operations of reduction and bracketing could be those of the proscenium stage itself" (1). Such bracketing does not depend on the actual presence of a proscenium stage so much as it depends on a willingness to accept the possibility of a firm separation between onstage and offstage action.

Although Husserl eventually came to believe it possible for consciousness to extract itself from the world and exist as a transcendental cogito, his students and others writing after him emphasized the dependence of consciousness on embodied experience. Martin Heidegger, for example, understood phenomenology to provide a basic analysis of human existence as "being-in-the-world." For Heidegger such being-in-the-world is action-oriented and has to be understood in relation to our environment and the uses to which we put it and which it proposes to us. The availability of the world for interaction can be perceived when things appear *ready-to-hand*.

The importance of our environment and the things in it for human experience led Heidegger to reflect on the ways in which technology transforms how the world appears to us. The essence of technology, he famously claims, is not *technological* but is instead given in how technology reveals. For example, when a house or ship is being built, "this revealing gathers together in advance the aspect and the matter of ship, or house with a view to the finished thing envisaged as completed" (Heidegger 319). With this notion of revealing, Heidegger draws attention to the intimate connection between what technology does and knowledge.

More recently, Don Ihde, Mark Hansen, and others have argued for a shift in approach with regard to our understanding of the relationship between human cognition and technology. Hansen in particular urges moving from a focus on representation toward the practical, lived effects of technology as a physical reality in the world. Technologies alter the very basis of our sensory experience and therefore affect what it means to live as an embodied human agent. Contemporary media developments foreground that the relation between humans and technology cannot be understood in terms of something added on to some "natural" core of embodied life. Instead, Hansen observes, "the irreducible bodily or analog base of experience [...] has always been conditioned by a technical dimension and has always occurred as a co-functioning of embodiment with technics" (8–9). Here, phenomenology meets with theories of extended cognition, drawing attention to the relationship between cognition and environmental elements. Tools and technologies facilitate cognitive processes as a result of how they afford interaction with them. They are not merely extensions of our body; they become part of how we do things, how we perceive, even how we perceive ourselves.

Writing in 1945, Merleau-Ponty describes already how for a blind man using a stick to find his way this stick ceases to be an object for him: "its point has become an area of sensitivity, extending the scope and active radius of touch" (143). Merleau-Ponty further developed the idea of action-orientedness in terms of an embodied relation in which our capacity for bodily movement necessarily plays an essential role. By insisting that our experience of the world derives from our involvement with it, Merleau-Ponty took away the possibility of the *epoché* and an overhead view: there is no commanding prospect from which to report on the world. He insisted that a proper phenomenology "must plunge into the world instead of surveying it, it must descend toward it such as it is instead of working its way back up toward a prior possibility of thinking it—which would impose upon the world in advance the conditions for our control over it" (Merleau-Ponty, *The Visible and the Invisible* 38–39). This plunge into the world embraces the possibility that experience cannot be solved—it is inexhaustible, incomplete, and mysterious. And yet we can still encounter it—cannot help but be involved with it—and find meaning in it.

PHENOMENOLOGIES OF PERFORMANCE

Phenomenology has provided contemporary performers with a language for thinking about how bodies operate and create meaning between each other. Concerned primarily with the structures of experience and perception, phenomenology speaks to fundamental concerns of performance-making, starting with questions about how audience members encounter performances. It has furnished us with ways of thinking about what it means to touch another body and what it means to push into a body and what kinds of bodies we have. Susan Kozel and Phillip Zarrilli—both of whom have chapters in this volume—are two of the most prominent performers to record how their work has been informed by phenomenology. Formal performance—here understood as the enactment of collaborative practices meant for other people to witness—has benefited from phenomenology by moving according to, with, and against the reflections on embodied being undertaken by phenomenologists.

Similarly, *writing* about formal performance has benefited from new vocabularies and conceptions of embodiment originating from phenomenology, and phenomenological approaches to questions of our material experiences and our relations with others have featured prominently in writing about performance since the 1980s. Phenomenology provided an alternative and a complement to (structuralist) semiotic approaches while shifting from a generalized affirmation of "the body's" experiences during performance towards thinking about *bodies'* construction of being and meaning. As a result of this development, phenomenology and semiotics no longer appear as opposite approaches dealing with meaning and experience as similarly distinct entities (States, Fischer-Lichte) but rather as inextricably intertwined. Meaning reveals itself in experience rather than in or as an isolated object (Kattenbelt).

Grappling with this realization sparked a determined focus on the materiality of theatrical experience and many naïve first-person accounts of attending or making performance followed. And yet, simply foregrounding the author's experience is not itself phenomenology, notwithstanding how popular this move has become. Phenomenology in performance studies has evolved into several varieties of sophisticated analysis of embodied relationships structuring performance making and reception. Stanton Garner surveys some of the paths these analyses have taken in his article "Theatre and Phenomenology," in which he ranges from Max Scheler's discussion of tragedy in relation to structure of consciousness in 1915 to Mikel Dufrenne's *The Phenomenology of Aesthetic Experience* in 1953 and from Bruce Wilshire's exploration of theater's "fictive variations" to Bert O. States's dialogues between theater semiotics and phenomenology in the 80s. From the 1990s on, theater studies' integration of phenomenological methodologies and interests began to focus more on praxis, action, and spatiality (Rayner, Garner) and on the embodied perception of movement onstage and on screen (Fraleigh, Sheets-Johnstone, Sobchak).

Following Garner's detailed coverage of the phenomenological development in theater and performance in the premillennial era, it is worth reflecting on the postmillennial activity of phenomenological enquiry. The use of technology within performance practice has led a number of scholars to revisit the notion of subjectivity through phenomenology either to negotiate how the "corporeal turn" relates to the digital in performance (Broadhurst), to rethink subjectivity when the human and non-human create "an open site for the development" of cyborgean formations (Parker-Starkbuck), or to expand on the virtual experience of the user/player/participant (Popat), and to reflect on the function and use of locative media and mobile interfaces in relation to space, body, and community (Farman). These analyses not only examine the constitutive role of technology in experience, they also foreground the historical and cultural specificity of how our perceptual relationships are staged. Critically, they also shift away from the tendency to account for materiality and experience in terms of immediacy, shifting instead towards the ways in which materialization and perception emerge as situated and relational phenomena.

This attention to cultural specificity reflects the relatively recent consensus that the term performance accounts for far more than the artistic enactment of practices for others to witness. Following a "performative turn" partially spurred by Erving Goffman's works *The Presentation of Self in Everyday Life* and *Frame Analysis: An Essay on the Organization of Behavior*, researchers in the humanities and social sciences increasingly used a theatrical concept of performance to understand social rituals and everyday interactions. Of course, the term performance predates Goffman, and his work continues a much older tradition that entertained the idea of the *theatrum mundi* in which everyday life can be understood as the playing out of parts. However, performance's emergence as a key concept in the second half of the twentieth century is part and parcel of more general transformations that Jon McKenzie describes as the rise of the performance stratum. This refers to the simultaneous emergence of performance as a key term in at least three different fields, namely of organizational management (striving to maximize workers' performance), technology (measuring the performance of machines and apparatuses) and performance studies (taking a wide range of cultural performances as its object of study).

The use of performance as a key term in these divergent fields not only indicates an increased interest in performance as object of study but also represents fundamental changes with regard to knowledge: what it is, how we obtain it, and what legitimizes it. Researchers from a variety of disciplinary fields, including anthropology, communication studies, and cultural theory took up performance as a perspective applied to a wide variety of cultural practices, from an individual's gait to political demonstrations. Theater provided a model to understand social rituals and everyday interactions in terms of role playing, scripting, and rehearsing of social interactions, as it is famously demonstrated in the work of Goffman, among others, while vice versa anthropological concepts of liminality and rite of passage as discussed by Arnold van Gennep and Victor Turner became a model to theorize what Richard Schechner and Peggy Phelan identified as the transformative power of theater and performance.

These developments entered a new phase in the 1980s as performance shifted from being a model for studying human behavior towards a model for knowledge itself. The insight from John Austin's speech act theory, that saying something is actually doing something with words, allowed for an expansion of what can be studied as performance while also drawing attention to the power of performance (in language or otherwise) to bring into being, or challenge, that what it names or shows. Among others, Judith Butler has demonstrated the importance of this understanding not only for studying how performance embodies symbolic systems but also, more radically, how these systems construct and constitute bodies and their behavior, and how they come to matter through practices of doing and knowing. More recently, Karen Barad has argued that performativity is situated at the very heart not only of the humanities but also of research and what counts as knowledge in the sciences. The crumbling credibility of what Lyotard identified as the grand narratives that purportedly legitimized how and what we know brought back into focus the contingency of perception and meaning, making that phenomenology rigorously questioned since its inauguration by Husserl in the early twentieth century.

THE NORMATIVE TENSIONS OF PERFORMANCE AND PERCEPTION

Alva Noë writes that, "the task of phenomenology, or of *experiential art*, ought to be not so much to depict or describe experience, but rather to catch experience in the act of making the world available" (176). This phenomenology—this art—does not limit itself to bringing to conscious experience what goes unnoticed in the so-called natural attitude; it also includes what happens beyond or beneath the registers of human sense experience. It not only provides a perspective on the body and experience in how the world becomes available to us, but also acknowledges the body as the very possibility of having a perspective and therefore also as a constraint to perceptual consciousness. Furthermore, phenomenology and performance posit an approach that can account for consciousness and experience from the relationship between action, perception, and environment.

The constitutive primacy over the world carried by embodied consciousness does not mean that the world is only a projection of consciousness, or that the phenomenological reduction would be a solipsistic or subjectivist move. Nor does it mean that phenomenology would bring us to an understanding of how the world comes to exist for us as the result of features of our embodiment only. The constitution of the objective world

> has two irreducible constitutive sources: world constitution is bound to the embodied abilities of the individual members of the intersubjective community, on the one hand, and to a generative inherited normality on the other. The relationship between them is one of "normative tension."
>
> (Taipale 15)

Part of phenomenology and performance's political potential lies precisely in exposing this tension. In *Social Works: Performing Art, Supporting Publics*, Shannon Jackson notes "phenomenology's 'synchrony' of space and self" (7) and describes how challenges to this rapport come for the foreground of our attention when we feel "privately inconvenienced rather than publicly grateful" for our self/milieu relation. The political essence of phenomenology can thus be situated in the "synchrony" —and disruption— of a social *infrastructure* of the individual and its environment. Before Jackson, scholars such as Elizabeth Grosz, Rosalyn Diprose, Sara Ahmed, and Silvia Stoller clearly outlined the potential of Husserl's and primarily Merleau-Ponty's work to describe the institution and support of difference across gender, race, sexuality, and ability. Even earlier, Simone de Beauvoir's and Frantz Fanon's work had established crucial concepts for understanding how something as seemingly "natural" as "bodily ability" was formed both by a social field and was accountable as much to the (always trained and habituated) body as to its circumstances.

While it is certainly true that, as Vivian Sobchack writes, "the normative practices of our culture [can] estrange us *phenomenologically* from our own bodies and the bodies of others" (204), this does not mean that these practices are themselves the phenomenological basis of non-normative behavior. Reflecting on her seminal 1980 essay, "Throwing Like a Girl: A Phenomenology of Feminine Body Comportment, Motility, and Spatiality," Iris Marion Young corrected her original claim that women experienced "inhibited intentionality" compared to men; such a claim assumes that male intentionality is both uninhibited and the basis of all other movement and this of course is not the case. Both post-Husslerian phenomenology and performance studies suggest that the extent to which our own bodily abilities are experienced as non-normative is precisely the extent to which we are estranged from the shared ground of being established uniquely by each body in its own movement. During these moments we are both embedded in embodied existence and disoriented enough by it to understand it differently. After all, unfamiliarity and a sense of estrangement defines our relationship with our body when we practice something for the first time, and it daily colors the experience of people whose normal lies outside the habits of the majority of others.

Performers come across momentary bodily "estrangement" when their bodies are stretched beyond their familiar and routinely practiced limits. The same can be observed of audience members attending performances that push past previous artistic or even societal norms, particularly when the performers are themselves disabled (Petra Kuppers) or during body-based performance art events (Amelia Jones). The interaction of audience members with each other and the performers reiterates an essential claim of post-Husserlian phenomenology: our foundational experience of the world is always and already socialized because it takes place in a world shared with and formed by others. Phenomenology considers our experience and any understanding of it to be located in actions that acquire meaning through repetition, and can thus be said to imagine a world that is fundamentally performative. The world must be *done* in order to be experienced. The repetition of socially conditioned and located perceptions produce a world that can in turn be further transformed by acts of performance that address and disrupt the action of perception.[1]

Krikor Belekian has offered the provocation, "the proper response to phenomenology is theatre" (Personal Interview). Of course phenomenology can offer a response to performance, but by making the claim in the opposite direction, Belekian draws attention to performance as phenomenological analysis in action: a demonstration of the means by which we perceive, experience, and think about the world. Embodied reflection of the kind proposed by performance involves accepting that there is no perceiving the world without altering it *and* being altered by it. Performance stages this reflective emphasis because of its inherent contingency, its manner of appearing dependent on the shifting and malleable experiences of both performers and audience members. Performance, regardless of how broadly or narrowly we understand it, only takes place through the attendance of others; it can only begin to exist through the involvement of others *to whom it can respond*. There are many means by which performance persists, but as a phenomenon it arises utterly embedded in a perceptual world dependent on others.

Since its formalization by Husserl in the early twentieth century, phenomenology has been driven by the claim that what this means above all is that we exist *among others who also experience the world*. Phenomenology insists that the embodied nature of being means more than having a body in a world; it means we exist through the experience of intersubjectivity. Performance stages this each time an act requires or acquires a witness in order to come into being *and to come into meaning*.

STAGING PHENOMENOLOGY

The first contribution to our volume examines not only how performances configure the act of perception, but also how Husserl relied on theater in developing his ideas about the epoché. Pannill Camp, in "The Stage Struck

Out of the World: Theatricality and Husserl's Phenomenology of Theatre, 1905–1918," elaborates on how the theater confronts the spectator with a situation of perceptual analogy between objects, persons, texts, and so forth presented on and off stage and therefore requires from the audience a mode of perceiving that is similar to that of the phenomenological bracketing to the extent that "the thing under view is temporarily unbound from what ties it to the world as an actually existing thing" (page 32 of this volume). In the theater—and in particular in the kind of dramatic theater Husserl is referring to—this results in the situation that spectators are able to perceive an actor not only as the human being standing right in front of us but also as the character he plays, and both at the same time. Theater consciousness, Camp observes, thus functions as the mirror image of phenomenological reduction. In both, a kind of bracketing suspends the natural attitude through deliberate abstention from positing empirically the observed world as real. Whereas in phenomenological analysis this serves the world and things being interpreted as an "establishment" of consciousness and how the world becomes conscious as existing, in the kind of theater described by Husserl suspending the natural attitude serves what Husserl describes as the production of an image. With this he refers to how the theater mediates in a perception of what is on stage as being part of an imaginary world.

Maaike Bleeker in "Movement as Lived Abstraction: The Logic of the Cut" examines how movement as an object of perception may alert us to perception as something that is (at least partly) implicated in what we encounter. In particular, she considers Yvonne Rainer's choreographies in which Rainer confronts her audiences with the difficulty of seeing movement. Bleeker argues that Rainer's experiments with strategies of "sculpting spectatorship" (Lambert-Beatty) directed attention to how movement as an object of perception and thought is abstracted out of the continuity of concrete, lived experience as a phenomenon of "lived abstraction" (Massumi). Rainer's strategies of sculpting spectatorship confront the audience with the difficulty of actually perceiving movement and direct attention to the perception of movement as a phenomenological problem. Moving is an immediate bodily sensation. In order to become objects of perception, movements have to be abstracted out of the continuity of sensory impressions. Rainer interferes with these processes of abstraction and draws attention to perception as something that is not only a matter of our bodily capacities intentionally directed towards the world, but also of how the world *affords* interaction. Understanding how our perception of movement comes into being therefore involves taking into account how modes of perceiving and what appears as an object of perception are implicated within what we encounter, an awareness that became more and more important with the rise of media culture and how media affords new kinds of abstractions. Rainer's choreographies that addressed these processes of abstracting mark a turning point in what Bleeker (after Rosalind Krauss) proposes understanding as a "reformulation of the choreographic enterprise." This manifests itself in an expansion of the kind of movements that can be the objects of choreography and includes movements not performed but abstracted from what is presented on stage.

Movement poses a paradox central to the entire enterprise of phenomenology: how can we perceive ourselves perceiving without losing contact with what we are perceiving? To pay attention to listening distracts us from what we are listening to, and to pay attention to ourselves moving is to lose track of what we are moving towards. For Renaud Barbaras, the approach to this problem involves locating movement itself at the heart of perception. Because we are never entirely coincident with what we perceive we have to approach it. To perceive is to approach a thing and in so doing, "wrest it [the manifestation of an object] from the background of the world in which it is inscribed" (Barbaras 97). Without movement there can be no contact with anything other than ourselves. Susan Kozel's contribution to this volume, "Process Phenomenologies," takes up the problems and processes of making movement and of making meaning out of movement. Kozel points out that understanding doing phenomenology as a performance does not mean that the aim of performing phenomenology would be to display ourselves in the performance. She thus distinguishes herself from a tradition of phenomenological writing (about performance and other things) that does precisely that. The aim of phenomenology is not to disclose what the phenomenologist is experiencing but to understand the experience as a phenomenon "that is not born whole" but "messy and uncooked at first." In tracing the contours of experience as it comes into being phenomenology may help to counter and overcome "philosophical anaesthesia." At this point, she argues, phenomenology not only meets with the practice of performance but also with process philosophy. A second innovation that she proposes is the connection to theories of affect as part of what Merleau-Ponty has described as the great domain of the invisible supporting the visible.

Phillip Zarrilli's chapter also offers the perspective of the performer/scholar interrogating practices that often escape attention or critique. In "The Actor's Work on Attention, Awareness, and Active Imagination," Zarrilli combines acting theory with cognitive science—a field recently benefiting directly from phenomenological insights—and transcendental meditation practices. His interest in a phenomenological approach to acting stems from his career-long interest as an actor, actor-trainer, director, and scholar in understanding acting as a psychophysical phenomenon and process that he aims to examine from the actor's position "inside" the experience of performing. He is particularly concerned with the ways in which imagination intertwines with attention to create a world sensible to the performer and in turn to audience members. Through a mix of breathing exercises, stream-of-consciousness descriptions of performance, and engagement with multidisciplinary approaches to awareness and attention, Zarrilli outlines both the ideas and the feeling of creative attention.

Actor training provides a vantage point from which to consider another favored problem of phenomenology: bodily habits. Merleau-Ponty and

Heidegger both undertook sustained analyses of how our normalized ways of moving in and with the world shaped our understanding of it and ourselves. In "Playing the Subject Card, Strategies of the Subjective" Philipa Rothfield looks at a particular modality of body-based actor training that encourages movement—figurative and actual—beyond habit. She presents Alexander technique as a practice that not only may change our modes of moving, but also invites a rethinking of philosophical understanding of the relationship between bodies and subjectivity. This relationship might extend beyond the integration of the body with subjectivity proposed by Merleau-Ponty and towards a Deleuzian pursuit of difference in the body, beyond the forces established by and associated with training, technique and habit. "We imagine ourselves as the authors of our actions. This is the façade of human agency, the tendency to posit oneself at the center of thought and action. It is the drive to subjectivity, manifest writ large and represented in the phenomenological project," observes Rothfield. Alexander technique is a bodily practice that aims to overcome bodily habits and to generate movement beyond the habitual every day and thus holds the promise of the possibility of actively making space for something new to occur in the body. She elaborates such understanding through a confrontation of Merleau-Ponty's notion of the *lived body* (bringing subjectivity and the body together and focusing on what a body does within the subject's existential milieu) with Friedrich Nietzsche's attempts to extract the body from subjectivity. Whereas for Merleau-Ponty the philosophical (and existential) value of subjectivity is given, the thrust of Nietzschean philosophy is to move beyond subjectivity towards new corporeal terrain.

The boundaries of corporeal experience are tested in Peta Tait's chapter, in which she explores how experiences of bodily revulsion in performance may inspire a moral phenomenology that is not only transhuman but also forges our responsibilities to animals in all states of life and death. Extreme sensory repulsion may upset how the world is bodily perceived and potentially cut through patterns of social avoidance, like for example the human habit of obscuring the exploitation of animals. In "Fleshing Dead Animals: Sensory Body Phenomenology in Performance," Tait discusses two examples that evoke such extreme sensory repulsion through the inclusion of dead animals in live performance. Our accounts of embodied perception in live performance usually presume an involvement with the living. Accounting for the impact of an encounter with death-ness therefore requires a reconsideration of how we make things live. Here movement appears to be a key term. Merleau-Ponty's "philosophy of the sensible" requires a human body attuned to *moving* phenomena in the world (*The Visible and the Invisible* 252). In Tait's examples however, movement connects us to the dead, in particular to dead animals, and reconfigures our responsibilities to others beyond the living human.

Joslin McKinney similarly pushes the boundaries of human responsibility in her consideration of the possibility that objects have agency. In

"Vibrant Materials: The Agency of Things in the Context of Scenography," McKinney explores the roles of objects and materials in performance and looks at new aesthetic encounters where agency moves from humans to materials. Starting from Merleau-Ponty's attempts to approach the relationship between subject and object as non-hierarchical she sets out to expand the "chiasmic" encounters between materials and seers/participants. The pursuit of the concerns around "new materiality" in the discussion of objects in scenography leads her to stir her discussion from the Merleau-Pontian encounter between the seer and the seen, to Tim Ingold's and Jane Bennett's exploration of the vitality and power of materials, regardless of the human agent. Through the analysis of the scenographic environment of *Beneath the Forest Floor*, which McKinney herself designed, this chapter poses questions regarding the role, potentiality, and agency of the objects and materials in the context of a participatory performance. In these different actions, interactions, and encounters between the bodies, materials, and objects, the power and vitality of the materials lay in the assemblage of them all.

Participatory performance, increasingly common in small- and large-scale productions and the subject of recent, sustained scholarly analysis, offers potent moments for considering how our inter*actions* with others create the worlds we perceive. The next chapters in this volume continue an exploration of performances that must be "done" by their attendants. In "Doing Time with the Neo-Futurists," Jon Foley Sherman approaches participatory performance by placing it in the context of Merleau-Ponty's reflections on time. Merleau-Ponty began from the classic phenomenological perspective that time must be experienced by a consciousness in order to appear as time at all. From there, Merleau-Ponty sought to understand how time could appear to advance while we never leave the present. This brings him to a concept of time that continually advances while always remaining, so to speak, in the present. Foley Sherman proposes that Merleau-Ponty does not go far enough, and that time cannot be understood simply as the encounter of one consciousness with its experience of change and movement.

Foley Sherman takes as his subject the Chicago and New York Neo-Futurists, a company popularly known for their signature late night piece, "Too Much Light Makes the Baby Go Blind," in which they perform thirty plays in sixty minutes. Each week a random number of plays—determined by audience members rolling a dice—are ejected from the show and replaced with newly written and rehearsed pieces. Foley Sherman's chapter considers the constraints of this format—in which the roughly two-minute time limit for each play produces particular temporal tensions—and examines a three-minute pause in darkness near the end of one of their "primetime" shows, *The Complete & Condensed Stage Directions of Eugene O'Neill, Volume 1: Early/Lost Plays*. The performance of a pause by an entire audience provides the grounds from which to consider that time arrives through its performance with and for others. We "do" time, but we never do it alone—there must always be someone present or imagined who can respond to our performance and provide us with the witness that creates time.

Eirini Nedelkopoulou's chapter complicates the proposition that audiences can act together through a consideration of the status of publics in KMA's participatory open-air performance *Congregation*. She takes up Claire Bishop's critique of "relational aesthetics" and Jean-Luc Nancy's reconsideration of community in order to analyze isolated—and isolating—moments of public performance.[2] The chapter reflects on the current debates and tensions regarding participation and "socially turned" art (Bishop) and discusses solitude as a mode of participation, which is constitutive of the in-common condition of being-with identified by Nancy. Through Nancy's negotiation of being-in-common, the chapter expands on new and current areas of "living through" and *with* in social encounters. The discussion of participation in *Congregation* is anchored in the exploration of community, which can only be possible as a "*désoeuvre*," as an "inoperative" collection of singularities. *Congregation* stages a place where participants are in-common, "only to discover that this 'in-common' cannot always be controlled by them and so eludes them" (Nancy and ten Kate 37). The chapter proposes that, without ignoring the ever-present risk of exclusion and loneliness, collective and participatory performance requires solitude as a mode of engagement in interactive performance.

The phenomenological idea of situated embodiment both as a site of oppression and transformation is addressed in Shirley Tate's "Transracial Intimacy and 'Race Performativity': Recognition and Destabilizing the Nation's Racial Contract." Tate considers the potential of performance to cut through usual patterns of doing and perceiving while acknowledging the political limits of these interventions. Focusing on the case of a Black British Caribbean man from the Windrush Generation and his White British wife, she elaborates on a phenomenology of the micropractices of their daily life. Tate draws attention to how, on the one hand their performance of quotidian personal intimacy transgresses the essentialist race binary by engaging in a relationship that was unthinkable and actively resisted in the colonial past, while on the other hand their transgressive intimacy meets with the performative force of the race binary, and thus illustrates Taipale's "normative tension." The couple's intimacy, Tate argues, establishes a "*third space*" (Bhabha) or Edward Soja's "*critical thirding*," which moves past binaries while also being overlapped by them. This moving-past-but-contained dynamic is what instantiates the productive tension between an intimate performance of race and the normative performativity of the race binary.

The tensions between the normative and non-normative provide the context for Gayle Salamon's chapter, considering the limits—and possible abuses—of phenomenological analysis in the context of a hate crime. In "Passing Period: Gender, Aggression, and the Phenomenology of Walking," Salamon shows how "walking like a girl" became a central issue in the court case of Lawrence King, a gender-transgressive 15 year old who was shot to death in his Oxnard, California school by a classmate. In the subsequent trial, the defense argued that it was actually Larry's inappropriately gendered movement—his walking "like a girl"—that had incited the murder, thus turning him from a victim into the perpetrator. Salamon uses a phenomenological analysis to understand how this happens in a careful construction of Larry's self-presentation—in particular his way of walking—as a potential projectile: as something that Larry could be "throwing at people." The extent to which his behavior differs from the presumably normal behavior and ways of walking of his classmates is thus constructed as something he does to them, whereas they are the ones verbally harassing and physically intimidating him. Nevertheless, according to the defense, it is Larry's behavior that counts as sexual harassment on the ground that it is "behavior that makes other people feel uncomfortable." The question at stake in the Lawrence King court case touches the core of phenomenology: grappling with the relationship between the world and the experiencing subject.

This relationship finds expression in the experience of empathy, a concept that has preoccupied both phenomenology and performance. How people experience others as people "like" themselves stands at the center of phenomenological accounts of perception as well as centuries of assumptions and theories concerning the connection between audience members and performers. In particular, empathy, the sense of feeling what someone else feels, poses epistemological, ontological, and ethical problems for performers and phenomenologists. Sigrid Merx, in her contribution to this volume, discusses an example of a performance that literally invites us to perceive like someone else, 'W' *(Double U)* by the Flemish company CREW. Merx refers to Don Ihde's call for a "post-phenomenology" that serves as research praxis in which performance serves as an experiment to investigate how technologies extend the bodily and perceptual capacities of human bodies and can help us to experience beyond the limits of our experiential horizons (110). This is what CREW aims to do: during the experience of the performance, two participants don headgear fitted with external cameras and an internal monitor. The images from one unit are projected inside the other, providing each participant with a visual representation of the other person's visual field. Crew's "experience-experiment" engages with the perspective inherent in how the world comes to exist for us and how the very possibility of having a perspective is also a constraint to perceptual consciousness. In her chapter, Merx investigates what CREW's "head-swap" could mean for a phenomenological understanding of a technologically induced experience of empathy.

The volume closes with Mark Hansen's chapter on the arresting ways in which technology conditions what is possible to experience beyond perception. In "Performance as Media Affect: The Phenomenology of Human Implication in Jordan Crandall's *Gatherings*" Hansen develops a "phenomenology of implication" as a way of explaining the reconfiguration of the embodied performativity in response to technical environments. Twenty-first-century media operate predominately beneath or beyond the registers of human sense experience and for purposes other than storing such experience. Doing so, they present us with the challenge to rethink, and to radicalize, some of our assumptions concerning the functioning of the phenomenal body and its correlation with the environment/world. What does it mean to theorize performance as the production of an event that implicates the body without making it the center or agent of sensory processing? This, Hansen argues, requires *reversing* the phenomenological method: to move from intentionality to implication, understood as a fundamental non-differentiation of body and world that necessarily underlies any intentional distance. Like intentionality, implication designates a relation between an experiential event and an objectivity informing that event, but it differs fundamentally from intentionality on the question concerning the status of that objectivity. *Gatherings* shows how this involves an understanding of the body as a participant in a larger operation of environmental eventuality, and not as the agent of the presencing of an event. The body's experience, then, would no longer ground experience, but serve as one part the larger operation of the environmental event, in some cases beyond perception if not imagination.

Drew Leder, writing in 1990, observed that "[w]hile in one sense the body is the most abiding and inescapable presence in our lives, it is also essentially characterized by absence" (1). According to Leder, bodily states of experiential absence present a key to understanding structures of embodiment. Intentionally directed outwards, our bodily investment in this world easily escapes our attention. Our bodies are the blind spot in our experiences, the blind spot that is constitutive of a point of view or "I" inside this world as it is laid out for us by our senses. Leder introduces the term *dys-appearance* to denote a mode through which explicit awareness of the body is awakened. The dys-appearing body is the body whose appearance undermines disappearance as an unquestioned, and therefore apparently normal, condition. No longer absent from experience, the body surfaces as an absence within normal experience (Leder 86–87).

The chapters in this volume have taken up Leder's challenge to think embodiment through the perception of absence—the absence of memory, habit, of ourselves or our sense of ourselves, even the absence of life. Our responses move phenomenology and performance into revised political, social, cultural and technological terrain where they meet with a wide range of approaches and ideas, including process philosophy, posthuman theory, new materialism, animal philosophy, and radical empiricism. Taken together they share an interest in decentralizing the human subject and thinking beyond the differentiation of the body and the world, beyond the registers of human perception. We—as in everyone—have bodies, and not simply one. Each of us has virtual and imagined and seen and seeing bodies, bodies in action and constrained and displaced and dominant and dominated. Experience arrives through, and as, these relationships with the world. And yet, those relationships are themselves part of systems beyond human perception, are indeed dependent on our inability to grasp them. It turns out that the advent of new technologies and new phenomenologies that take us beyond the human can be understood to rearticulate an ancient task at the heart of philosophy and performance: reaching for the invisible in order to learn from our failure to grasp it.

NOTES

1. See for example, Butler (*Bodies that Matter*).
2. The term "relational aesthetics" was coined by Nicolas Bourriaud, who later wrote a book of the same name.

WORKS CITED

Ahmed, Sara. *Queer Phenomenology: Orientations, Objects, Others*. Durham: Duke UP, 2006.
Austin, John L. *How to Do Things with Words. The William James Lectures*. Cambridge: Harvard UP, 1962.
Barad, Karen. "Posthumanist Performativity: Toward an Understanding of How Matter Comes to Matter." *Signs: Journal of Women in Culture and Society* 28: 3 (2003): 801–31.
———. *Meeting the Universe Halfway. Quantum Physics and the Entanglement of Matter and Meaning*. Durham: Duke UP, 2007.
Barbaras, Renaud. *Desire and Distance: Introduction to a Phenomenology of Perception*. Cultural Memory in the Present. Stanford: Stanford UP, 2006.
Belekian, Krikor. Personal Interview. 13 April 2008.
Bhaba, Homi K. *The Location of Culture*. Abingdon: Routledge, 2004.
Beauvoir, Simone de. *The Second Sex*. 1952. Trans. H. M. Parshley. New York: Vintage Books, 1989.
Bishop, Claire. *Artificial Hells: Participatory Art and the Politics of Spectatorship*. London, New York: Verso, 2012.
Bourriaud, Nicolas. *Relational Aesthetics*. Dijon: Les presses du réel, 2002.
Broadhurst, Susan. *Digital Practices: Aesthetic and Neuroesthetic Approaches to Performance and Technology*. London: Palgrave Macmillan, 2007.
Butler, Judith. *Gender Trouble: Feminism and the Subversion of Identity*. 1990. 10th anniversary ed. New York: Routledge, 1999.
———. *Bodies That Matter: On the Discursive Limits of Sex*. New York: Routledge, 1993.
———. "Performative Acts and Gender Constitution: An Essay in Phenomenology and Feminist Theory." *Theatre Journal* 40.4 (1988): 519–31.
Deparaz, Natalie and Shaun Gallagher. "Phenomenology and the Cognitive Sciences: Editorial Introduction." *Phenomenology and the Cognitive Sciences* 1:1 (2002): 1–6.

Derrida, Jacques. *Speech and Phenomena and Other Essays of Husserl's Theory of Signs*. Trans. David B. Allison. Evanston: Northwestern UP, 1973.
Diprose, Rosalyn. *Corporeal Generosity: On Giving with Nietzsche, Merleau-Ponty, and Levinas*. Suny Series in Gender Theory. Albany: SU of New York P, 2002.
Dufrenne, Mikel. *The Phenomenology of Aesthetic Experience*. 1953. Trans. Edward S. Casey. Northwestern UP, 1973.
Fanon, Frantz. *Black Skin, White Masks*. 1952. Trans. Charles Lam Markmann. New York: Grove, 1967.
Farman, Jason. *Mobile Interface Theory: Embodied Space and Locative Media*. New York: Routledge, 2012.
Fischer-Lichte, Erika. *The Transformative Power of Performance: A New Aesthetics*. 2004. Trans. Saskya Iris Jain. New York: Routledge, 2008.
Fraleigh, Sondra Horton. *Dance and the Lived Body: A Descriptive Aesthetics*. Pittsburgh: U of Pittsburgh P, 1987.
———. "A Vulnerable Glance: Seeing Dance through Phenomenology." *Dance Research Journal*. 23.1 (1991): 11–16.
Franko, Mark. "What Is Dead and What Is Alive in Dance Phenomenology." *Dance Research Journal*. 43:2 (winter 2011): 1–4.
Garner, Stanton B. *Bodied Spaces: Phenomenology and Performance in Contemporary Drama*. Ithaca: Cornell UP, 1994.
———. "Theatre and Phenomenology." *Degrés* 29: 107-08 (2001): b1–b17.
Gennep, Arnold van. *The Rites of Passage*. London: Routledge and Kegan Paul PLC, 1977.
Goffman, Erving. *Frame Analysis: An Essay on the Organization of Experience*. Cambridge, MA: Harvard UP, 1974.
———. *The Presentation of Self in Everyday Life*. 1959. Woodstock, N.Y.: Overlook Press, 1973.
Grosz, Elizabeth. "Merleau-Ponty and Irigaray in the Flesh." *Thesis Eleven* 36 (1993): 37–59.
Hansen, Mark. *Bodies in Code*, New York and London: Routledge, 2006.
Heidegger, Martin. *Being and Time*. 1927. Trans. John Macquarrie and Edward Robinson. New York: Harper and Row, 1962.
Ihde, Don. "Stretching the In-Between: Embodiment and Beyond." *Foundations of Science* 16.2 (2011): 109–118.
Jackson, Shannon. *Social Works: Performing Art, Supporting Publics*. New York; London: Routledge, 2011.
Jones, Amelia. *Body Art/Performing the Subject*. Minneapolis: U of Minnesota P, 1998.
———. *Self/Image:Technology, Representation, and the Contemporary Subject*. New York: Routledge, 2006.
Kattenbelt, Chiel. "Intermediality in Performance as a Mode of Performativity." *Mapping Intermediality in Performance*. Eds. Sarah Bay-Cheng, et al. Amsterdam: Amsterdam U P, 2010. 29–37.
Kozel, Susan. *Closer: Performance, Technologies, Phenomenology*. Cambridge, MA: MIT P, 2007.
Krauss, Rosalind. *Passages in Modern Sculpture*. Cambridge Mass.: MIT P, 1981.
Kuppers, Petra. *Community Performance: An Introduction*. London: Routledge, 2007.

———. *Disability and Contemporary Performance: Bodies on Edge*. New York: Routledge, 2004.
Leder, Drew. *The Absent Body*. Chicago: U of Chicago P, 1990.
Lyotard, Jean-Francois. *The Postmodern Condition: A Report on Knowledge*. Minneapolis: U of Minnesota P, 1979.
McKenzie, Jon. *Perform or Else: From Discipline to Performance*. New York and London: Routledge, 2001.
Merleau-Ponty, Maurice. *Phenomenology of Perception*. 1945. Trans. Donald A. Landes. London: Routledge, 2012.
———. *The Visible and the Invisible; Followed by Working Notes*. 1964. Trans. Alphonso Lingis. Northwestern University Studies in Phenomenology & Existential Philosophy. Evanston: Northwestern UP, 1968.
Nancy, Jean Luc. *The Inoperative Community*. Ed. Peter Connor. Trans. Peter Connor et al. Foreword by Christopher. Fynsk. Minneapolis: U of Minnesota P, 1991.
Nancy, Jean Luc, ten Kate, Laurens. "'Cum'. ... Revisited: Preliminaries to Thinking the Interval" in *Intermedialities: Philosophy, Art, Politics*. Eds. Henk Oosterling and Ewa Plonowska Ziarek. Lanham MA: Lexington Books, Rowman & Littlefield, 2011. 37–44.
Noë, Alva. *Action in Perception*, Cambridge, Mass: MIT P, 2004.
Parker-Starbuck, Jennifer. *Cyborg Theatre: Corporeal/Technological Intersections in Multimedia Performance*. Basingstoke: Palgrave, 2011.
Phelan, Peggy. *Unmarked: The Politics of Performance*. London; New York: Routledge, 1993.
Popat, Sita. "Keeping It Real: Encountering Mixed Reality in Igloo's SwanQuake: House." *Convergence: The International Journal of Research into New Media Technologies*. 18.1 (2011): 11–26.
Popat, Sita and Pitches, Jonathan, eds. *Performance Perspectives: A Critical Introduction*. Basingstoke: Palgrave, 2011.
Rayner, Alice. *To Act To Do To Perform: Drama and the Phenomenology of Action*. Ann Arbor: U of Michigan P, 1994.
Schechner, Richard. *Performance Theory*. 1988 New York: Routledge, 2003.
Sheets-Johnstone, Maxine. *The Phenomenology of Dance*. London: Dance Books Ltd, 1979.
Sobchack, Vivian Carol. *The Address of the Eye: A Phenomenology of Film Experience*. Princeton: Princeton UP, 1992.
———. *Carnal Thoughts: Embodiment and Moving Image Culture*. Berkeley: U of California P, 2004.
States, Bert O. *Great Reckonings in Little Rooms. On the Phenomenology of Theater*. U of California P, 1987.
Soja, Edward W. *Thirdspace*. Malden: Blackwell, 1996.
Stoller, Silvia. "Reflections on Feminist Merleau-Ponty Skepticism." *Hypatia* 15.1 (2000): 175–82.
Taipale, Joona. *Phenomenology and Embodiment. Husserl and the Constitution of Subjectivity*. Evanston, Ill.: Northwestern UP, 2014.
Turner, Victor. "Liminality and the Performative Genres." *Studies in Symbolism and Cultural Communication*. Ed. F. Allan Hanson. Lawrence, KS: U of Kansas P, 1982: 25–41.
Wilshire, Bruce. *Role Playing and Identity: The Limits of Theatre as Metaphor*. Bloomington: Indiana UP, 1982.

Young, Iris Marion. "'Throwing Like a Girl': Twenty Years Later." *Body and Flesh: A Philosophical Reader*. Ed. Donn Welton. Malden: Blackwell Publishers, 1998. 286–90.

Zarrilli, Phillip. "Toward a Phenomenological Model of the Actor's Embodied Modes of Experience." *Theatre Journal* 56.4 (2004): 653–66.

1 The Stage Struck Out of the World
Theatricality and Husserl's Phenomenology of Theatre, 1905–1918

Pannill Camp

Edmund Husserl's place in theatre and performance studies has shifted since phenomenology first made inroads in the field. Early phenomenological scholarship asked what Husserl's approach to conscious experience could reveal about theatre. Some supposed that through the phenomenological reduction—the procedure Husserl devised to unlock a realm of pure consciousness—live performance could be seized from the flux of perception and rigorously described, rather than flattened into a piece of culture to be read. Once installed in the critical repertoire of theatre studies, however, phenomenological approaches to performance gradually distanced themselves from Husserl. Martin Heidegger's pivot to the question of being and Maurice Merleau-Ponty's focus upon embodied perception helped frame foundational concepts in the field, while Husserl's reduction drifted to the margins. In a sense, this trend recapitulated the history of continental philosophy. Phenomenologists of performance moved beyond Husserl's terminology and transcendental aims just as Heidegger and Merleau-Ponty had done in the mid-twentieth century.

But just as Husserl's legacy informed the work of even those thinkers who largely left his methods behind, his phenomenology, in recent decades, has continued to percolate in some areas of performance theory. One such area concerns theatricality, a term that in common parlance might denote exaggerated or preening style, but that in scholarship has lately come to signify theatre's audience-oriented posture. Theatricality has assumed a wide range of meanings even in its more considered applications (Davis and Postlewait 1–4, 16–34). One cogent theory of theatricality by Josette Féral draws on Husserlian thought. Féral argues that spectators can inscribe this quality upon objects by exercising a kind of active gaze, instigating theatricality by "instituting a Husserlian qualitative modification" (97–8). Though she does not elaborate, Féral's citation of Husserl suggests that a similarity links her understanding of theatricality to Husserl's core technique of phenomenological reduction, also known as bracketing or *epoché*. For Husserl, phenomenological research begins with a calibrated modification of the way one posits the world to exist. Without denying the existence of the world, the phenomenologist willfully converts positing in the mode of belief into bracketed, or parenthesized positing (Husserl, *Ideas* 65). Both this subjective mental action and the "active gaze" to which Féral ascribes theatricality are brought about with complete freedom on the part of the subject.

A more sustained examination of Husserl's significance to the field of theatre studies appeared in Julia Walker's essay on the text/performance split and twentieth-century philosophy. Walker identifies a common theme in twentieth-century poetics and philosophy: a controversy over whether meaning is something fundamentally restricted to text—a position that typifies both poetic theory associated with New Criticism and the analytic or Anglo-American tradition in philosophy—or whether it is irreducibly constituted in the body owing to the conscious mind's links to the body's sensorium and capacity for expression. Walker aligns Husserl with those who embrace "experiential knowledge," both in the realm of poetics and philosophy (26). Like the actor who incorporates a text to express the central meaning in a theatrical performance, the Husserlian knowing subject exists "inside the object of its investigation" (32).

Considered alongside other work that identifies sympathies between Husserlian phenomenology and enduring concerns of Western theatre theory and practice—the dividing line between staged and non-staged states of affairs, the body's capacity of expression, the outlook of spectators—it is now possible to speak of a new moment in phenomenological writing about theatre. Theatre scholars formerly adopted Husserl's reduction as a critical framework that could reveal new insights into the nature of the performance event and its reception. But more recent studies like Féral's and Walker's have pointed out correspondences that suggest something quite different: theatre practice and Husserlian phenomenology set up the relationship between the mind and the world in similar ways.

The basis for a historical understanding of these "theatrical" tendencies in Husserl's thinking, I would like to argue, can be found in Husserl's own thoughts about the art of the stage. In extensive notes written between 1905 and 1918, Husserl examined theatre itself. These writings were not intended for publication and show Husserl's thinking in process, but they nonetheless contain both an early and unstudied corpus of phenomenological writing about theatre and a foundational study of the consciousness of theatrical appearances. What makes theatre a special case for Husserl is that it challenges the distinction between form and medium in mimetic art. He is concerned foremost with theatre because of its unique capacity to base fictional images in the medium of the things the images themselves represent.

Indeed, the fact that theatre may be seen as, in Bert O. States's terms, "a kind of language whose words consist to an unusual degree of things that are what they seem to be," is critical to Husserl's understanding of the stage (*Great Reckonings* 20). Assessing Husserl's views of theatre requires taking note of the particular problems that led him to engage with the art. Rather than elaborating a theory of drama within a project dedicated to imitative or fine arts, Husserl examines the nature of image consciousness, a mode of awareness that he contrasts with both ordinary perception and with pure—or inwardly generated—fantasies. Theatre produces image consciousness, for Husserl, because it offers an image of something not actually present. But theatre also carves out a special place within that category of consciousness. Theatre's unique tendency to appropriate the forms, materials, and perceptual content of ordinarily perceived objects reveals, more so than painting or sculpture, facets of image consciousness that are elsewhere obscured. Stage consciousness factors out certain media-specific image qualities, revealing aspects of the distinction between image consciousness and ordinary perception in a sharper way that would, say, meditations on the difference between the experience of a real and painted lake.

For Husserl, theatre's salient properties are its dynamic, human scale spatiality, the identity between its materials and the things they represent (chairs on stage represent chairs) and the conspicuously non-depictive nature of theatrical representation. This essay outlines Husserl's cursory phenomenology of theatre with a view toward the way the specificity of theatre informed his evolving theory of imaging in general. As I will hope to demonstrate, it is precisely because Husserl employs theatre as a limit case for what he calls perceptual fantasy—the sort of imaginative play that images like those on stage engender—that his discussions of theatre remains an important part of the canon of phenomenological writing about theatre. In the course of exploring the boundaries that separate—but also fail to separate—stage consciousness from the experience of ordinary things, Husserl acknowledges that theatre engenders a promiscuous sort of imaginative play not restricted to aesthetic stages. This suggests both that Husserl's thinking on theatre helped inaugurate a central theme in phenomenological criticism—one concerned with the extra-discursive elements of theatrical representation—and supports the contention that theatrical thinking was fundamental to Husserl's elaboration of the *epoché*.

IMAGE CONSCIOUSNESS

The consciousness of theatre spectators occupies a specific place in Husserl's broad taxonomy of experience. Husserl in the first place distinguishes presentation (*gegenwärtigung*), which designates consciousness of perception, from re-presentation (*vergegenwärtigung*), which encompasses memory, expectation, imagination (phantasy), and image consciousness.[1] This last category includes aesthetic experiences of a mimetic and predominantly visual kind such as painting, sculpture, photography, and theatre, but also applies to duplicative images such as waxen figures and mirror images. In keeping with his desire to subject consciousness to logical thinking, Husserl attempts to discern certain attributes that pertain to these various modes of consciousness. Perception stands as a default or background mode; it persists and looms behind other modes and bears several essential markers. Ordinary perceptual consciousness finds its objects to be present "in person" (*leibhaftig*), factually existing or actual, and, when not actively in doubt, in a mode of belief (Husserl, *Phantasy* 88, 109, 214, 601).

Husserl believes that the essential features of perceptual consciousness are necessary, but not sufficient or exclusive to it. Both remembered and expected objects, for example, appear actual and are invested with belief, though not presently. Pure fantasy on the other hand, however lively, is consciousness of objects that are neither present, nor actual, nor believed in; fantasy objects are given "as if" actual (Husserl, *Phantasy* 345). Nonetheless, Husserl in many places considers memory, expectation, and fantasy together under a single heading distinct from "image consciousness." All are considered reproductive, or inwardly generated, re-presentation; they have no immediate perceptual ground and are thought up with the aid of reproduced impressions (Husserl, *Phantasy* 565).[2] But this does not mean that fantasy is walled off from image consciousness. Husserl both distinguishes between fantasy on the one hand and memory and expectation on the other, and associates fantasy with the way we experience representational images. In a 1918 text, Husserl claims that memory amounts to a form of reproduction that is given "as it were," as opposed to fantasy, which is given "as if" (Husserl, *Phantasy* 606). Memory is constituted as a "quasi-actual," "unmodified reproduction" unlike fantasy, which is given as non-actual. The "as-if" of fantasy, furthermore, prevails also in our experience of art including theatrical performance. Husserl distinguishes between "reproduced fantasy," which is purely imagined, and "perceptual fantasy," which is prompted by the perception of art's physical stratum. Pure fantasy thus is classed as a "reproductive re-presentation," while the imaginative processes that produce it are also apparently available for image consciousness (Husserl, *Phantasy* 605–7).

In contrast with memory, expectation, and pure fantasy, image consciousness has a basis in something actually perceived, like a photograph or stage image. Such objects provoke "perceptual re-presentation," or "pictorial exhibiting" because they have an actual, in-person, perceptual ground (Husserl, *Phantasy* 565). Images of this sort instigate a sort of conscious experience unto themselves. Husserl explains image consciousness as the interaction of three sorts of objects: a *physical image*, a representing *image object*, and a represented *image subject*. Physical images are real things with material existence in the world. They are made up of canvas, paper, stone, pigment, bodies, etc., but support appearances different from themselves (Husserl, *Phantasy* xlv, 20, 49, 118, 646). In these physical substrates, image objects are seen. These ideal, non-actual "figments" or "semblances" are neither actual in the manner of artistic materials like paint, nor in the manner of whatever image subject to which they might refer. Yet image objects are the only things that are genuinely present in image consciousness. Husserl explains that in the example of an engraving, the image object prevails in the mode of image consciousness because it "uses up" the "apprehension contents" supplied by the paper and lines belonging to the physical object

(Husserl, *Phantasy* xlv–xlvii, 49). Image objects, finally, point toward an image subject that is meant only and does not really appear. Image subjects in Husserl's view may be real entities, such as the subjects of portraits, or they may refer to things in an "illusory world" like those generated by purely fictional plays (Husserl, *Phantasy* 617). We will see that the nature of what theatre in particular presents as its subjects evidently led Husserl to revise his opinion of the representational structure of image consciousness in general.

As this schema suggests, image consciousness embraces, and in fact arises from the multiple conflicts that these three sorts of objects produce (Husserl, *Phantasy* xlvii–xlviii). A "little figure in bronze" presents the figure of a non-present human being, but the conspicuous color and texture of sculptural media conflict with the image object it supports. Tension also arises between the distinct space in which an image object is ensconced and the space of the abiding perceived reality around it. Photographs, for example, generate "a conflict of the image space with actual space" outside their border (Husserl, *Phantasy* 581). A third sort of conflict appears: variances between image objects and the real subjects to which they refer. These conflicts are not clashes between completely opposed perceptions—as in the case of a mirage—where the conflict must be settled on one side or another. "Conflict belongs to the essence of a perceptual image" (Husserl, *Phantasy* 588). Such images do not need to overthrow the perceived reality around them, but merely contest ordinary perception so long as the viewer holds the image object in view.

While this tripartite scheme prevails in much of Husserl's thinking about images, his views on the last sort of conflict—those arising between image objects and the actual things to which they refer—evolved over the course of time. He at first ascribed a depictive function to all fine arts; all art images referred toward non-present but actual things. By 1918 he had reversed this view. As we will see, this revision in his theory of imaging may have arisen specifically from Husserl's investigations into theatre.

THE FIRST PHENOMENOLOGY OF THEATRE

Husserl did not address theatre systematically as part of a work of dramatic theory or a treatise on fine arts. He considered it sporadically in the course of research into categories of re-presentation, especially image consciousness. Theatre helped him think through the ways that memory, expectation, and fantasy—both pure and rooted in perceptible images—come about. While this approach has deprived us of a holistic early phenomenology of theatre, it allows us both to discern what Husserl believed set theatre apart from other variants of image consciousness, and to elicit some of the broader implications that the case of theatre posed for his thought. Theatre comes to bear in Husserl's thinking mainly around two issues. First, how is our consciousness of the physical image as an objective existing thing essentially distinct from our apprehension of the image object that it supports? Second, what essentially is the relationship between these two interrelated and simultaneous sorts of appearance?

Husserl's use of theatrical examples in these investigations suggests that he ascribes three distinct features to the stage that are absent or less evident in other arts: theatre space bears a high degree of resemblance to and contiguity with space ordinarily perceived; theatre synthesizes different sorts of perception into a unified manifold in a more expansive way than other arts; theatre, finally, is overtly non-depictive—it does not necessarily refer to anything outside of itself. Thus because it more closely resembles the ordinary perception of things in the world, theatre serves as a limit case, an instance in which only essential points of conflict separate image consciousness from everyday experience.

Husserl contends that our experience of artistic images subsists in intuitions that "quarrel" with reality in numerous ways, but that do not cause us to fall into illusion (*Phantasy* 582). The primary sort of discord is spatial. Image space "somewhere borders on the real space," and the "unseen parts" of image space conflict "with parts of the space of actual experience" (Husserl, *Phantasy* 610–11). Discussing the limits of "image intuition" in 1912, Husserl examines a series of objects that assume progressively more congruity with ordinarily perceived space. Photographs bear spatiality that is "approximate, imperfect," and plainly anomalous with respect to "ocular-motor unity" and dynamic orientation that we experience in ordinary spatial consciousness (Husserl, *Phantasy* 581). Photographic image space and actual space therefore vie openly with each other; "the one ousts the other from intuition" (Husserl, *Phantasy* 581). Sculptures present a more faithful facsimile of ordinary space, but not without prompting their own acute conflicts. Husserl notes that a white plaster bust impedes his ability to see the "image head" without effort. "I cannot hold on to the space as actually seen and color [the bust] differently" (Husserl, *Phantasy* 582). The scale of even uncannily mimetic sculptures can also engender further potential spatial incongruities (Husserl, *Phantasy* 582).

Theatre, however, achieves a closer analogy between aesthetic and ordinary spaces: "The space of the stage, with its sets, and so on, analogizes actual space ..." (Husserl, *Phantasy* 584). The effect of this uniquely natural spatiality is felt not only in a close resemblance between the spaces proper to theatre's physical images and image objects, but also in the harmony between these spaces and the actually perceived space beyond the theatrical frame. Theatre is unique also in that it deploys an "enveloping pictoriality," a field that surrounds individual performers and objects, sustaining the credibility of the representation (Husserl, *Phantasy* 585). While theatre space's boundaries, unlike those of painting or photography, are not sharply delineated by virtue of the medium itself, they nonetheless have an indistinct outer limit. Theatre is "not a panorama picture;" its border is partly articulated by theatre architecture (Husserl, *Phantasy* 585). Husserl refers once to the "nexus of further experiential realities,"—that is, the reality that stage consciousness provisionally suspends—as something that can be found "beyond the rostrum through the orchestra and into the audience" (*Phantasy* 618). Theatre space is not uncontained, but it blends into the space outside of it in a way that subdues the spatial conflicts that define other arts.

Theatre also casts off perceptions saturated with natural color, and Husserl alludes to additional perceptual convergences: "[T]here is even more in drama: it goes much further. Human beings, living human beings, analogize, depict human beings without illusion" (*Phantasy* 584). Though he does not elaborate upon the other perceptual components that draw theatre closer to the appearance of actual and present reality, he elsewhere suggests that they include movement, sound, and the physical behavior of objects and bodies. Husserl thus anticipates States's observation about the identity between theatrical materials and referents. A candle on stage represents, precisely, a candle. For Husserl, it merely appears in the "as-if" mode of positing. In the same way, actors' bodies stand, in a sense, for themselves, though they are also fixed to a role. "The king on stage is indeed an actual human being with actual garments—except that in reality, of course, the King is Herr actor so-and-so and not the king, his robe is a part of the theatrical wardrobe and not a coronation robe, and so on" (Husserl, *Phantasy* 611). Husserl, throughout his analyses of theatre, seems to assume that what Michael Kirby calls matrixed performances are integral to the constitution of stage consciousness (3–20). Persons and objects on stage mean to belong to a fictional world. But this representation is carried about against a background of intimacy between physical things and the images they produce.

Theatre's manifold perceptual analogy produces a robust, multi-sensory synthesis that accords in many ways with actual experience of off-stage phenomena. In an early text concerning image consciousness, Husserl claims that image objects and the physical things that support them are "built on the same presentational foundation." A note here claims that images can be only visual or tactile, which is to say oriented toward the senses that specialize in space, "[b]ut the church bell rings in the theater, and so on" (Husserl, *Phantasy* 155). In other words Husserl invokes theatre to suggest that the category of image might transcend space and visual perception. The toll of a bell in a playhouse produces something like the image of a sound. Passages like this, on the one hand, show that Husserl considered the theatre to have characteristics all its own that promote image consciousness in special ways. Theatre doesn't simply deploy objects that work narrowly upon individual senses, but a "whole image situation" whose infinite, if bounded, appearances correspond with an unusually expansive range of possible judgments (Husserl, *Phantasy* 277). On the other hand, Husserl thinks of theatre not as something that stakes out a categorically distinct sort of experience, but rather an instance that is uniquely equipped to disclose what is essential about image consciousness as a whole (*Phantasy* xliv).[3]

The unique way that theatre construes its image subjects—the entities to which its image objects refer—impelled Husserl to reconsider the fundamental conditions of image consciousness as a whole. In earlier thinking, Husserl had given credence to the idea that artistic representations necessarily indicated definite and actual entities. The subjects of painted portraits and photographs, for instance, amounted to the actual but non-present referents of present but non-actual images (Husserl, *Phantasy* 20–2). Husserl was not oblivious to the fact that paintings and sculptures could present wholly fictional subjects, but he nonetheless understood images to point to something "represented or depicted" and in some way actual (*Phantasy* 21). By 1918, Husserl had revised this understanding, and theatre, again, seems to have most clearly elucidated the salient principles: "In the case of theatrical performance, we live in a world of perceptual phantasy; we have 'images within the cohesive unity of one image, but we do not for that reason have depictions.'" Even in the case of history plays such as *Richard III,* where depiction clearly operates on some level, "depictiveness is not the *primary* concern" (Husserl, *Phantasy* 616). Husserl does not argue, then, that we see Richard III portrayed on stage and doubt that what is meant is the last Plantagenet king. It is rather that no actuality is ascribed to the image itself seen on stage. Confronted with a play, "no consciousness of depiction whatsoever needs to be excited, and what then appears is a pure perceptual figment. We live in neutrality; we do not carry out any actual positing at all with respect to what is intuited" (Husserl, *Phantasy* 617). Husserl, however, does not attribute a completely distinct modality to stage consciousness. By 1918, he has come to believe that even painted portraits constitute a sort of fiction.

There is thus a pattern to the way that Husserl employs theatre to think through imaging phenomena. Theatre allows him to test whether different sorts of conflicts that mark images as unreal are essential to image consciousness. Theatre presents an unusually attenuated version of the spatial and other perceptual disharmonies that cleave artistic images from the sphere of actuality. It also shatters the presumption that we encounter such images as pictures of real things. This, in turn, undermines the idea that conflicts between image objects and the subjects to which they refer are necessary to the way we see images in general. If image subjects are pure perceptual figments, they lack empirical standing, and therefore the discord between them and the images that refer to them is weakly intuited. Thus because theatre tends to quell some conflicts that prevail amongst the components of image consciousness in other art forms, Husserl searches on stage for the essence of the unreality of images. In considering the theatre, he finds an acute version of yet another sort of conflict that seems to operate even in the absence of depiction.

Husserl contends from 1905 forward that images prompt a peculiar tension between competing apprehensions of the same experience. An artwork's physical component produces intuitions of an image that is different from it, and which, being "built along with it on the same presentational foundation," stand "in partial conflict" with it (Husserl, *Phantasy* 155). When we view a painting by Chardin, the same experience leads us to perceive an arrangement of artistic materials and the semblance of a wine carafe, goblet, and fruit. These two apperceptions are not completely mutually incompatible; it is not like the case of a mirage or other true illusion, where we "take sides with what is experienced against what is illusory, which we actively negate, cancel" (Husserl, *Phantasy* 618). Nonetheless, image object apprehensions trade off with the consciousness of the actual things that support them. Husserl explains that in the example of an engraving, the image object prevails in the mode of image consciousness because it "uses up" the "apprehension contents" supplied by the paper and lines belonging to the physical object (*Phantasy* xlv–xlvii, 49). This is the case for image consciousness in general, since the content of perceptual fantasies "can be exactly the same as the content that is intuited in actual empirical experiences."[4] But it is particularly evident in the theatre, where the contents of images presented are made up of perceptions of precisely the things they pretend to be.[5] In the theatre, Husserl observes, "The same perceptual sensations are assigned" to both the physical actuality on stage and the image object, "but an illusionary conflict [...] does not come about" (*Phantasy* 585). Instead, what prevails is a competition between apperceptions of the physical image thing and apperceptions of the image object. Consciousness directs itself to either one or the other in a given act. We turn our regard "from what is perceptually given to the figment interpenetrating with it" (Husserl, *Phantasy* 585).

How, then, can the same sensory perceptions, the same set of intuitions, support consciousness both of the actual and physically present things of the theatre and the semblances they produce? Husserl contends that in image consciousness, both of these types of objects are constituted in a way that is distinct from the process of ordinary objectification. First of all, the image object, the "pure perceptual figment" of the play, "lacks 'belief,'" even when we are fully immersed in it; "it lacks the characteristic of reality" (Husserl, *Phantasy* 584). This appearance thus has the quality of nullity—it is "a nothing" in the way of other image objects. In the case of a play, the figment "is annulled intrinsically and not only by being in conflict with the space of the theatre" (Husserl, *Phantasy* 50, 585). Husserl takes pains to explain that the type of nullity characteristic of image objects is not like that which belongs to disillusionment. It is not that we posit belief in what we see staged and then "take a position" against that belief. The image figment that comes to us on stage is "annulled in itself" (Husserl, *Phantasy* 586). The conflict with reality "is there from the beginning" and there is no need for us to "carry out any cancellation understood as active negation" (Husserl, *Phantasy* 612–14, 617–18).

The absence of active cancellation allows the image figment to manifest without the disruptive awareness of a contrary apprehension (of reality) rooted in the perceptual content. It follows that the competing apprehension (which would state "all of this is a merely a play") is also held in check in some way. Reality and image consciousness are not symmetrically matched. The intentional nexus that corresponds to the consciousness of reality is unrestricted in a way that the figment worlds of image consciousness are not. Consciousness of reality can topple the consciousness that roams the world of images, while the apprehension of perceptual figments can only "annoy" consciousness of actuality by infringing upon it at the margins (Husserl, *Phantasy* 614). Immersion in the appearances of the stage thus requires image consciousness to hold the full awareness of the really existing world at bay. Husserl maintains that while image consciousness holds sway, consciousness of background reality "also has its inhibition" (*Phantasy* 612–13).

Husserl suggests that immersion in images requires that we suspend questions directed toward existing things. In 1912, Husserl writes that when "living in aesthetic consciousness," "we ask no questions about the being or non-being of what directly appears or appears in an image." Similarly, in a discussion of perceptually based "phantasms" including theatre, he declares, "*now let us exclude the consciousness of reality*" (Husserl, *Phantasy* 459–60). This facet of image consciousness, more than any other, reveals the similarity between Husserl's understanding of theatre and his elaboration of the phenomenological reduction—his central methodological instrument. It is consequently crucial to understanding why Husserl's thought has sustained the interest of theatre and performance theorists.

REDUCTION AND STAGE CONSCIOUSNESS

Husserl implicitly assigns specific distinguishing features to theatre. Its specificity lies in its unusually expansive and natural style of spatiality and its synthesis of multiple perceptual elements. But it also requires a special vigilance on the part of the spectator. Theatre, unlike painting and sculpture, cannot rely upon the sensate qualities of its medium to continually announce its unreality. It calls upon us to abstain from positing its appearances as real in ways that are not required of other imitative arts. This suspension—without active negation—of the normal operation of consciousness has a close relative in the phenomenological *epoché*, which is instanced through deliberate abstention from positing an empirically observed world as real. Husserl described the *epoché* as a way for the phenomenologist to escape "the natural attitude." In opposition to this quotidian "waking consciousness," wherein one finds the world, "the one spatiotemporal actuality to which I belong," "as factually existing," the *epoché* suspends certain position-taking regarding the world (Husserl, *Ideas* 62–5). Husserl argues that we can suspend our positing of any object as existing, since this is a preliminary step in the "attempt to doubt," which we are free to carry out. Extending this "putting out of action" to cover "the general positing which belongs to the essence of the natural attitude," Husserl excludes all beliefs about the world, all sciences, in short, as Dermot Moran puts it, all "commitments to this world" (Moran 188).

What's more, just as the phenomenological reduction can be willfully directed to isolate any particular object, Husserl's indicates that a version of theatrical image consciousness can be imposed onto anything—even non-staged objects. The phenomenologist seems to be able to view all sorts of objects through a theatrical lens. In 1909, Husserl wrote that a subject could fantasize "into" real perceived things: "[...] I alter the appearance fictionally, but in such a way that the material of the sensation remains untouched. I imagine, for example, that a theatrical scene rather than the house is actually there, and so forth" (*Phantasy* 99). The act of perfect freedom that attends the reduction, it would seem, has an analogue in image consciousness, which manifests in what one might call a "theatricalized" reality.

It is important to note that Husserl does not uniformly use theatrical language to describe transpositions of aestheticized consciousness. He would likely consider what Féral calls theatricality to be an instance of a freely instanced ability to fantasize into objective experiences, a "change from the attitude of actual experience into the attitude of perceptual phantasy" that can also be thought of as painterly:

> Perhaps one can say that precisely the same thing is not impossible even in the case of uninterrupted and uninhibited actual experience— as when we contemplate a beautiful landscape aesthetically, and the landscape and even all of the human beings, houses, and villages that we see in our experience of it are "accepted" by us as if they were mere *figures in a painted landscape*. [...] The reality changes into reality-as-if for us, changes into "play"; the objects turn into aesthetic semblance: into mere—though perceptual—phantasy objects.
> (Husserl, *Phantasy* 615)

Nonetheless, since theatre approaches what Husserl calls "the style of the intuition of nature" in synthetic and multi-sensory ways that surpass the capabilities of painting, the phenomenologist might consider theatricality to be a more expansive category of aesthetic contemplation (*Phantasy* 585).

Husserl's account of the play of fantasy in image consciousness accentuates the subtractive as well as the additive aspects of stage consciousness. According to Husserl, to confer a theatrical appearance on something brings with it a certain diminishment of potential. This may be understood as the result, on one level, as a consequence of Husserl imputing the status of fantasy to stage appearances. Reproductive or "pure" fantasy, for Husserl, is a hollow sort of object. It can take on any and all of the appearances of actual experience, but is encountered as "emasculated," having taken on "the impotent form of the as-if" (Husserl, *Phantasy* 606). Though they are built upon genuine sensory perception, "perceptual phantasies" like those of painting and theatre exhibit a similar modification. At best, this attitude toward of imaged or staged appearances forecasts the etiolated condition that J. L. Austin later ascribed to utterances said on stage (22). At worst, Husserl seems to inscribe a sexist bi-polarity upon this distinction, implicitly feminizing what he sees as a deficit associated with objects of theatrical representation.

While I would reject the patriarchal logic behind this use of language, I do not believe that the transactional nature of theatricality ought to be disregarded. Husserl's characterization of theatricalized perceptions cannot be reduced to the adoption of the "veil or fog" that overlays reproductive re-presentations such as memory and pure fantasy (Husserl, *Phantasy* 241). Real things on stage also take on modifications associated with the phenomenological reduction. One of the attributes of the natural attitude—the mode of encountering the world that precedes the reduction—is that it presents the world "a practical world" filled with objects that have value and uses. The things in the actual world are "objects on hand" (Husserl, *Ideas* 61). This element of the quotidian actuality—the practicality of things—is one casualty of the conflicting apperceptions Husserl identifies in the mode of stage consciousness. Though many materials of stagecraft are objectively no different from their real counterparts, under the "fictionalizing experience," or "in the attitude in which we live in the 'image' world," the "real world of actual experience" is "a suspended world" (Husserl, *Phantasy* 619).

Seeking to trace the distinction between ordinary and theatrical apperceptions of the very same objects, Husserl focuses upon stage furniture. A perfectly suitable chair, for stage consciousness, is useless. "The use to which the furnishings are subject and for which they are there is annulled by conflict" (Husserl, *Phantasy* 620). This means not only that for spectators immersed in the world of the play, a chair on stage becomes non-actual, but also that for an actor its availability for use has been in a certain sense struck away.

> It is use presented in the figment, which is use for the persons who belong to the figment, who sit on the furnishings, and so on—in which case the sitting is not actual sitting but phantasy sitting, although the actor does also actually sit (which, however, only means that he performs all the movements, that he has the feelings in his muscles, that the corresponding physiological processes run their course in the muscles—all of which, surely does not amount to "taking a seat").
> (Husserl, *Phantasy* 620)

Here Husserl explains the odd sensation one feels stepping onto an empty stage at intermission, or the repulsive force an otherwise inert stage prop exerts on a non-actor. Such things exude a residual unreality; however practical in an absolute sense, they lack the sense of being "on hand."

The analogy between the acts of consciousness that constitute a theatrical object as theatrical—which is to say struck out of the world—and those that deliberately instance the reduction, suggests a way out of a deep-seated prejudice about theatre: that it isn't real. This is an enduring theme in anti-theatrical thought—the anxiety about false seeming that goes back to Plato—and it runs right through twentieth-century analytic thought—J. L. Austin's idea that the performative utterances on stage are withered or parasitic. For Husserl, what is on stage is certainly real, objects and actors stand there as themselves. But they have been modified in such a way that they cease to belong to the world in a common way. An actor sits in a chair on the stage, but he or she doesn't take a seat. The critical distinction between anti-theatrical denigration of theatre's ontological status and Husserl's treatment of theatrical representation is that for Husserl, the way in which staged things can be thought of as outside of the world is similar to the way in which we encounter them when they are disposed to reveal something else about what belongs to them essentially.

Husserl's legacy in our field does not rest solely on the fact that theatre scholars in the 1980s found his way of thinking about consciousness to offer a vital complement to semiotic and other essentially discursive models of interpretation. It also derives from the fact that Husserl discovered in theatre a uniquely productive phenomenological problem. The unique extent to which theatre's underlying medium and its images coincide leads him to see that the consciousness that embraces it 1) negotiates between two distinct modes of apprehension, 2) that neither of these two modes or attitudes is deluded, and thus neither has to be definitively excluded in order to let the other hold sway—as would be the case of a mirage, and 3) that the negotiation between them is to some extent a matter of willful conscious activity.

The implications for this way of analyzing perceived things were potentially enormous for Husserl. The task of articulating the distinction between *common* consciousness and *image* consciousness of one and the same thing on stage leads Husserl to formulate a fresh conception of what it means for an object to exist in the world. An actor on stage finds and maneuvers his or her body into a chair, but doesn't "take a seat." This means that the persistent natural given-ness of the world is suspended for the performer and for those who regard him or her as such. But rather than concluding that the chair and actor forfeit their genuine status as beings while on stage, Husserl sees two distinct modes of constitution competing to prevail without abolishing the other—one that belongs to a persistent and natural given-ness, and another that steps outside of it while in service of producing an image. Theatre consciousness is thus the mirror image of phenomenological reduction. Whereas the object on stage is struck out of the world in a provisional way, the phenomenological reduction suspends the presumption of the facticity of the world around the object. In both cases, the thing under view is temporarily unbound from what ties it to the world as an actually existing thing. In other words, theatre for Husserl is not a domain of false objects; it prompts a conscious exercise that puts what's true about objects into relief.

The homology between Husserl's description of theatrical image consciousness and his elaboration of the method of bracketing may be one manifestation of a profound spectatorial tendency in his thought. To prove this claim would require an investigation of Husserl's writing well beyond the scope of this essay. But to whatever extent this is the case, Husserl's writing on theatre supports two conclusions for the way we understand the relationship between phenomenology and the field of theatre and performance studies. One is that, while the 1980s did see a decisive turn toward phenomenological critical methods, the intellectual convergence between these theatre and phenomenology is much older; arguably it is as old as twentieth-century phenomenology itself. Well before recent generations of theatre and performance scholars turned their attention to phenomenology, Husserl identified theatre as a unique instance of an important kind of conscious activity.

Secondly, the initial convergence between phenomenology and theatre demonstrates an overlooked reason why these two self-reflexive exertions of consciousness are disposed to illuminate each other. Husserl's writing about theatre compounds the reasons to think of phenomenology as a way of thinking or a critical apparatus inherently disposed to engagements with theatre and performance. It might even be said that the special type of awareness that allows us to see certain situations as theatre, or that marks any kind of behavior as performance, entails conscious acts that implicitly or explicitly interrogate the ways that particular things belong to the world. In other words, consciousness of theatrical performance is in itself a kind of phenomenological investigation.

NOTES

1. In the present essay, "re-presentation" refers to this category of objects in Husserl's phenomenology. I also use "representation" without a hyphen in the colloquial sense.
2. See also the text from 1918 in which Husserl repeats that every phantasy "in the ordinary sense is an example of a reproductive fantasy" (605).
3. The fact that image consciousness, in turn, became the basis of Husserl's explanation of other types of re-presentation including fantasy and memory corroborates the idea of theatre a significant place within phenomenology as a whole.
4. Husserl, however, notes that this statement is somewhat misleading since fantasies of "transcendent objects" like numbers would have no concrete space and time, and thus could not completely coincide with an empirical experience. (*Phantasy* 607, 607n).
5. On stage, Husserl states, "everything [...] in the way of things and persons, everything said and done [...] has the characteristic of the 'as-if' (*Phantasy* 617)."

WORKS CITED

Austin, John L. *How to Do Things with Words*, 2nd ed. Cambridge, MA: Harvard UP, 1975.

Camp, Pannill. "Theatre Optics: Enlightenment Theatre Architecture in France and the Architectonics of Husserl's Phenomenology." *Theatre Journal* 59:4 (2007): 615–33.

Davis, Tracy C. and Thomas Postlewait. "Theatricality: An Introduction." *Theatricality*. Eds. Tracy C. Davis and Thomas Postlewait. Cambridge UK: Cambridge UP, 2003.

Féral, Josette. "Theatricality: The Specificity of Theatrical Language," *SubStance* #98/99, 31:2&3 (2002): 94–108.

Garner, Stanton B. *Bodied Spaces: Phenomenology and Performance in Contemporary Drama*. Ithaca and London: Cornell UP, 1994.

Husserl, Edmund. *Ideas I. The Essential Husserl: Basic Writings in Transcendental Phenomenology*. Ed. Donn Welton. Bloomington: Indiana UP, 1999.

———. *Phantasy, Image Consciousness, and Memory (1898–1925)*. Trans. John B. Brough. *Edmund Husserl Collected Works*, Vol. XI. Dordrecht: Springer, 2005.

Kirby, Michael. *A Formalist Theatre*. Philadelphia: U of Pennsylvania P, 1990.

Moran, Dermot. *Edmund Husserl: Founder of Phenomenology*. Cambridge: Polity Press, 2005.

Rayner, Alice. *Ghosts: Death's Double and the Phenomena of Theatre*. Minneapolis: U of Minnesota P, 2006.

States, Bert O. *Great Reckonings in Little Rooms: On the Phenomenology of Theater*. Berkeley: U of California P, 1985.

———. "The Phenomenological Attitude." *Critical Theory and Performance*. Eds. Janelle Reinelt and Joseph Roach. Ann Arbor: U of Michigan P, 1992.

Walker, Julia A. "The Text/Performance Split across the Analytic/Continental Divide." *Staging Philosophy: Intersections of Theater, Performance, and Philosophy*. Eds. David Krasner and David Z. Saltz Ann Arbor: U of Michigan P, 2006: 19–40.

Wilshire, Bruce. *Role Playing and Identity: The Limits of Theatre as Metaphor*. Bloomington: Indiana UP, 1982.

2 Movement as Lived Abstraction
The Logic of the Cut

Maaike Bleeker

"The choreographer as phenomenologist" reads the headline of a short article in the May/June 2014 issue of the intellectual glossy *Intelligent Life* announcing a new work by British choreographer Alexander Whitley, titled *The Measures Taken*. The work, the text explains, is "driven with a fascination with phenomenology" and "what is moving about movement"; it uses motion tracking devises to investigate the difference between a computer's response to movement and that of the human eye (Kavanagh 19). On the homepage of the website created for the project, *The Measures Taken* is described as a work that has at its core "questions of the role of technology in society and the contrasting ways we come to view the world in a culture highly mediated by digital technology."[1] Philosophy and technology are part of staging these works as fresh, exciting, and upbeat, and as quite different from the work of choreographers like George Balanchine or Frederic Ashton who, according to the author of the text in *Intelligent Life*, were "warning against overloading dance with ideas" and kept the thoughts behind their choreographies secret, even to their dancers (Kavanagh 19).

The choreographer becoming a phenomenologist, I argue, is symptomatic of transformations in the practice of theatre and dance in which the focus expands from what is (re)presented or expressed on stage to include also what happens in between stage and spectator. This shift did not come about with Whitley but is a prominent feature of the development of theatre and dance throughout the twentieth and early twenty-first century. The same could be said about the fascination of dance with what is moving about movement and with how technology has become part of how we perceive and think. These three are intimately connected and intertwined with the rise of media culture. From the early avant-garde on, theatre and dance makers have expanded the practice of their art through other media by literally incorporating other media in their work as well as by redefining their creative practice. Invested in "resensibilising perception," they made use of "techniques of fragmentation, juxtaposition, repetition, duplication, speeding up, and slowing down in order to emphasize and intensify the experience of the continuity of the performance itself" (Kattenbelt 35). With the end of the "Gutenberg Galaxy" and the advent of newer communication technologies, "the mode of perception is shifting: a simultaneous and multi-perspectival form of perceiving is replacing the linear-successive" (Lehmann, *Postdramatisches Theater* 16). As the linearity and unity of dramatic representation begins to break apart or disappears altogether, attention is drawn in new ways to how the spectator makes sense of what happens on stage. Erika Fischer-Lichte (in an article aptly titled "Discovering the Spectator," reprinted in her *The Show and the Gaze*) similarly observes how in the avant-garde theatre of the twentieth century the interaction between stage and auditorium increasingly becomes the focus of interest.

Elsewhere I have elaborated on how these developments observed by Hans-Thies Lehmann, Fischer-Lichte, and others draw attention to visuality as a culturally specific and embodied phenomenon (Bleeker, *Visuality in the Theatre*). In this text I will focus on movement as the object of perception and thought. Starting from Yvonne Rainer's work from the 1960s (and Carry Lambert-Beatty's excellent reading of this work), I will show how choreographers as phenomenologists draw attention to movement as a matter of what Brian Massumi has termed "lived abstraction." With this expression Massumi describes how the concrete and the abstract converge in the constitution of experience.[2] Movement never *is* at any one moment. It exists in continuous transformation and must be lived through in a succession of impressions. Yet to become an object of perception, movement has to be abstracted out of the succession of impressions in which it is experienced because movement is always more than the individual impressions. Lambert-Beatty's analysis of Yvonne Rainer's *Trio A* (1966), as well as other works by her, draw attention to how Rainer's work confronts spectators with the characteristics of movement as an object of perception. Rainer confronts spectators with the fact that "Dance is hard to see" (qtd. in Lambert-Beatty 1). The ways in which she does so, I will show, point to how movement is a phenomenon of lived abstraction. Abstraction here does not mean disembodiment but refers to the difference between the immediate experience of concrete feelings and sensations of living bodies and what is abstracted out of these experiences. Abstraction allows making a distinction between movement as immediately felt and experienced, and movement as an object of perception and thought, and allows making this distinction without erasing the important relation between the two. Abstraction, I will argue, is also the point of connection between the rise of media culture, transformations of the practice of choreography, and choreographers becoming phenomenologists.

MOVEMENT, MEDIA, AND ABSTRACTION

In *Dance Film: Choreography and the Moving Image*, Erin Brannigan traces the relationship between dance and cinema from the very beginning of modern dance and shows cinema to be a structural influence and a key reference for twentieth-century dance. She shows how the work of Loïe Fuller and Isadora Duncan is expressive of concerns, aims and fascinations similar to those expressed in early cinema as discussed by Gilles Deleuze in his *Cinema* books. Brannigan thus challenges the centrality of cinema in relation to the kinetics of modernity and points to the importance of taking into account dance as expression of and reflection on the cultural transformations discussed by Henri Bergson and Deleuze. In *Moving Without a Body: Digital Philosophy and Choreographic Thought*, Stamatia Portanova also takes us back to early cinema and the beginning of modern dance and how both emerge as sites of experimentation with a new understanding of movement. She points to the relationship between the idea of movement as continuous flow and that of movement "intended not as a form composable from preexisting immobile poses (such as with ballet)," but as "infinitely decomposable into 'mobile sections' or images" (Portanova 21). She thus draws attention to the connection between the continuity of movement as it found its expression in early modern dance and early cinema, and the "intuitive logic of the cut."[3]

The logic of the cut is integral to how recording media, from photography and film to audio tape and video to the digital camera, cut what is captured out of the continuity of that which it is part and allow what is captured to be played back, combined, and recombined. This logic would become central to the development of montage in film and, in more recent times, gain even more prominence with the rise of digital culture. This logic, Portanova observes, requires a rethinking of what movement itself is and in particular the relationship between movement, the concrete physical body, and abstraction.

The relation between movement as sensation and movement as abstraction is the basis for Deleuze's explanation of how the technology of cinema, and in particular the moving camera and montage, mediate new modes of thinking space, time, and movement. The moving camera and montage transformed cinema from a technology to show images of bodies moving into a technology to create what Deleuze calls *movement-images* and *time-images*. In watching film, Deleuze argues, our sensorimotor schemata make it possible to grasp the continuity of movement and actions shown on screen. We are capable of grasping the movement of, for example, a character on screen as a continuity unfolding over time because of how we bring to bear our sensorimotor schemata—as they are also constitutive of how we enact perception in everyday life—on what is depicted in the image. Film, however, can also make us perceive movements that are not shown. This potential of film would become important with the discovery of the moving camera and montage. For example, when a camera moves through a room, we see an image of an immobile room while we perceive the movement of the camera. We perceive movement while we do not see a body moving in the image. Here too our sensorimotor schemata are instrumental in understanding the logic of the successive sensory impressions. In perceiving a succession of images from different points of view, our sensorimotor schemata make it possible to grasp connections between them as the effect of movements that we actually abstract out of the images. Our experience with the effects of movement and changing points of view makes it possible to follow the changing point of view of the moving camera or to grasp the logic of the cuts and jumps of montage and abstract the movement of the point of view out of the succession of images.

The mobile camera and montage demonstrate how we are capable of interpreting changes in point of view, and even cuts from one point of view to the next, in terms of movement, and thus how we are capable of abstracting movement out of images that *do not depict* this movement. This capacity is given in the structure of our embodiment. The technology of cinema takes this possibility in new directions and this way, cinema allows for time and space to unfold in new ways. Mediatization, therefore, starting with cinema and increasingly so in our current digital times, requires a rethinking of an understanding of movement as a continuity as it points to an implicit tendency already present in movement, namely "motion as a multiplicity of potential cuts" (Portanova 3). Cinema and other recording media allow recordings of movement to literally be cut and recombined. This possibility, Deleuze explains, makes it possible for cinema to take us along in new kinds of movements: movements that are not shown in the image but result from how the montage takes viewers along by means of a succession of cut out sections ("mobile sections"). Movements perceived in watching a cinematic montage are not a matter of continuous motion shown in the image but result from how mobile sections have been cut out and are combined. In our perceptual encounter with montage, these movements have to be abstracted out of the immediate sensory impression evoked by the succession of cinematic images.

Deleuze explains how this invites a rethinking of movement in cinema towards an understanding of movement not merely as something that can be shown in images but also as emerging from how cinema takes us along in perception. This new understanding points to movement as a radical relational phenomenon: an abstraction that emerges from the relation between the cinematic images and the perceiver.[4] Rainer's work demonstrates that this capacity for abstraction that is so crucial to how cinema mediates in new modes of perceiving movement is actually also part of how we perceive movement that happens right in front of our eyes. In order to become an object of perception, movement has to be abstracted out of the continuity of direct sensory impressions, and this requires a logic similar to what Portanova calls the logic of the cut.

SCULPTING SPECTATORSHIP

The prevalent interpretation of Rainer's work has been that it is all about the body of the performer and that she, as Roger Copeland (commenting on *Trio A*) puts it, "remains coolly oblivious to this watching" (qtd. in Lambert-Beatty 7). However, Lambert-Beatty observes: "Rainer's area of exploration in the 1960s was not exactly 'things in themselves' but things-in-themselves *to watch.* Eyeing this difference, I have come to see Rainer as not only a shaper of dances and a mover of bodies but a sculptor of spectatorship" (9).

In *Watching Dance*, Lambert-Beatty shows that the site of Rainer's most crucial interventions in the 1960s was not the body of the performer but the relationship between this body and the eye of the viewer. Rainer engages with the difficulty of seeing dance as an artistic problem, and the various artistic strategies she uses have to be understood from how they are means of sculpting spectatorship. Like Merce Cunningham before, she removed from dance performance story, character, and emotional expression. On top of that, she also resisted everything that could mark the dancer's body and its movements as extraordinary, like special clothing and virtuoso movements. Rainer describes the movement quality she was looking for as task-like and had her dancers develop this quality by interacting with simple objects like for example mattresses. She also does not want her performances to be understood as expression of emotions or artistic intentions of a maker, as associated with Modern Dance of Wigman, Graham, and others.

These strategies are not (as has been assumed) meant to deny or undo the fact of showing but instead highlight this condition. As Lambert-Beatty rightly observes: "[d]isplaying the moving body for you without any attempt to seduce or affirm you does not remove dance from the condition of exhibition, after all. It reduces the performance situation to the fact of display" (8). Reduced to the fact of display, Rainer's performances draw attention to what happens in seeing movement. In particular, they draw attention to "the difficulty of seeing and understanding an ephemeral art that moved through time" (Lambert-Beatty 107).

Lambert-Beatty shows how this difficulty of seeing dance is a central motive in Rainer's work that manifests itself in different, sometimes even opposed choreographic strategies:

> As Rainer saw it, an artist who acknowledged this difficulty had two options. She could try to make performance less ephemeral, as she herself had done in 1961, when in her dance *The Bells* she repeated a short sequence of movement while facing different directions "in a sense allowing the spectator to 'walk around it" like an object. Or she could exaggerate the problem of dance's disappearance, as she had just done with an elided continuum of unique movements in what would become her most famous dance (which is *Trio A*, MB) (1).

These choreographic strategies can be considered ways of sculpting spectatorship in that they are about making movement appear as an object of perception and question how movement is seen, or not seen. Rainer's strategies of sculpting spectatorship confront the audience with the difficulty of actually perceiving movement and direct attention to the perception of movement as a phenomenological problem, that is to say, one that addresses the ways in which we constitute the world from what we experience of it.

By repeating sequences of movement while facing different directions, for example, she allows movement to be perceived both by hindering what happens in these processes and by highlighting that. Repeating sequences of movement while facing different directions "in a sense allowing the spectator to (imaginarily) 'walk around it'" like an object, as in *The Bells*, she allows movement to be perceived in an object-like way. At the same time she draws attention to the difference between such perception of movement and our usual modes of perceiving movement. In other works, and most famously in *Trio A*, she exaggerates the problem of dance's continuous disappearance by means of strategies that aim to prevent the spectator from recognizing its components as part of phrases and larger structures.

In an essay written in the same year, she observes that in a typical dance phrase "there is always maximal output or 'attack' at the beginning of a phrase, recovery at the end, with energy arrested somewhere in the middle" (qtd. in Lambert-Beatty 133). In dances constructed according to this principle "one part of the phrase—usually the part that is most still—becomes the focus of attention" (33). In *Trio A*, Rainer sought to prevent such reading by means of a phraseless continuum of movements, an inorganic continuity, and thus destabilize the constitution of discrete movements as objects of perception. Lambert-Beatty quotes Jean Nuchtern's review of *Trio A* for the *Soho Weekly News* in 1976, in which Nuchtern attempts to re-create the effect for her readers in typographical terms:

Thereisnopartofthisarticlethatisanymoreimportantthananyotherpart eachwordsentenceparagraphcarriesthesameweightasanyotherandits smoothnessliesnotonlyintheequalweightednessofeachwordsentence- andparagraphbutinthejuxtapositionofoneparagraphtoanotherwhich- causesthereaderreacttothearticleasawholeratherthanassegments.

(qtd. in Lambert-Beatty 133–134)

Similarly, in *Trio A* movements follow one another without being organized in phrases. The result is continuous motion that at the same time is hard to perceive precisely as discrete movements.

THE RELATIONALITY OF PERCEPTION

Rainer undertook her explorations in close collaboration with other artists, some of them dancers, others visual artists, among them well-known minimalist sculptors like Robert Morris. At first glance, it may seem that, with their object being sculpture and not dance, their artistic problem has to be quite different from Rainer's difficulty of seeing and understanding an ephemeral art that moves through time. A closer look however reveals that notwithstanding the differences, they meet in a shared engagement with spectatorship, rather than a material object, as that which is sculpted. Using simple shapes, often prefab materials, avoiding signs of "artistic handwriting," and limiting themselves to geometrical compositions, the works of these sculptors aimed to prevent an understanding of these objects as autonomous art and instead drew attention to the relation between the object and the context, between the object and the viewer.

These works, Rosalind Krauss explains, defy the idea that the meaning of a shape is to be found in its abstractness or separability, in its detachment from an actual situation, in the possibility that we can transfer it intact from one place to another (239). Instead they demonstrate a sensibility she compares to Merleau-Ponty's phenomenological approach: they draw attention to how what the work is comes into being as a result of our perceptual engagement with it. For this reason, Krauss argues, they mark a turning point in what she describes as "a reformulation of the sculptural enterprise" (242). Throughout the twentieth century, she observes, sculpture has been in the process of reinventing itself. This can be seen reflected in fundamental transformations in what is considered the object of sculpture: from an autonomous understanding towards a relational one. Minimalist sculpture—drawing attention to the constitutive flow of experience and the relationality of perception as fundamental to what the work is—marks a turning point in this reformulation.[5]

In the "reformulation of the sculptural enterprise," theatricality played an important role as "an operational divide between the sculptural object and the preconceptions about knowledge that the viewer might have about both it and himself" (Krauss 240). Theatricality emerged as a means to destabilize seemingly self-evident modes of perceiving and trigger reflection about what actually the object of sculpture is, how we know it, and what it means to know it (Krauss 242). Krauss refers to Michael Fried's (in)famous text "Art and Objecthood," in which he uses theatricality to criticize Minimalist art (or Literalist art as he calls it) for how it addresses the spectator in ways that make the spectator aware of her being implicated in her perception of the work. He opposes this experience to that of modern art characterized by instantaneousness and what he calls *presentness*. "Presentness is grace," reads the final line of his text, for presentness lifts us above the perverted "theatrical" mode of being we are confined to most of our lives (Fried, *Art and Objecthood* 147).

Fried's anti-theatrical prejudice is not directed against the theatre per se. In his usage, theatricality does not denote the essence, or even a quality of the theatre as an art form. Instead he uses theatricality to describe "the wrong sort of consciousness of an audience" as he puts it in a 1987 review of his 1967 essay. What is wrong about it is that:

> The beholder knows himself in an indeterminate, open ended—and unexacting—relation *as subject* to the impassive object on the wall or floor. In fact, being distanced by such objects is not, I suggest, entirely unlike being distanced by the silent presence of another *person*; the

experience of coming upon literalist objects unexpectedly [...] can be strongly, if momentarily, disquieting in just this way.

(Fried, "Theories of Art" 128)

Theatricality here manifests itself as the effect of how, in response to the address presented by the work, Fried begins to make a distinction between self and self-as-spectator. Making this distinction is not a matter of a deliberate choice but the result of the address presented to him by the artwork.[6] His account of his own experience shows how this address undermines the appearance of the artwork as autonomous. Instead, his attention is directed to how the work comes to exist for him as spectator and how he is *implicated* in his perception of the work.

Both Krauss and Lambert-Beatty point to the shared sensibilities of Minimalist sculpture and the kind of dance developed by Rainer and other Judson Church dance makers. However, there is also an important difference. Aspiring to the condition of sculpture, Rainer's choreographies expose something about how objects come to exist for us that is easily overlooked in the work of the sculptors. In many Minimalist sculptures, the movement of the spectator (like walking around an object, or through it in case of an installation) draws attention to the fact that the way an object appears to us depends on our relation to it, and that this relation unfolds in time. Yet, since these movements happen in relation to a fixed object, it is still possible to understand these successive appearances as ever-partial perceptions of a world that is posited to preexist these perceptions. Rainer's choreographies—where the object is movement—make clear that such objective existence is not prior to appearance but instead can only be constituted in the process of appearing.

Rainer's choreographies draw attention to how we perceive movement and do so by means of strategies that destabilize what in phenomenology is referred to as the natural attitude in which consciousness is directed towards the world and things, and in which the existence of the world is taken for granted. In her modes of sculpting spectatorship theatricality functions as a kind of phenomenological bracketing similarly to Krauss's description of the "operational divide" between artwork and viewing subject in Minimalist art. Theatricality is used to highlight the relationship between perceiver and perceived, to how the work comes to exist for a spectator, and in so doing performs a task that is central to phenomenology. Phenomenology investigates how the world is grasped as receiving its sense in and through experience. This does not mean that the world is only a projection of consciousness, or that the phenomenological reduction would be a solipsistic or subjectivist move, nor does it mean that phenomenology would bring us to understanding of how the world comes to exist for us as the result of features of our embodiment only. The constitution of the objective world, Joona Taipale points out: "has two irreducible constitutive sources: world constitution is bound to the embodied abilities of the individual members of the intersubjective community on the one hand, and to a generative inherited normality on the other" (15). The relationship between them is one of "normative tension:" "As it is gradually appropriated, the normality of the tradition gains a normative status, which means that the tradition comes to orient our experiences and actions from within: culture becomes our 'second nature'" (Taipale 161).[7] I argue that choreographies of Rainer and others draw attention to this second nature, in particular the ways in which this second nature takes shape in interaction with media technology and mediatization.

INTENTIONALITY VS. IMPLICATION

Lambert-Beatty observes that, "a key aspect of the historicity of Rainer's work is the complexity with which it engages mass media spectatorship—even though (or especially because) this was not often a consciously intended effect" (11). She mentions the rise of television culture and increased awareness of television broadcasting as a mode of sculpting spectatorship that makes us participate in a seeing that is not ours. Media sculpt spectatorship for us. She also mentions the ubiquity of recording technologies in the postwar area and how audio recording emerged as a means not only to record but also to reorder sound and music; how this mediated in new ways of structuring and perceiving time, and how this appeared as a means of structuring the experience of a listener. And she refers to an essay in which Rainer opposes what she describes as the photographic tendency in dance. Rainer describes these tendencies as "getting from one point of still registration to another" and observes how the unmoving center of the dance phrase seems frozen before the viewer's eyes "registering like a photograph or suspended moment of climax" (qtd. in Lambert-Beatty 133). For Rainer, these kinds of dances, like photographs, direct attention to focal moments and to an understanding of movement as structured around such moments.

Rainer's essay, as well as her attempt to prevent her choreographies from having these photographic tendencies, can be usefully situated in Deleuze's account of cinema. Deleuze's starting point was Bergson's critique in *Creative Evolution* of how movement has come to be imagined in modern times in terms of a trajectory of positions within space as a stable and unitary container. Movement is thus "understood" by adding to these positions in space the abstract idea of a succession. However, Bergson observes, what is absent from such a series of instants is actually precisely movement. He mentions as an example the photographic experiments of Muybridge, who attempted to capture movement by means of a succession of still images (Deleuze, *Movement Image* 5).

Deleuze observes a close connection between Bergson's philosophy of movement in terms of flow and duration and the simultaneous emergence of cinema. Deleuze also notes that similar reconfigurations of movement can be observed in other arts and here he is explicitly referring to dance, ballet, and mime. Dance, in his text, figures both as an example of what he (after Bergson) calls the ancient understanding of movement, and as an example of how modernity moves beyond such understanding and towards an understanding of movement in terms of flow and duration. In the ancient understanding, movement is understood in terms of a succession of poses or instants. These instants "are supposed [...] to characterize a period of which they express the quintessence, all the rest of this period being filled by the transition, of no interest in itself, from one to another form (Bergson qtd. in Deleuze, *Movement Image* 4).

Bergson sees this understanding continued in cinema as a technology that produces the illusion of movement by means of a succession of static images. Deleuze takes these ideas from Bergson as his starting point but disagrees with Bergson's rejection of cinema as producing merely an illusion of movement. The new modes of thinking movement made possible by cinema are not a matter of cinema's capacity to depict movement (to show images of movement), nor to present an illusion of movement by means of a succession of still images (as Bergson argues), but of how cinema affords movement to become an object of perception in new ways. This is what makes the movement image different from images like those of Muybridge. Muybridge's images invite us to imagine the movements performed by the body seen in the image. They invite us to fill in the movement that is not shown to produce an illusion of movement. The novelty of cinema is that the moving camera and montage take us along in movements that we do not see, nor fill in, but abstract out of what we see. With this explanation, Deleuze directs attention away from cinema as a means to show or represent movement towards cinema as a mode of sculpting spectatorship.

This capacity for abstraction is fundamental to how media shape spectatorship and how viewers are able to make sense of what media presents to them. Yet, the perceptual possibility to abstract objects of perception out of a continuity of impressions is given in the structure of our embodiment and did not come with the invention of cinema. With her modes of sculpting spectatorship in dance, Rainer shows that abstraction is also part of how we perceive movement that is not mediatized but happens in front of our eyes. She does so precisely by interfering with this process of abstraction, subverting it. She places the moving body in full view, and all that could distract from seeing movement is taken away. And yet, even then (or, precisely then) movement appears to be difficult to see—difficult because the movements in her choreography lack the kind of logic that would afford abstraction to proceed easily. Movements that are clearly phrased are much easier to perceive as movement because the phrasing supports abstracting the movement as an object of perception from the continuity of impressions.

Rainer as a choreographer becoming phenomenologist destabilizes the natural attitude in which we take for granted that we perceive movement as continuity because it is there. The problem with which her audience finds itself confronted is not to fill in movement that is not there (as Muybridge's photographs invite to do) but to perceive the continuity of movement that is there. Her work invites a reconsideration of an intuitive understanding of movement as continuity and points toward what Portanova terms "the intuitive logic of the cut." This logic would become more and more important with the rise of media culture. However, Rainer's phraseless compositions point to the fact that the dialectic of the continuity of movement and the logic of the cut is actually also part of how we perceive movement that is not mediatized. Her phenomenology of movement thus confirms Mark Hansen's observation that new technological developments "foreground the constitutive or ontological role of the body in giving birth to the world" (5). The modes of sculpting spectatorship made possible by the technology of cinema foreground aspects of our bodily capacities for perceiving movement and takes these in new directions. This does not mean that therefore the way cinema shows movement is something more natural than, for example Muybridge's chronophotography. Rather, the way cinema expands on our bodies' capacities for perception makes us aware of these capacities in ways we were not before and makes us aware of how the way in which these capacities give shape to perception is *triggered from the outside*.

Rainer's choreographies draw attention to perception as something that is not only a matter of our bodily capacities intentionally directed towards the world but also of how this outside *affords* interaction. The term affordance was introduced by Gibson to describe the ways in which environments hold the potential for actions.[8] Nowadays, the term is used in a diversity of fields, including cognitive psychology, design, media theory, and philosophy of technology. Rainer's modes of sculpting spectatorship point to the role of affordances in perception: how the way in which movement is structured affords modes of perceiving it. With *Trio A* she makes us aware that movement, even when performed fully visible right in front of us, is a phenomenon of lived abstraction. In order to become objects of perception, movements have to be abstracted out of the continuity of sensory impressions and how they will be abstracted out (or not) depends not only on the intention of the perceiver but also on how that which this perceiver engages affords abstraction.

Trio A thus suggests that understanding how our perception of movement comes into being involves understanding of perception as something that is (at least partly) implicated in what we encounter. This does not mean that modes of perceiving are imposed on us by someone. The world does not sculpt spectatorship the way the technology of cinema does. Nevertheless, the way in which media technologies (of cinema as well as newer developments) build on our capacities for abstraction of movement alert us to the fact that what we perceive is neither simply the world as it is, nor the product of our intentional directedness towards the world, but emerges from the interaction between our capacity for perception and how what we encounter affords our engagement with it. And Rainer's work shows how in this context choreography emerges as a means to explore and investigate the implications of what Bernard Stiegler, Hansen, Katherine Hayles, and others describe as "technogenesis:" the co-evolution of humans and technology.[9] Such an exploration becomes all the more important now that technological possibilities to capture, store, and manipulate movement abstracted from the body and transformed into a data flow can activate new kinds of physical, mental, technical, and creative processes. Rainer's denaturalization of the natural attitude, making us aware that how we perceive movement is (at least partly) implicated within that which is the object of our perceptual engagement, also points to how mediatization sets the stage for new encounters between the fields of phenomenology and process philosophy. In particular media developments draw attention to perception as a matter of prehending relationships and differences as a result of which entities and occasions are abstracted out of the continuity of impressions.

REFORMULATION OF THE CHOREOGRAPHIC ENTERPRISE

Rainer's choreographies that addressed these processes of abstracting mark a turning point in a reformulation of the choreographic enterprise analogous to the reformulation of the sculptural enterprise observed by Krauss. As is the case with the reformulation of the sculptural enterprise, this involves a transformation of what is considered the object of, in this case, the choreographic enterprise. This transformation manifests itself in an expansion of the kind of movements that can be the object of choreography, to include movements not performed but abstracted from what is presented on stage.

This does not mean that prior to this reformulation the term choreography was used to describe only one clearly defined practice and is used to describe another clearly defined practice afterwards. The term choreography, as Susan Foster shows, has been used in different places and times to describe different practices and is currently used as referent for a structuring of movements of various kinds, human and non-human. The reformulation that is the subject of this text describes a specific transformation: one in which choreography as the structuring of movement begins to engage with movement as lived abstraction, and include this in what is the object of choreography. Similar to Krauss's observations on sculpture, this reformulation also entails the emergence of new understandings of how we can know this object as a radical relational phenomenon.

As is the case with sculpture, this reformulation did not happen overnight but was the result of a development over time, which can be traced back to shared fascinations of dance, technology, and philosophy since the early days of modern dance, and how these meet with a fascination with the kind of movement dance can be about and "what is moving about movement" (Whitley) that have also been important for dance makers since the late nineteenth century. Resisting the tradition of ballet, they started to develop alternative modes of working that included their own movement languages.

At that time Foster observes, the term choreography came to name "the creative act of formulating new movement to express a personal and universal concern" (45), and this new understanding of choreography was supported by the emergence of a new kind of dance pedagogy that promoted exploration of the body's kinesthetic responsiveness, as well as an understanding of dance as translation of emotional experience into external form. Instead of assuming the image of the correct position (or pose, in Bergson and Deleuze's terms), students now were stimulated to investigate their own impulses to move, to improvise, and to understand movement as malleable material that can be reshaped and reformed.

In this context and in relation to these practices John Martin presented his *Introduction to the Dance* as a theoretical account of what these dances are about in terms of movement and feeling. Dance for Martin is essentially movement, and this centrality of movement pertains not only to that what is seen on stage. Movement, Martin argues, is central to our ways of responding to what we see. Martin describes how looking involves an active "mimicking" of what is seen, in which the motor responses of the body seeing connect this experience to previous experiences and thus awaken earlier sense perceptions and the feelings, emotions, expectations, and so on related to them. In this process, movement sense receptors play a role that Martin describes in terms that seem to anticipate Merleau-Ponty's much later philosophical elaborations, as well as the discovery of mirror neurons and enactive approaches to perception like those of Alain Berthoz and Alva Noë's.[10] Martin develops his theory at the same time that cinema is becoming the new potential for movement that is the subject of Deleuze's *Cinema* books in which he too observes that "all perception is primarily sensori-motor perception" (*Movement Image* 64).

When we are watching dance, Martin famously claims: "We cease to be mere spectators and become participants in the movement that is presented to us, and though to all outward appearances we shall be sitting quietly in our chairs, we shall nevertheless be dancing synthetically with all our musculature" (53). In Martin, this moving along is part of his explanation of movement as (to speak with Foster) an expression of a personal and universal concern. He understands these movements of the spectator as a means to relate to the emotions and feeling expressed by the artist in the choreography. The moving along, therefore, is not itself considered to be part of what the choreography is about. This changes with Rainer. In her work, what is the object of choreography shifts from a focus on what is shown and seen on stage to include the abstractions performed in perceiving. Rainer's work and that of the Judson Church therefore marks a turning point in this development in how it invites an expansion of our understanding that the object of choreography is to include also movement that is not performed but is abstracted out of what is presented.

Rainer's work engages with these questions through "a challenge to attentiveness" (Lambert-Beatty 98). In *Trio A* this challenge resulted from the phraseless composition. In *Parts of Some Sextets*, she used continuous, simultaneous task-like movements, changing abruptly according to a rigid time structure to create a dance that was, in her own words, "completely visible at all times but also very difficult to follow and get involved with" (qtd. in Lambert-Beatty 98). The result was an attentional structure that, in the words of Lambert-Beatty:

> though full of cuts, [...] was without montage. Its principles were interruption—movements cut off on the thirty-second cue–and repetition–the same movement recurring time and again, on different bodies [...] *Parts of Some Sextet* did not flow, but neither did it leap. It had no correlate for the editorial process that allows film to go beyond the "real time" of the moving bodies or scenes it depicts, but it did stack those actualities together in a sequence (107).

Although Rainer is explicitly deploying the logic of the cut, the way she does so prevents the smooth abstraction usually afforded by filmic montage. The result was a structure "built on continuous stopping" (Lambert-Beatty 107).

This principle of stopping is a recurring choreographic strategy in Rainer's work and that of her Judson Church colleagues. Surprisingly here, Muybridge's work, rejected by Bergson for how it fails to capture movement, returns as an image of suspension, stuttering, and discontinuity, as well as an inspiration for the seriality so characteristic of minimalist sculpture. For Dan Graham, Muybridge's visualizations of moving bodies offers an alternative to the idea of temporal flow: in these images "things don't happen; they merely replace themselves in space" (qtd. in Lambert-Beatty 114). Robert Morris used Muybridge images in the performance *Waterman Switch*, which he performed together with Rainer. Early in the piece, the audience witnessed Morris running in circles while hearing a tape recording of his voice saying: "I hope eventually to have slides made of this dance. Perhaps if anyone is photographing now they will let me know later. I will then show the slides of this section, for example, near the beginning" (qtd. in Lambert-Beatty 117).

A media recording thus invites the audience to perform the logic of the cut characteristic of media recording and to imagine how using these cut-out moments will transform future performances. The performance consists in how the audience is invited to abstract out of the performance the fact that they are witnessing a future performance that includes slides of the performance they are seeing now. The actual movements performed on stage are only the starting point for a choreography that unfolds through how the audience is invited to abstract future performances out of imagined media specific mediations of the movements performed.

"[I]s it possible for choreography to generate autonomous expressions of its principles, a choreographic object, without the body?" wonders William Forsythe in his essay "Choreographic Objects," written four decades after

Trio A. He observes that historically choreography has been indivisible from the human body in action. However, he asks: "Are we perhaps at the point in the evolution of choreography where a distinction between the establishment of its ideas and its traditional forms of enactment must be made?" In the time that has passed since *Trio A*, choreographers have explored a great number of strategies to incorporate in their choreographies movements that are not enacted by bodies. The examples are too numerous to mention, but one might think of Anne Teresa de Keersmaker's *Fase* (1982), in which minimalist strategies of repetition, sometimes in phase, at other times gradually shifting out of phase, redirect attention from the movements performed themselves to the gradually transforming patterns and shapes produced by them. Or Jonathan Burrows and Matteo Fargion's duet *Both Sitting* (2002) in which they perform, both sitting, the score of Morton Feldman's *For John Cage* by means of small repetitive hand and arm gestures that convey not only the movements we see them perform but also how these movements take us along in the much more abstract movement that the musical score is about. Or Ivana Müller's *While We Were Holding It Together*, a choreography in which six performers do not move for almost an hour in a performance that is nevertheless emphatically about movement generated in perception. Or Forsythe's CD ROM *Improvisation Technologies*, which elaborates a logic of spatial relationships that requires dancers to simultaneously execute movement and undertake a process of abstraction in which the movement performed becomes something related to as an idea.

Through the inclusion of movements that are not performed on stage, these choreographies (and many others with them) invite a further rethinking of movement as object of perception and thought. With his essay on "Choreographic Objects" Forsythe shows how this has resulted in radically new approaches to choreography. Beyond that, with his proposal to conceive of choreography in terms of a choreographic object, Forsythe invites a reconsideration not only of what choreography is about, how it relates to movement and what kind of movement, but also beyond that: what objects are and how they relate to movement.

"Choreographic Objects" is made available on the website of *Synchronous Objects* on which one can explore the outcome of an interdisciplinary research that aimed to answer the question "What else can physical thinking look like?" (which is actually a question posed in the essay "Choreographic Objects"). The website offers 22 different visualizations of aspects of Forsythe's choreography *One Flat Thing, reproduced*.[11] These visualizations are based upon two sets of data: spatial data taken from a video recording of a performance of the choreography and attribute data gleaned from dancers' accounts. Each visualization deals with a different aspect of the organizational structures of *One Flat Thing, reproduced* as it can be derived from these sets of data. These organizational structures are turned into visualizations that show how these structural principles develop over time. What is visualized, therefore, is not bodies, nor the movement of the individual dancers (although some of the visualizations do include recordings of the dancers), but aspects of the structure of the performance as it unfolds over time.

The performance is thus shown as source of potential abstractions. Each abstraction is a kind of grasping of sets of relationships as they develop over time. Like for example, the Cue Score, a graph showing the cues given and received between dancers over time. Or the Motion Volume Visualization that shows a visualization of the outer edge of the dancers' motions transformed into volumes that emerge and disappear over time. Or the Movement Density Map, showing how much time dancers spent in any location during the execution of the choreography and how this develops during the performance. Together, the 22 visualizations of *Synchronous Objects* show the choreography as an object that can be known under a potentially endless number of aspects and that therefore it can never be known in its totality. With this proposal to conceive of choreography in terms of a choreographic object, Forsythe invites a reconsideration not only of what choreography is about, and how it relates to movement, but beyond that, what objects are and how they relate to movement. *Synchronous Objects* shows how the choreography *One Flat Thing, reproduced* appears as an object depending on how this object is abstracted out of the continuous unfolding and how this unfolding affords abstractions. *Synchronous Objects* suggests that a phenomenology of the object in the digital age should start from movement as lived abstraction.

NOTES

1. Web. 31 July 2014. <http://themeasurestaken.com/about.php>.
2. In *Semblance and Event*, Massumi explains abstraction as "a technique of extracting the relational-qualitiative arc of one occasion of experience—its subjective form—and systematically depositing it in the world for the next occasion to find, and to potentially take up into its own formation" (15). From this perspective, what we call objects are actually lived relations. He quotes Deleuze, observing that "The abstract is lived experience. I would almost say that once you have reached lived experience, you reach the most fully living core of the abstract […] You can live nothing but the abstract and nobody·has lived anything else but the abstract" (qtd. in Massumi 15). *Technologies of Lived Abstraction* is also the title of a book series edited by Massumi and Erin Manning with the MIT P. The Book Proposal is available at <http://static.squarespace.com/static/51fda0f4e4b024582fd94132/t/5242743ee4b0c4a5c2a2b0fa/1380086846724/Book%20Series%20Proposal.doc.>. Web. 31 July 2014. pdf.
3. The idea of the intuitive logic of the cut is fundamental to Portanova's argument throughout her book *Moving Without a Body*. The expression is also the second part of the second chapter of the book: "Digital Abstractions: The Intuitive Logic of the Cut."
4. This understanding of relationality distinguishes itself from what Nicolas Bourriaud has termed "relational aesthetics," a type of art that he himself defines as "a set of artistic practices which take as their theoretical and practical

point of departure the whole of human relations and their social context, rather than an independent and private space" (113). Relationality as I use it here is not a type of esthetics but describes the fact that nothing exists in itself but only within relations, and can only be known from within relations.
5. Krauss refers to Lessing's famous categorization of the arts in his *Laocoön*. Lessing attempts to define norms (or objective criteria as he understands them) by which to understand the essential differences between different art forms, and this brings him to his definition of sculpture as essentially an art concerned with the deployment of bodies in space. The underlying premise of Krauss study of twentieth-century sculpture is that even in a spatial art like sculpture, space and time cannot be separated, and that this is precisely what the development of twentieth-century sculpture draws attention to.
6. Useful here is the distinction made by Tracy Davis ("Theatricality and Civil Society"), between theatrical (referring a characteristic of what is perceived: to something being of the theatre or like the theatre) and theatricality, describing a communicative affect that emerges from a situation in which a spectator takes a certain distance and begins to distinguish between actor, role, and situation; self and other; and between self and self-as-actor or spectator. This can be the result of a conscious choice on the part of the spectator (comparable by what Camp after Feral argues, elsewhere in this volume), but also the effect of the address presented to a spectator, as it happens as I will argue in Rainer's work. For a further elaboration of this understanding of theatricality, see Bleeker "Theatres of/or Truth."
7. In our encounter with others, our own body as our primordial centre of orientation is constituted as "over there" for others. This way, through others, we constitute ourselves as intersubjective objects in the world and our system of orientation as one standpoint among others. "[T]his does not imply that the other's system of orientation is constituted as the absolute point of reference, to which our system is relative: we still perceive this alien standpoint from our point of view, and only in relation to it does the alien standpoint have a sense to us as such"(Taipale 157). These two are normative poles at work in each concrete experience and the relationship between them provides a perspective on how normality and normativity orient our experiences from within and reveal themselves in our experiences, actions, and particular ways of being.
8. Gibson introduced this idea in "Theory of Affordances" and further elaborated this idea in his *The Ecological Approach to Visual Perception* (Boston, MA: Houghton Mifflin, 1979).
9. Hayles, N. Katherine. *How We Think. Digital Media and Contemporary Technogenesis*. Chicago and London: Chicago UP, 2012; Hansen, Mark. *Embodying Technogenesis. Technology Beyond Writing*. Ann Arbor: U of Michigan P, 2003; Hansen, Mark. B.N. *Bodies in Code*. New York and London: Routledge, 2006; Stiegler, Bernard. *Technics and Time 1: The Fault of Epimetheus*. Trans. Richard Beardsworth and George Collins. Stanford: Stanford UP, 1998; Stiegler, Bernard. *Technics and Time 2: Disorientation*. Trans. Stephen Barker. Stanford: Stanford UP, 2009; Stiegler, Bernard. *Technics and Time 3: Cinematic Time and the Question of Malaises*. Trans. Stephen Barker. Stanford: Stanford UP, 2011.
10. Berthoz, Alain. *The Brain's Sense of Movement*. Trans. Giselle Weiss. Cambridge, Mass.: Harvard UP, 2000; Alva Noë. *Action in Perception*. Cambridge, Mass.: MIT P, 2004.
11. Web. 20 Aug. 2014. <http://synchronousobjects.osu.edu/>.

WORKS CITED

Bergson, Henri. *Creative Evolution*. Trans. Arthur Mitchell. London: Macmillan Press, 1954.

Berthoz, Alain. *The Brain's Sense of Movement*. Trans. Giselle Weiss. Cambridge, Mass.: Harvard UP, 2000.

Bleeker, Maaike. "Theatres of/or Truth". *Performance Paradigm* 2 (2007). <www.performanceparadigm.net>.

———. *Visuality in the Theatre: The Locus of Looking*. Basingstoke: Palgrave Macmillan, 2008.

Brannigan, Erin. Dancefilm. *Choreography and the Moving Image*. Oxford: Oxford UP, 2011.

Davis, Tracy. C. "Theatricality and Civil Society." Eds. Tracy Davis and Thomas Postlewait. *Theatricality*. Cambridge: Cambridge UP, 2003. 127–155.

Deleuze, Gilles. *Cinema 1: The Movement-Image*. Trans. Hugh Tomlinson and Barbara Habberjam. Minneapolis: U of Minnesota P, 1986.

———. *Cinema 2: The Time-Image*. Trans. Hugh Tomlinson and Robert Galeta. Minneapolis: U of Minnesota P, 1989.

Fischer-Lichte, Erika. *The Show and the Gaze of Theatre: A European Perspective*. Iowa City: U of Iowa P, 1997.

Forsythe, William. "Choreographic Objects." Web. 31 July 2014. <http://www.williamforsythe.de/essay>.

Foster, Susan Leigh. *Choreographing Empathy. Kinesthesia in Performance*. London: Routledge, 2011.

Fried, Michael. "Art and Objecthood." *Minimal Art, A Critical Anthology*. Ed. Gregory Battcock. New York: E.P.Dutton & Co. 1968. 116–147.

———. "Theories of Art After Minimalism and Pop." *Dia Art Foundation. Discussions in Contemporary Culture*. Ed. Hal Foster. Seattle: Bay Press. 1987. 55–58.

Gibson, J.J. "The Theory of Affordances." *Perceiving, Acting, and Knowing: Toward an Ecological Psychology*. Eds. Robert Shaw and John Bransford. Hillsdale NY: Erlbaum, 1977. 67–82.

Hansen, Mark B.N. *Bodies in Code*, New York and London: Routledge, 2006.

———. *Embodying Technogenesis. Technology Beyond Writing*. Ann Arbor: U of Michigan P, 2003.

Kattenbelt, Chief. "Intermediality in Performance as a Mode of Performativity." *Mapping Intermediality in Performance*. Eds. Sarah Bay-Cheng, Chiel Kattenbelt, Andy Lavender and Robin Nelson. Amsterdam: Amsterdam UP, 2010. 29–37.

Kavanagh, Julie. "The Choreographer as Phenomenologist." *Intelligent Life* May-June 2014:19.

Krauss, Rosalind. *Passages in Modern Sculpture*. Cambridge: MIT P, 1981.

Lambert-Beatty, Carrie. *Being Watched. Yvonne Rainer and the 1960s*. Cambridge: MIT P, 2008.

Lehmann, Hans-Thies. *Postdramatisches Theater*. Frankfurt am Main: Verlag der Autoren, 1999.

———. *Postdramatic Theatre*. London: Routledge, 2006.

Martin, John. *Introduction to the Dance*. A Dance Horizons republication. 1939. New York: W.W. Norton & Co, 1965.

Massumi, Brian. *Semblance and Event. Activist Philosophy and the Occurrent Arts*. Cambridge, Mass.: MIT P, 2011.

Portanova, Stamatia. *Moving Without a Body. Digital Philosophy and Choreographic Thoughts*. Cambridge: MIT P, 2013.
Taipale, Joona. *Phenomenology and Embodiment. Husserl and the Constitution of Subjectivity*. Evanston: Northwestern UP, 2014.

3   Process Phenomenologies
Susan Kozel

> *the idea that the thinking person has to be a kind of dead person on holiday is inseparable from the ancient European culture of rationality*
> (Sloterdijk 3)
>
> *I reach down into my handbag to take out my book so I can take some quick notes in the dark when suddenly the house lights come on.*
> (Srinivasan 160)
>
> *I could make something up.*
> *Do you want me to?*
> *It is so easy to surprise you.*
> (Lilja 30)
>
> *breadth of thought reacting with intensity of sensitive experience stands out as an ultimate claim of existence*
> (Whitehead qtd. in Sherburne 202)

Phenomenological reflection sets in motion a process of translating, transposing, or transgressing lived experience into writing. Usually writing, I should say. Sometimes a phenomenology first produces drawings, scribbles, murmurs, or gestures. Or a big blank of confusion. A nothing that is something.

My contribution to this collection on performance and phenomenology opens up a phase of the phenomenological process that is less polished, less complete, and almost always overlooked. I examine closely the transition from raw experience into scholarly writing. Occurring between live performance and philosophical presentation of text, it usually exists only in a performer's personal journals or notes shared with collaborators as part of a working process. It is an essential part of enacting a phenomenology, and is frequently what those new to this methodology miss when they seek to understand and implement it for themselves. Phenomenologies are not born whole and complete; they are rather uncooked and messy at first.

In revealing the intermediary space between raw motion or affect and academic writing, I confront the accusation that academic writing deadens, dampens, or diminishes experience into the accepted discourses academic research. Philosopher Peter Sloterdijk aptly characterizes the problem with the mode of writing most often used for scholarly journals, books, or catalogues as adopting the detached intellectual style of "a dead person on holiday." "Naturally," he elaborates, "we do not mean dead according to undertakers, but the philosophically dead who cast off their bodies and apparently become pure intellects or impersonal thinking souls" (Sloterdijk, *The Art of Philosophy* 3). Jean Luc Nancy identifies a similar problem, calling it "philosophical anaesthesia" (31).

Fine. So phenomenology, an embodied and situated methodology for conducting scholarly enquiry ideally suited to performance research, might help us overcome the dead-person-on-holiday problem. But there is more. My secondary intention for this chapter is to reveal the process of enacting a phenomenology and to locate this, not simply within the *work-in-process* phase of performance creation, but within a wider contemporary current of philosophy called *process philosophy*.[1] This implies that the interim phases of thinking, devising, and creation are significant parts of the phenomenological process at the same time as they are embedded in a wider philosophical movement. It also emphasizes a breadth of performative perspectives, not just that of the conventionally defined performer on stage. I suggest that a phenomenology itself is performed; it is not simply a methodology applied to performance.

> Process philosophy, explained in fairly simple terms, is an effort to think clearly and deeply about the obvious truth that our world and our lives are dynamic, interrelated processes and to challenge the apparently obvious, but fundamentally mistaken, idea that the world (including ourselves) is made of things that exist independently of such relationships and that seem to endure unchanged through all the processes of change.
> (Mesle 8)

Phenomenology and process philosophy are sometimes set off as oppositional currents in philosophical circles, but this is a brittle dualism that does not hold up in the face of contemporary revisions of phenomenological method. Nor does it hold up when Alfred North Whitehead's work *Process and Reality* (1929), the text generally considered to ground of process philosophy, is examined closely. Whitehead laments that philosophy has been too detached for too long and seeks to embed philosophical thinking in both practice and imagination (203–204). Processural thinking, call it speculative or phenomenological, twists free from yet another pernicious duality in much performance scholarship: the contrast between the ephemerality of live performance (the argument around liveness as disappearance) and the permanence of documents (the artificial construction of archives as closed and enduring). This opposition between "stage and page," as dance scholars Susan Manning and Lucia Ruprecht call it, is superseded by contemporary phenomenological approaches (4).[2] Process philosophy is consistent with the dynamic processes of devising, performing, interpreting, and re-enacting that occur in many arts. With relevance beyond manipulation of artistic content, it accounts also for the processural transformation of aesthetics, concepts, performance techniques, technologies for representation and documentation, and relations between performers and audience members.

This chapter is composed of six examples of process phenomenologies and one methodological interlude. The six processes are brief and highly pragmatic glimpses into how various phenomenological notes were written: under what circumstances, from what perspective, what they felt and looked like. I call these *stories of notes* because I am telling a partial and idiosyncratic tale based on several phenomenologies performed by myself and by others. Often these notes do not yet have the formal structures of language. More akin to poetry, they might be scribbles, fragments of sentences, traces, or drawings. One story of notes below captures the act of taking notes rather than the notes themselves. Such interim stages of the phenomenological process may come from very tight cycles of action and reflection, reflecting while doing in rapid succession, or they may emerge out of periods of relatively unreflective performance followed by more structured phases of reflection. This latter coincides with many rehearsal processes during which there is a period of improvisation or performance followed by reflection, or director's notes. A familiar mode of phenomenological process is to write in fragments in the moments between focused movement or engagement with participants/audience.[3] The open improvisational qualities of many installations and performances offer the flexibility to take notes almost in mid flow, but this is not always the case. A longer, strictly framed dance or theatre piece offers less scope for diving out of the action and into reflection, but reflection occurs throughout action and can be accumulated and held in memory until it can be noted down. Inevitably this holding process means that some details are lost but other qualities are gained.

The approach to phenomenology in this chapter, emphasizing the interim phases of phenomenology as performed by multiple actors and locating these within the dynamics of process philosophy, contributes to the "radicalization of the phenomenological voice" (Nancy 28). Not a disinterested procedure of bracketing out the noise of context (the Husserlian life world) in order to get at the essence of lived experience, the phenomenologies in this chapter are reflective processes attending to the sensory and affective layers of embodied life. The thick descriptions sustaining these stories of notes deepen and expose the complexity and richness of experience, with little interest in producing generalizable truths. In short, when I refer to phenomenology I mean a reflective process that is subjective, embodied, and situated, but also exploratory and critical.[4] A critical phenomenology is not a simple process of negation, instead it palpates the edges of what exists and the categories already in place for understanding the matter of experience. This mode of reflection exists "beyond affirmation and denial," and does not permit "a withdrawal into disinterestedness" (Sloterdijk, *You Must Change Your Life* 14). Sloterdijk does not frame his extensive exploration of practice in this book as a phenomenology, but the mode of investigation he describes is highly consistent with what I call phenomenological reflection: "the matter itself entangles its adepts in an inescapable self-referentiality by presenting them with the practicing—the ascetic, form-demanding and habit-forming—character of their own behaviour" (*You Must Change Your Life* 14). The radicalization of the phenomenological voice can mean many things, but for now it can be glimpsed as phenomenology in transition from the models of the early-to-mid twentieth century first phenomenologists (Husserl, Heidegger, Sartre, Merleau-Ponty) into modes for the current times as a reflective process closely entwined with practice and criticality.

Given that this is a collection of essays on phenomenology and artistic or theatrical performance, it is worth reiterating that phenomenological reflection in this discussion does not just come from the perspective of the performer. Audience members and participants of all sorts have meaningful phenomenological experiences in the wider context of performance. Further, the temporal dimension is something to play with rather than hide. All reflection is reflection of past events, even if that event happened 10 seconds ago, and events from 10 years ago are not necessarily phenomenologically or experientially stale. This opens the suggestion that phenomenology relies on a sort of corporeal, experiential archiving. Or storytelling. The point of view, voice, and general situatedness of each story of notes below differs: performer, ethnographer, audience member, choreographer, workshop participant, and somatic practitioner.

FIRST STORY OF NOTES—A PERFORMER'S PERSPECTIVE

> *This one is a memory. I once choreographed and performed in a piece called Liftlink, set in a lift, and recall buying a long thin spiral notebook to use for the devising process. It was shaped like an elevator shaft. I have no idea where it is, but I know it existed. I can even recall physically writing and drawing in that book. My fingers remember the thick creamy texture of the paper, the extreme narrowness making long sentences impractical, forcing me into short notes and pictures. Drawings travelled up and down the page.*[5]

Memories of that notebook combine with its ambiguous physical status as an object. Is it lost? Destroyed? Mislaid amongst other things in the cluster of boxes that have survived my many moves over the years? Torn into pieces with only fragments remaining? Damaged by damp or mice? Perhaps someone else has it, one of the collaborating dancers or the producer. These notes exist in memory, or in the hybrid archive that spans physical reality and embodied memory. As such they point to qualities of this phase of the phenomenological process, often lost or forgotten once the final products of performance or publication are achieved. This interim phase is frequently written out of the officially preserved history of process.

SECOND STORY OF NOTES—AN ETHNOGRAPHER'S PERSPECTIVE

> *"The pace of the evening has picked up. Even though the* padam *(within the Bharata Natyam Indian dance repertoire) was slow the fact is that she had already completed several pieces in quick succession. These pieces did not require the sustained energy and focus of the* varnam, *for example, which came before intermission. I reach down into my handbag to take out my book so I can take some quick notes in the dark when suddenly the house lights come on."*
>
> (Srinivasan 160)

Caught in the act of recording thoughts and ideas, and describing impressions, Priya Srinivasan evokes the clandestine sense of taking notes while contained in the audience of someone else's performance. The lights came on, and we almost sense that she froze in mid motion, hand halfway down to her bag or perhaps pen poised above the page. As if the role of spectator should be free from transcriptions of any sorts. Cameras are still prohibited in most theatres, as per conventional theatre etiquette, but also very few people take notes. Not many scholars discuss the act of taking notes. Of course note taking and transcription have huge roles in much ethnography, but Srinivasan's description captures the phenomenological process of actually translating into words her experiences of sitting in the audience of a Bharata Natyam performance. Throughout *Sweating Saris*, she dances across a wonderfully fine line between ethnography and phenomenology. Her descriptions, memories, and stories are embodied, at times dripping with sweat or cramped with pain; they comprise what she calls the methodological perspective of "unruly spectator." She takes the reader on a journey from a small, airless theatre in Southern California to recollections of purchasing in India the sari worn by the dancer. The dancer's foot bleeding on the stage exists in counterpoint with the thumb of the sari seller and the hands of the woman who weaves bells, a street vendor in New Delhi (Srinivasan 154). Dancing, bleeding, weaving, and writing are all embodied processes. Elspeth Probyn captures this simply and profoundly when she says "We work ideas through our bodies; we write through our bodies, hoping to get into the bodies of our readers" (76). Probyn does not say we write *with* our bodies, we write *through* our bodies; this implies immanence and process.

Being an unruly spectator means, for Srinivasan, inserting herself into her observations—her thoughts, memories, histories, and sensations. It also seems to imply taking notes at inappropriate or unruly moments, working against the conventional order that dictates when one dances, when one watches, or when one transcribes thoughts. It is clear that her process questions what is appropriate. Thoughts spill over and must be captured or they might be lost. Consistent with process philosophy there is no fixity of practice or of protocol. All can be questioned. All can be transformed.

THIRD STORY OF NOTES—AN AUDIENCE MEMBER'S PERSPECTIVE

Small Acts (2011) was an unusual performance. Commissioned by Skånes Dansteater in Malmö, Sweden, it was a restaging of a piece by British choreographer Ben Wright. Deciding to avoid entirely the theatre with raked seating, Wright dispersed the choreography throughout the SDT building: the rehearsal studios, workshop, backstage area, small dancers' rest areas, and corridors became locations for small clusters of dancers performing while audience members wandered from site to site, in search of dance.

I was an audience member, but it became clear immediately that the autonomy and spirit of exploration granted to all of us made us more than a passive group of watchers. We were explorers. We were given maps showing how to find our way around the building, but not revealing when we might find dance in the various places. It was both frustrating (so difficult to see the choreography when there were 15 people already blocking my view to the small space where dancers performed a duet) and delightfully intimate (I decided to stay put in a studio and without warning two dancers joined me and began a wonderful duet just an arm's length from where I was sitting). It was clear that the choreography included the constant reconfiguration of the audience members in relation to the dancers, and I was suddenly hit by the need to write down what I was thinking, seeing, and feeling. My thoughts burst out of me. I had a pen, but I had no paper. I had the map. I began to scribble.

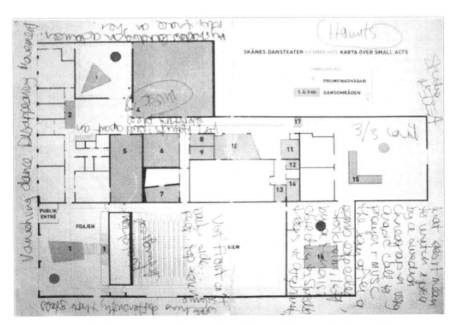

Figure 3.1 Scan of notes taken during *Small Acts* (2010) on the front side of the map given to the audience members to navigate the performance.

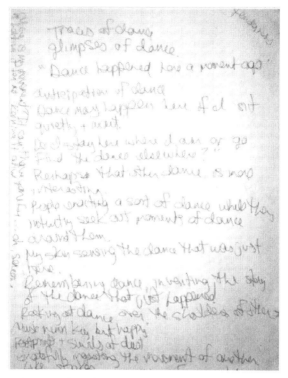

Figure 3.2 Scan of notes taken during *Small Acts* (2010) on the back side of the map given to the audience members to navigate the performance.

As an audience member I had what can be called a strong phenomenological moment, both sensory and conceptual, demanding that I write down traces of it prior to the thoughts and sensations disappearing. This addresses two critiques of phenomenology of performance: first that it is only relevant to revealing the experience of the performer, and second that by committing something to words, the experience is necessarily deadened. *Small Acts* demonstrated the opposite. All positions of perception and reflection on a performance can invite phenomenological reflection, and the words helped to deepen and enrich the strange social and aesthetic experience. The more I jotted down my thoughts the more I appreciated what I was experiencing, and further reflection was invited.

The notes include observations that did not make it into the scholarly article I subsequently wrote about the performance (Kozel, "Relational Choreographies"). Writing sideways and upside down, I filtered the thoughts through a new project I was formulating and made an observation about a different performance, a re-enactment of Kenneth Kvarnström's choreography from 1996 *no-no*, through contemporary political events.[6] Process phenomenologies are not linear, from experience to final performance or publication, but ripple outwards to include other creative and life experiences. E. Robert Mesle describes an "urgency" behind the process-relational philosophy inspired by Whitehead. More than just a commentator on another philosopher, it is clear by Mesle's writing that he has an ethical and personal commitment to this philosophical world view: "there is an urgency in coming to see the world as a web of interrelated processes of which we are integral parts, so that all of our choices and actions have consequences for the world around us" (9). The decision to let audience members wander through sections of choreography has consequences, as does the decision to write about it.

FOURTH STORY OF NOTES—A CHOREOGRAPHER'S PERSPECTIVE

Figures 3.3 Drawing reproduced with kind permission from Efva Lilja, 2012.

Figure 3.4 Drawing reproduced with kind permission from Efva Lilja, 2012.

Efva Lilja is a unique choreographer and dance writer. She writes with a rawness and a directness that makes it feel as if her publications are close to the phenomenological notes she has taken. Her publications are oddly sized and produced more in the vein of art books than academic publications. You can feel the thought processes; you can feel the pulse of the words; you can feel the motion and affect. Barely veiled. Pulling at the flesh of the paper.

She probes at the edges of dance writing and in doing so circles the practice of phenomenological expression. She speaks of the opportunities and insights of "losing oneself" when moving beyond what is established and accepted. "Transformed into action through artistic methods and practices, it creates images and tales that make us question what we hitherto believed was true and curiously explore an alternative. Our ideas of what a performance is are upended and new forms of expression make us share desirable events and sequences that mirror our different realities" (Lilja 107).

The early phase of transposing movement into words frequently requires sketching or drawing. Even dancers, notoriously wary of drawing because their skills gravitate to kinaesthetic or physical expression, not the expression of ink on paper, find themselves using lines, dots, or colors to capture a fleeting motion or intensity or spatial relation between people.[7] Lilja's drawing above is used as an example of notes, but I am aware this is the version included in a published book—perhaps there were earlier sketches, rougher drawings, weeded out in the publication process. Does she have them still? The drawing in the book points backwards to its (possible) earlier versions, ones we never see but can imagine. It calls attention to processes over time. The little figures also suggest a narrative of trembling and loss of control, sliding out of the shadows of bodies. They are a foreshadowing of the discussion of affect and somatics found at the end of this chapter.

METHODOLOGICAL INTERLUDE

Emphasizing the processural quality of phenomenology opens an alternative to the usual formulation of doing a *phenomenology of performance*; this alternative is the act of performing a phenomenology, or *phenomenology as performance*. This does not mean we display ourselves in the performance of a phenomenology, but calls attention to the necessarily processural and dynamic qualities of performance based on an understanding of performance as emergence (Kozel, "AffeXity").

There are practical implications to this, influencing how we do a phenomenology, or in more formal terms, how we implement the phenomenological method. Previously the way I answered the question "How do you do a phenomenology?" emphasized attention, or even the sort mindfulness familiar to anyone who does meditation. Here is an extract:

- Take your attention into this very moment.
- Suspend the main flow of thought.
- Call your attention to your body and what it is experiencing.
- Witness what you see, hear, and touch, how space feels, and temperature, and how the inside of your body feels in relation to the outside.
- Take a break (a moment, a day, a week, a year).
- Describe what you experienced. Take notes, record sounds or images.
    Initial notes can be a sort of "brain dump." Do not worry about style, grammar, or relevance at this stage. This stage may occur immediately following your immersion in a specific sensory experience, or it may happen after an interval. Memory and imaginative reconstruction are involved regardless of the lapse of time between experience and documentation of the experience, but obviously too much time passing can dull the recollection.
                                                    (Kozel, *Closer* 52–55)

Latent in this rather simplistic description are the qualities of process phenomenology I now want to emphasize: first, in performing a phenomenology we continuously modify our own practices and methods, sometimes without realizing it. Second, we *create* sensory and affective content though our awareness; we do not just *describe* what already exists. Third, this process is relational across other bodies and objects. Phenomenology, like all philosophical ideas, develops through "limitations, adaptations and inversions" (Whitehead 196). I am not prepared to offer new step-by-step instructions for how to do a phenomenology, given how inadequate my first attempt now seems. However, to stir things up even further, I will introduce Nancy's instructions on how to do a phenomenology of listening, based on his deep reflections on music, sound, and resonance. Nancy's writing on music aims not to be restrained by the primacy of language. He has some recommendations for how to do this in relation to music and listening:

- treat "pure resonance" not only as the condition but as the very beginning and opening up of sense
- treat the body as being wholly a resonance chamber or column of beyond meaning (like the part of the violin that transmits vibrations)
- envisage the "subject" as that part, in the body, that is listening or vibrates with listening to—or with the echo of—the beyond-meaning (31).

His instructions, necessarily quite abstract because sound and the experience of music are his material, open the conditions for the translation into language of that which originates beyond language. His consideration of resonance also provides a clear dynamic of relationality. He writes, somewhat obliquely, that "sense reaches me long before it leaves me, even though it reaches me only by leaving in the same movement" (Nancy 30). If we think of experience as enveloping us, then dissolving into something else, our writing about it is a play between it arriving, making sense of it, and it transforming. Frequently, we only really understand what we experienced once we set a phenomenological process of reflection and writing in motion. Then it changes.[8]

The process phenomenologies that fascinate me, only 6 of which I have included in this chapter, exist between sound, visuals, poetry, sketches, and ethnographic field notes. They exude a form of corporeal listening and translation. They can be euphoric or frustrating, full of insight or fraught with uncertainty. These notes can fall completely flat, missing what they try to capture. They palpate the borders of what we have known or thought before.

Prior to this methodological interlude I included four stories of notes from the perspectives of performer, choreographer, and those who are mobile or "unruly" spectators. The two remaining stories of notes come from expanded constructions of performer and performance; the fifth comes from the experiences of participants in a workshop and the sixth from practices immersed in somatic awareness or affective qualities. These are part of a programme of expanding phenomenological processes so that they are refined enough to assist the exploration of more subtle and affective domains. Such subtlety is not outside the domain of existing phenomenological reflection. Witness two resonating fragments: "ashes of movement," a fragment from my *Small Acts* notes, and Lilja's poetic disintegration of the little dancing figure into particles, or indeed, ashes.

Process Phenomenologies 65

Figure 3.5 Crop from *Small Acts* notes.

Figure 3.6 Reproduced with kind permission from Efva Lilja, 2012.

FIFTH STORY OF NOTES—WORKSHOP PARTICIPANTS' PERSPECTIVES

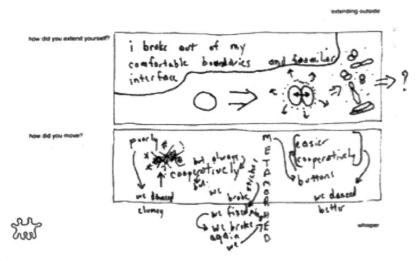

Figure 3.7 Drawing from participants of the *heart(h)* workshops for the *whisper(s)* wearable project (2004).

66 *Susan Kozel*

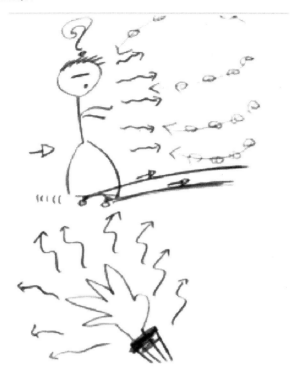

Figure 3.8 Drawing from participants of the *heart(h)* workshops for the *whisper(s)* wearable project (2004).

Figure 3.9 Drawing from participants of the *heart(h)* workshops for the *whisper(s)* wearable project (2004).

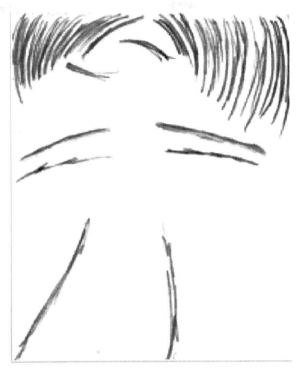

Figure 3.10 Drawing from participants of the *heart(h)* workshops for the *whisper(s)* wearable project (2004).

These drawings came from the *heart(h)* workshops in 2004. They were part of the devising phase of a large performance project in wearable computing that came out of a collaboration between dancers, fashion designers, engineers, software designers, and sound artists. For this project, called *whisper(s)*, garments embedded with electronics that could sense non-verbal bodily communication and transmit this to others were designed and constructed. The public presentations of this research project occurred as participatory performances; the *heart(h)* workshops were used to help us clarify and deepen the poetic and performative dimensions of the concept so that embodied qualities could lead the engineering and programming.[9]

Thecla Schiphorst, Camille Baker, and I lead the workshop participants through a series of improvisational exercises, with an emphasis on sensing between bodies and deepening the sense of space around bodies. Participants were asked to respond to questions in written form. This was similar to design ethnography in the field of interaction design and basic ethnographic practices, but diverging somewhat from standard ethnographic practices there was also a blank page in the questionnaire asking participants to draw their experiences of performing their sensations in space. A bridge between ambiguous corporeal experience and language can occur by means of inscription other than words: drawing, moving, vocalizing. As we saw with Lilja's sketches, and know from the way choreographers work, drawing is not just mere notation. Nor is it a reduction, or a telegraphic way of acting as a placeholder for words. Drawings can be condensations of phenomenological experience. Details of bodies, space, relations, and affect can be present in a few lines. These lines are generally not intended to be seen by audiences or readers.

Increasingly, experimental performances are constructed around various phases of workshops. The model of the workshop may come from theatre games, pedagogy, interaction design, or ethnography, but it still can have strong phenomenological grounding and provide phenomenological insight. It is significant that the workshop format intends to flatten the creative hierarchy somewhat: creative actions and agency are not just the domain of the director or dominant artist of the project; they are opened to other groups. Reflecting a process philosophical view, it is possible to discover something from the smallest sliver of one person's experience, no matter how insignificant or eccentric (Mesle 42–43).

SIXTH STORY OF NOTES—A SOMATIC PERSPECTIVE

indigo
ultraviolet
cramps in my gut

somatic blur

rats in a barrel
pain ricochets through my body
brittle edges, like ice

holding till I'm burning with fever or pain
radiant burst of sunshine

dark dark electric purple

(personal notes, autumn 2012)

There are far fewer words in my notebooks when I try to capture affective or somatic experiences. And fewer drawings. The narratives are almost painful in their intensity, with much reliance on color. Or they are the opposite: the somatic zone of affect is beyond not just my words but my ability to integrate internal perception into anything resembling previous categories of comprehension or articulation. Still, affect is performed. It is set in motion and it unfolds, taking oneself and others on a journey we participate in but do not fully control.

Some context is useful. I am in the process of expanding phenomenological "tools" to capture not actions or senses but affect and somatic awareness.

In order to do this I am exploring various somatic practices, yoga, meditation, and other means of accessing internal body states through visualization, physicalization or other sensing techniques. These are performances of perception; the tools are variations on a theme of attention, reflection, breath, and multi-sensory perception. Currently I am exploring affect within somatic practices, but it is clear that all performances have affective and somatic layers. Generally these are unaddressed or are filtered through other forms of description or critical judgment. Performances that move us, those that are traumatic or euphoric for example, are imbued with affect but frequently are discussed in terms of narrative, technique, dramaturgy, musicality, or composition. Affect is part of the great invisible domain that supports and sustains the visible, to use the formulation that gives the title to Maurice Merleau-Ponty's posthumous collection, *The Visible and the Invisible*.

Phenomenology is well established as a methodological approach for capturing, questioning, sharing, and even problematizing sense experience, but affect exists in a different spectrum from the senses. Affect inhabits bodies and the spaces beyond them. Bodies, objects, architecture, imaginations, memories, even meteorological or atmospheric qualities, make up the affective clouds within which we live. More like particle systems or fields, affect is an ever-fluctuating exchange of forces. It is most commonly reduced to emotion, but philosophical thought contributing to the area of affect theory reveals it is much more subtle and expansive than simply human emotion.[10] It can be seen as a shimmering, or rippling of material and immaterial forces (Kozel, "Somatic Materialis" 90–92). A wider question is whether it is possible to do a phenomenology of affect. Elsewhere I have begun to address this question—with the suggestion that approaches to phenomenology in the twenty-first century have rendered it less a faithful reproduction of early twentieth-century method and doctrine, than an expanded and subtle means for understanding that which is beyond comprehension, but which is still experienced (Kozel, "Somatic Materialism"). As such, phenomenology can be useful to contemporary performance, as performers tackle wider and more nuanced questions relating to bodies, cultures, artistic practices, politics, environmental issues, and scientific knowledge.

Continuing to navigate within the focus of this chapter—process phenomenologies and stories of notes from the interim phase of transposing experience into words—this final story asks what affective notes look like. I suggested above that colors and intensities played a stronger role, but these color sensations are not always directly pinned to clearly defined physical or emotional qualities. Returning to Nancy's nuanced take on phenomenology, we learn that when it comes to affect the expected relation to experience is reversed: "no longer a question so much of letting a fundamental affect come to expression but of shaping such an affect, of forming it and conforming it to a measure not yet registered in nature or in history" (56). This relates to a quality of somatic experience I have encountered occasionally: noticing something that is so unusual that it at first registers as nothing. Or a ripple in something-ness. It is possible to feel nothing and something at the same time. A nothing that is something (Kozel, "Somatic Materialism" 164–167).

In addition to affect materializing as internally perceived colors and the play between something and nothing, this research into performing a phenomenology of the somatic yields one other observation: the first attempts at taking notes often read like stories. Small extrapolations of narrative spiral into being as a way to fill in the gaps in more concrete sensory description. There is a fine line between my writing or telling these little stories, and their seeming to tell themselves. This sense of the story creating the affect is part of the reversal or "inversion of sense" Nancy identifies when affect comes to the fore. Shifting the agency of telling a story to the nebulous zone of affect, "the intimate and ineffable experience must give itself, recreate for itself, and forge for itself, its tonality, its voice, its sonority" (Nancy 56). The implication for phenomenology is that this method is not a passive description of experience. Phenomenological processes do not just describe what is there; they create meaning and deepen experience. In effect, we venture into a domain where meaning is not immediately accessible but has to be probed, palpated, and stirred into being. Notes from a recent experience in an anechoic chamber[11] provide a glimpse of this.

> *Infinite blackness.*
> *Like velvet*
> *I have never seen black like this. Blacker because of the silence.*
> *My eyes struggle for perceptual distinctions between floor, wall, and ceiling.*
> *Is this room round, I wonder?*
> *I like this black. At least at first.*
> *No sound, even though I know I am here with 3 others.*
> *I hear my body, it surges up to my attention like a fountain.*
> *Like vomit rising, I feel this rush of sound up the core of my body to my ears.*
> *I hear my breath, my heart—then my ears travel down but get lost somewhere around my navel.*
> *Then I begin to ... panic? Or float?*
>
> *(I feel an urgent need to touch you*
> *Where are you? You were next to me.*
> *I reach down: you are sitting on the floor.*
> *I touch your hair. Silky. Real. Comforting.*
> *You are there.)*
>
> *This means there are people in this world of blackness. This supposed social space that has suddenly become a space of sensory confusion and affective surges. I decide to act, to dampen the spiral of unease, the disintegration of all that is familiar. I quietly rub my fingers together near my ear. Comforting, soft cricket sounds. I let my hand float away from my ear in this deep utter blackness and there sound is taken from*

me. Swallowed up. At arms length I can barely hear my fingers. Fragile. Without resonance. The sound dies.

The door opens and we are let out into light and sound once more.

Something inside me releases.

We were in the anechoic chamber for one minute. It was part of Kimsooja's piece *To Breathe* at the Korean Pavilion of the Venice Biennale (2013). The anechoic chamber is a room quite simply, without echo. Without light. The chamber deprives us of resonance, the constant exchange of sound, gesture, and sight that makes up the texture of relational and dynamic life. Nancy would challenge my sense of deprivation, preferring to say "silence is not a privation but an arrangement of resonance" (21). Nevertheless, I retain the affective imprint of my experience in that chamber. It is archived deep within me.

Ending by returning to the beginning: recall that my notebook from the first story of notes was lost. For a long time I was delayed in writing this chapter because I dearly wanted to revisit and explore my old notebooks and drawings from past performances. I knew most of these were lost but refused, in some unacknowledged yet highly obstructive way, to accept this. Phenomenological nostalgia? Perhaps, but also a deeper understanding of the full arc of a phenomenology and a mourning for what was lost. Once I accepted that it was enough for the memory of the notebook to exist, I could write this piece. I was able to see that in past years I (and others) did not place as much emphasis on this stage of phenomenological process as on the end products of the performance, the documentation, or the scholarly articles. Yet when I examine the documentation of performances I did in the 1990s, I see how poor it is by today's standards: partial, badly lit, and blurry. The notebooks seemed to point forward to the performance, the documentation to point backwards, but both exist partially in memory, part in imagination, and across various materialities that include muscle memory, ancient and now unreadable VHS or Hi-8 tapes, missing notebooks, and imaginative reconstruction. The documentation of performance is an incomplete sketch, just as the notebooks that produce a performance are fragmentary and incomplete. And when I read what I have written, I see how the words and ideas could have been otherwise.

It is not that I want to transform the previously overlooked interim processes into products themselves, rather that I want to inject processural qualities into all phases of a phenomenology. Donald Sherburne notes how Whitehead believed that "the merest hint of dogmatic certainty as to finality of statement is an exhibition of folly," for we are in a perpetual process of setting thought, imagination, and experience into play so that we can generate ideas that will then be "capable of criticism and improvement" (204); and this edited collection demonstrates how phenomenology is currently critiqued, expanded, and applied to performances of all sorts. Attending to the interim processes of doing a phenomenology, rather than performing one formulaically or with only the end goal in sight, is a way of "letting breadth of thought" react with the "intensity of sensitive experience" (Sherburne 202). It seems that I am giving the last word to the dead male philosopher; certainly his words describe of the powerful combination of forces that artists and scholars have at their disposal, but there are many voices in this chapter. Dancers, writers, students, philosophers … words, drawings, and motions. Phenomenologies are rarely entirely solitary or isolated processes; they are multiple, they are populated, they are entangled performances.

NOTES

1. Traced back to Alfred North Whitehead's *Process and Reality* (written in 1929), this dynamic approach to thought and the world is experiencing a revival as both process philosophy and speculative materialism. See Whitehead, Sherburne, Mesle, Bryant et al.
2. Further, Manning and Ruprecht note a shift from broadly sociohistorical to broadly philosophical and phenomenological approaches to dance history, the catalyst for this being a more conceptual approach to dance and performance.
3. I described a process of writing in fragments in *Closer*, when I was partially inside the *Telematic Dreaming* installation and partially outside the camera view (Kozel, *Closer* 88–89). Other variations on fragmentary phenomenological writing include Maurice Merleau-Ponty's working notes from *The Visible and Invisible*. This book was incomplete at the time of his death in 1961 and the publishers wisely included his fragments (comprising a full third of the book) rather than ignoring them or asking someone to integrate them into a more fluid text. Contemporary phenomenologist Jean Luc Nancy includes an "interlude" and a "coda" into his book on music, *Listening*, which have a fragmentary feel to them, and of course Jacques Derrida made famous an attention to margins, footnotes, and voices from the gaps between texts.
4. Expanding somewhat my earlier writing on phenomenology, the approach proposed here emphasises the critical, exploratory, and emergent qualities of phenomenological reflection. I also argue for the ability to use phenomenology to access affect and not simply sensory experience (Kozel, *Closer* 127–35).
5. *Liftlink* was performed by Ruth Gibson, Annie Loh, Sterling Steward, and Susan Kozel. It is described in (Kozel, *Closer* 127–35).
6. From the top left corner of the map, a note reads: "What does it mean to watch a piece by a Swedish choreographer using Arabic call to prayer and music the day after a bomb explodes in Stockholm left by a terrorist objecting to Swedish troops in Afghanistan?" Kvarnström's choreography was performed as the second part of the double bill with *Small Acts* that day.
7. Video sketching can be used too but will not be discussed here because it opens up wider debates over the finished visual aesthetic invited by the camera and the gaze.
8. I contributed a video lecture for a Practice Based Research in the Arts course at Stanford University (taught by Helen Paris and Leslie Hill) called "Phenomenology in 5 Acts: A Short Lecture on Phenomenology." In it I provide

guidance for performing a phenomenology that is consistent with the discussion in this chapter. <http://medea.mah.se/2013/12/susan-kozel-phenomenology-practice-based-research-arts/https://www.youtube.com/watch?v=mv7Vp3NPKw4&feature=youtu.be>.
9. This project was a collaboration between Thecla Schiphorst, Sang Mah, Susan Kozel, Kristina Andersen, Robb Lovell, Pablo Mochcovsky, Jan Erkku, Gretchen Elsener, Brady Marks, and Camille Baker. http://whisper.iat.sfu.ca (Kozel, *Closer* Chapter 5) (Schiphorst)
10. There is much fascinating work on affect. See Gregg and Seigworth (2010), Sedgwick (2003), Barthes (2005), Massumi (2002), Clough and Halley (2007), and Sedgwick and Frank (1995) tracing affect back to Tompkins in the mid twentieth century.
11. An anechoic chamber is a room with no echo; walls, ceiling, and floor are padded so that sound is absorbed. It is completely dark.

WORKS CITED

Barthes, Roland. *The Neutral*. Trans. Rosalind E. Kraus and Denis Hollier. New York: Columbia UP, 2005.
Bryant, Levi, Nick Srnicek and Graham Harman, eds. *The Speculative Turn: Continental Materialism and Realism*. Melbourne: re.press, 2011.
Clough, Patricia Ticineto and Jen Halley, eds. *The Affective Turn: Theorizing the Social*. Durham and London: Duke UP, 2007.
Derrida, Jacques. *Margins of Philosophy*. 1972. Trans. Alan Bass. Brighton: The Harvester Press, 1986.
Gregg, Melissa and Gregory Seigworth, eds. *The Affect Theory Reader*. Durham and London: Duke UP, 2010.
Kozel, Susan. *Closer: Performance, Technologies, Phenomenology*. Cambridge, MA and London: MIT P, 2007.
———. "AffeXity: Performing Affect using Augmented Reality," in *Fibreculture Journal* Issue 21 on "Exploring affect in interaction design, interaction-based art and digital art," eds. Jonas Fritsch, Thomas Markussen and Andrew Murphie. 2012. Web. <http://twentyone.fibreculturejournal.org/fcj-150-affexity-performing-affect-with-augmented-reality/>.
———. "Somatic Materialism, or 'Is It Possible to do a Phenomenology of Affect?'" in *Site*, issue on Senses, no. 33, 2013. 153–167.
———. "Relational Choreographies," in *Artistic Research Then and Now: 2004–2013*, ed. Torbjörn Lind. Stockholm: Yearbook of the AR&D Swedish Research Council, 2013. 74–88.
Lilja, Efva. *Do You Get What I'm Not Saying? On Dance as a Subversive Declaration of Love*. Lund: Ellerströms, 2012.
Manning, Susan and Lucia Ruprecht, eds. *New German Dance Studies*. Urbana, Chicago and Springfield: U of Illinois P, 2012.
Massumi, Brian. *Parables for the Virtual*. Durham and London: Duke UP, 2002.
Merleau-Ponty, Maurice. *The Visible and the Invisible*. 1962. Trans. Alphonso Lingis. Evanston: Northwestern UP, 1987.
Mesle, C. Robert. *Process-Relational Philosophy: An Introduction to Alfred North Whitehead*. Conshohocken, PA: Templeton Press, 2008.

Nancy, Jean Luc. *Listening*. 2002. Trans. Charlotte Mandel. New York: Fordham UP, 2007.
Probyn, Elspeth. "Writing Shame." *The Affect Theory Reader*. Eds. Melissa Gregg and Gregory Seigworth. Durham and London: Duke UP, 2010.
Schiphorst, Thecla. PhD Thesis, "Planetary Collegium" U of Plymouth. *The Varieties of User Experience: Bridging Embodied Methodologies from Somatics and Performance to Human Computer Interaction*, 2007. Web. 10 Apr 2012 <http://www.sfu.ca/~tschipho/PhD/PhD_thesis.html>.
Sedgwick, Eve Kosofsky, ed. *Touching Feeling: Affect, Pedagogy, Performativity*. Durham and London: Duke UP, 2003.
Sedgwick, Eve Kosofsky and Adam Frank, eds. *Shame and its Sisters: A Silvan Tomkins Reader*. Durham and London: Duke UP, 1995.
Sherburne, Donald W., ed. *A Key to Whitehead's Process and Reality*. Chicago and London: U of Chicago P, 1981.
Sloterdijk, Peter. *The Art of Philosophy: Wisdom as a Practice*. 2010. Trans. Karen Margolis. New York: Columbia UP, 2012.
———, Peter. *You Must Change Your Life: On Anthropotechnics*. 2009. Trans. Weiland Hoban. Cambridge: Polity Press, 2013.
Srinivasan, Priya. *Sweating Saris: Indian Dance as Transnational Labor*. Philadelphia: Temple UP, 2012.
Tomkins, Sylvan S. *Affect Imagery Consciousness*, 4 vols. New York: Springer, 1962–1992.
Whitehead, Alfred North. *Process and Reality, Corrected Edition*. Eds. David Ray Griffen and Donald W. Sherburne. New York: The Free Press, 1985.

4 The Actor's Work on Attention, Awareness, and Active Imagination
Between Phenomenology, Cognitive Science, and Practices of Acting

Phillip Zarrilli

> *When you have reached the level of "no-mind," your concentrated mind will be hidden even from yourself, thus binding everything that comes before or after to these intervals of "doing nothing." This refers precisely to the intuitive power that binds all skills together with the concentrated mind.*
>
> (Zeami 141)

PREFACE

This essay is one step toward a phenomenology of acting written in the interdisciplinary territory between recent developments in phenomenology; cognitive science and the study of consciousness; and embodied practices with special reference to acting and Buddhist meditation as embodied phenomena/processes. Of special importance to this distinctive three-fold interdisciplinary program of research is the work dating from the early 1990s of such key figures as cognitive scientist, Francisco Varela and his various colleagues, especially phenomenologists Evan Thompson and Natalie Depraz. These researchers combine (1) an examination of our lived experience utilizing highly nuanced modes of phenomenological analysis with (2) insights from the specific branch of cognitive science known variously as "dynamic systems theory," "embodied dynamicism," or enactment theory, which builds on empirical brain-body research,[1] and (3) a grounding of research in the transformative possibilities for experience offered by a specific approach to mindfulness within centuries-old Buddhist traditions of meditation.[2]

My interest in considering acting from a phenomenological perspective stems from my career-long interest as an actor, actor-trainer, director, and scholar in understanding acting as a psychophysical phenomenon and process, examined from the actor's position "inside" the experience of performing. I use the compound term "psychophysical" to mark the constant dialectical engagement of the actor between the "inner" and "outer" processes and experiences that constitute acting as a phenomenon and process taking place in and through the immediate stream of consciousness and experience of the performative moment. From the perspective of the actor "inside" the phenomenon of acting, that process can be described as the lived "experience" (*Leib*) of enacting a performance score while responding to the immediate environment the actor inhabits in the moment of performance. In this view of acting, the actor-in-the-process-of-performing is not concerned with "character" or role, but with bodymind immersion in the tasks/actions at hand that constitute one's performance score. As a sentient being, one enacts/experiences each moment of a performance score. In the moment of performance the actor perceives, attends to, opens one's awareness to, feels, remembers, reflects, senses, and/or imagines as appropriate to the performance score, the aesthetic that has shaped the creation of a performance, and in response to what is available within the performance environment at each moment. Processes of perceiving, attending to, awareness of, feeling, remembering, reflecting, sensing, and imagining collectively constitute the embodied consciousness of the actor per se.

Unfortunately, the recent emphasis on "physical theatre" and studies of embodiment in the UK have tended to deflect attention from the actor's embodied consciousness (or bodymind) as a gestalt in which the "inner" and "outer" dimensions of embodied experience are equally considered. It is time to reconsider the embodied "mind" or inner dimensions of acting in reflecting on acting as a phenomenon and process, and thereby to carefully consider the complex issue of embodied consciousness in performance.

I begin with a brief discussion of the problem of "consciousness," and how embodied consciousness (such as the direction of attention) has been central to considerations of acting as a phenomenon and process in both Western and non-Western contexts. I then focus at length on a phenomenological examination of the specific issue of training the actor to psychophysically "attend to," and go on to explain how "attending to" is related to ancillary states/processes of opening the actor's awareness and the actor's work with active imagination. I conclude with a first-person account of my "work" as an actor on several specific moments in the performance score of *The Echo Chamber*, articulating specific examples of how my embodied consciousness in the moment of performance attends to, becomes sensorially aware of, and/or engages my active imagination.

"CONSCIOUSNESS," EXPERIENCE, AND EMBODIMENT IN ZEAMI AND STANISLAVSKY

Issues of consciousness have been addressed for centuries from a variety of cultural, philosophical, and scientific perspectives. I think it legitimate to argue that historically the issue of consciousness has always been central to acting *when it is considered as a phenomenon and process*. For example, although separated historically by centuries and vastly different sets of cultural, philosophical, and scientific/medical assumptions, two of the most notable practitioner-theorists of acting for whom issues of embodied consciousness and the experiential states of being/doing that constitute consciousness have been central are the actor/teacher/co-founder of Japanese *noh* theatre, Zeami (Hada no Motokiyo, 1363–1443), and the Russian actor/theater-director/teacher Konstantin Stanislavsky (1863–1938).

Zeami was equally a great actor/performer, a renowned playwright authoring between thirty and forty plays, an acting theorist steeped in the nuances of poetic and aesthetic theories of the time, a shrewd manager of a company of actors always with an eye on how he and his fellow actors had to constantly reinvent their practice of acting in order to attract and hold the attention of their contemporary audiences, and a teacher who authored twenty-one highly sophisticated treatises on the arts of acting and playwriting written over the course of forty years from his mid-career to the end of his life. Shelly Fenno Quinn describes Zeami's treatises as constituting "a nuanced and comprehensive phenomenology of the stage informed by a lifetime of artistic practice" (1).

Zeami's *Kyūi* ("A Pedagogical Guide for Teachers of Acting")—written when Zeami was approximately 65 years old and probably after he had become a Zen monk—describes nine different levels (*kurai*) of acting (Nearman 301). The highest three levels Zeami associates with the actor's ability to hold the spectator's attention through a process of actualizing ever-subtler modes of bodymind concentration. At the highest level of embodied practice the actor attains the type of consciousness or state of "no-mind" (*mushin*) described in the epigraph at the beginning of this essay. In his commentary on Zeami's text, Mark Nearman explains how this optimal, heightened state of "no-mind" is "open, perceptive awareness" that contrasts with "the analytical-conceptual intellect" (301). Attaining this state of "no-mind," the actor's technique per se disappears or is burned away completely. Zeami himself metaphorically describes the actor's inhabitation of this state as "The Mark of the Miraculous Flower" where "In Silla, at midnight, the sun is bright"—a level of accomplishment and mastery that "transcends praise," is "beyond [...] critical analysis and judgment," and where "its external mark is No-Mark" (Nearman 324).

For Zeami one of the most important beginning points for the young *noh* actor to progress toward this subtle, heightened, extraordinary state of optimal consciousness was to learn how to become attentive, in other words, how to channel and focus the vibrant energy (*ki*) of the young actor that is like a tree squirrel—excited but as yet unfocused and uncontrolled (Nearman 307).

Although separated by vast cultural and historical differences, Stanislavsky shared some similar concerns with Zeami when he attempted in his own way to address acting as a phenomenon and process. Jean Benedetti in his recent translation of Stanislavsky's *An Actor's Work* entitles Part I as "experiencing" (*Perezhivanie*) and Part II as "embodiment"—a reflection of Stanislavsky's fundamental concern with addressing acting as an embodied/experiential phenomenon/process of living a role (*An Actor's Work*). As Rose Whyman argues, Stanislavsky's ever-evolving approach to acting and acting pedagogy was influenced by the idealist philosophies of Johann

Fichte (1762) and Georg Hegel (1770–1831) who viewed "consciousness as the foundation of reality;" the emergent "new" science of psychology, especially Tikhon Faddeev's *Psychology* (1913), and the work of French psychologist, Theodule Armand Ribot (1839–1916); and late nineteenth century versions of key elements of yoga (10). Stanislavsky's central concern with the actor's consciousness is also evident in his specific discussions of "attention" (*Vnimanie*), the "circle(s) of attention" (*Krug Bvimaniya*) through which the actor's attention is focused or widened, the actor's work with his "inner eye" (*Vnutrenij Zrenie*), and the state of "I am being" (*Ya Esm*). Stanislavsky's primary concern with the actor's ability to inhabit the stage environment as a living/sentient being is reflected in his statement that

> all our acts, even the simplest, which are so familiar to us in everyday life become strained when we appear [...] before a public. [...] That is why it is necessary to correct ourselves and learn again how to walk, move about, sit, or lie down. It is essential to re-educate ourselves to look and see, on the stage, to listen, and to hear.
> (*An Actor Prepares* 73)

Although the study of consciousness was central to formative considerations of consciousness in the initial development of "psychology" as a distinctive discipline in late nineteenth century, especially in the work of William James, and has remained a central focus of Eastern and some Western philosophy (especially phenomenology), during much of the twentieth century the study of "consciousness was considered beyond the scope of legitimate scientific investigation" (Zelazo et al. 1). The study of consciousness has only recently reemerged as a focus of research in the Western sciences, especially cognitive science.

William Seager explains how "the term 'consciousness' possesses a wide-ranging and diverse set of meanings;" indeed, "it is not even obvious that there is any one 'thing' that all uses of the term have in common which could stand as its core referent" (9). Despite its diversity of meanings, I agree with Seager's argument that "the core problem of consciousness focuses on the nature of subjectivity" and that "consciousness is distinctive for its subjectivity or its first-person character," i.e., there is "'something it is like' to be in a conscious state" (10). In this essay I begin to examine a few of these conscious states of embodied being/doing in relation to acting as a phenomenon and process.

BETWEEN COGNITIVE SCIENCE AND PHENOMENOLOGY

The explosion of research in cognitive science over the past twenty plus years has led to differentiation between three major approaches to the study

The Actor's Work on Attention, Awareness, and Active Imagination

of mind and consciousness within the general field known as cognitive science, including

1. cognitivism where the mind is metaphorically (and highly problematically) conceived as a "digital computer" where there are inputs and outputs;
2. connectionism, where the mind is thought of as a "neural network;" and
3. embodied dynamicism, where the mind is thought of as "an embodied dynamic system" (Thompson 4–13).

Of these three approaches embodied dynamicism or an enactive view offers a complex view of bodymind-brain relationship, which, when combined with new perspectives offered by phenomenology, provides a model with the most explanatory power able to illuminate both processes of acting as well as the experience of the actor from inside a performance.

As noted above, one of the primary concerns of phenomenology is examining what it is like to experience specific phenomenally conscious states, in other words, with what it is like to perceive, attend to, imagine, feel, sense, remember, and so on. From a phenomenological perspective, consciousness is "intentional," meaning phenomenology always recognizes that consciousness is "of something, is always directed at something" (Gallagher 687). As Thompson and Zahavi explain, there are various types of intentionality identified by phenomenologists: "In a narrow sense, intentionality is defined as object-directedness. In a broader sense [...] intentionality is defined as openness toward otherness (or 'alterity'). In both cases, the emphasis is on denying that consciousness is self-enclosed" (71–72). A phenomenological examination of a specific state focuses on "the *first person givenness* of my experience," in other words, the qualitative nature of what it is like to be having that experience (Thompson and Zahavi 75). For some phenomenologists, this quality is known as *ipseity*—the constitutive way in which there is a sense that experience is always to or for "me" and not for someone else (Thompson and Zahavi 75).[3]

When Maurice Merleau-Ponty shifted from an examination of "I think" to the "I can" of the body, he laid the philosophical foundation for a more processual account of how our relationship to the world(s) we experientially inhabit is constituted by our phenomenal/inter-sensory and inter-subjective engagement with those worlds. Echoing Merleau-Ponty, a number of years ago Varela, Thompson, and Eleanor Rosch argued for viewing experience and its relationship to cognition as processual: "We propose as a name the term *enactive* to emphasize the growing conviction that cognition is not the representation of a pregiven world by a pregiven mind but is rather the enactment of a world and a mind on the basis of a history of the variety of actions that a being in the world performs" (9). Expanding on his earlier work with Varela and Rosch, Thompson more recently explained how living beings are "autonomous agents" for whom "cognition is the exercise of skillful know-how in situated and embodied action" (13). An enactive approach therefore attempts to "catch experience in the act of making the world available" (Noë, *Action in Perception* 176).

As explained in detail in *Psychophysical Acting*, in contrast to representational or mimetic theories of acting that are constructed from the position of the outside observer to the process/phenomenon of acting, an enactive approach to acting articulates a way of understanding acting and actor training as a phenomenon and process from the perspective of the actor as enactor/doer *from inside the act of performing*. In this view, *acting may be defined as that dynamic embodied/enactive psychophysical process by means of which a (theatrical) world is made available at the moment of its appearance/experience for both the actors and audience* (Zarrilli, *Psychophysical Acting* 41–60).

AN EXAMINATION OF ATTENDING TO AND ITS RELATIONSHIP TO PERCEPTION AND ACTION

For many practitioner-theorists of acting such as Zeami and Stanislavsky, focusing one's attention is often understood to play a central role in actor training and acting per se. I focus first on the phenomenon and process of "attending to" and its relationship to perception and action.

During the 1960s and 1970s in cognitive science the dominant view of how the mind worked was based on a "digital computer" model where there are inputs (perceptions/sensations) that are organized in the brain's motor cortex to produce outputs in the form of action (Ingold 3). In this old view perception (input) is distinct from action (output). This problematic notion of perception has been a primary focus of phenomenology since its inception, and especially so since the publication of Merleau-Ponty's seminal *Phenomenology of Perception*. Phenomenological analysis of perception usually begins by examining "innocent" modes of perception. From this perspective, "perceiving is an ongoing process of making the indeterminate and ambiguous determinate. The perceiver is presented with a vague something-or-other that invites further exploration" (Romdenh-Romluc 125). For example, in the act of completing an early draft of this essay and composing this sentence, I was in Singapore sitting at my computer when I experienced what was at first a vague, indistinct feel of the air in movement to my right. I then sensed a soft, vague "whirring" noise above and to my right. I tilted my head slightly to the right, and attended to the sound with my auditory awareness—the overhead fan was spinning. This vague "something or other" that *was* in the background took shape for me as a "fan" moving the air. Although still "available" to me as an object in my immediate environment, it disappeared into the background again as/when I refocused my thoughts and continued refining this paragraph.

For Merleau-Ponty "perception is the focus of one's attention; it is seen clearly and in detail. It stands out from the background, which is perceived indistinctly, as indeterminate" (*Phenomenology of Perception* 126). The background is always present because subject and world are inextricably intertwined. In this view, perceiving is "a conscious activity" where "conscious" does not refer to one's awareness of the object of perception—the fan and its whirring. Rather, "conscious" describes "the kind of activity that perceiving is"; in other words, as the subject I was "conscious *in* perceiving" the fan/whirring, "rather than conscious of" what I was perceiving (*Phenomenology of Perception* 166).

Carmen Taylor characterizes Merleau-Ponty's view of perception as an embodied experience and practice where "the (relative) *passivity* of sense experience" (sensing the movement of the air/whirring) "and the (relative) *activity* of bodily skills" (turning slightly to the right, opening my auditory awareness, and realizing it is the fan moving/sounding) are inseparably woven together as "a single, unified phenomenon"; therefore, perception is always "both passive and active, situational and practical, conditioned and free" (xii-xiv).

Implicit in Merleau-Ponty's understanding of the body as an "I can" is a theory of embodied perception-in-action. One proponent of this new view of the interdependence of perception and action is philosopher Alva Noë. Noë's primary thesis is that "perceiving is a way of acting (*Action in Perception* 1). Perception is not something that happens to us, or in our brains. It is not like sight, which *makes it seem* as if we are passive spectators to the world. Rather, perception "is something we do [...] the world makes itself available to the perceiver through physical movement and interaction" (ibid.). Perception is therefore more like the sense of touch than sight since in touching one actively engages and explores what is available to touch (Noë, *Action in Perception* 33). In the example above, my auditory awareness could therefore be said to have been "touched" by the air stirred by the fan, and to have "touched" what was at first an indistinct/unknown sound. Perception, therefore, is active and relational. What appears in perception is emergent in the moment of its appearance/sensing as we engage what arises out of the indeterminate horizon of my stream of consciousness in the immediate environment (Merleau-Ponty, *Phenomenology of Perception* 30; Csordas 135–156).

Perception is gained by having access to the world, and access is gained by "mastery and exercise of skills of access" (Noë, *Varieties of Presence* 12–13). By cultivating specific skills, specific "worlds open up that would otherwise be closed off. In this way we achieve for ourselves new ways of being present" (Noë, *Varieties of Presence* 12–13). For Tim Ingold the notion of skill incorporates, but should not be reduced to bodily based skills; rather, perceptual skills are "the capabilities of action and perception of the whole organic being (indissolubly mind and body) situated in a richly structured environment" (5). [A specific example of "perceptual apprenticeship" or skill training for the actor is provided below.]

VISUAL PERCEPTION AND "RECKON[ING] WITH THE POSSIBLE"

Studies of perception have often focused on the nature of visual perception—in the West what is often problematically assumed to be the most "innocent" (and dominant) mode of perception. It is commonplace to assume that

> To see [...] is to have picture-like representations of the world in consciousness; seeing is having a kind of mental picture. Vision in turn is thought to be the process whereby this kind of richly detailed internal conscious picture is produced [...] from pictures in the eyes, *retinal pictures*.
>
> (Noë, *Varieties of Presence* 82)

One of the limitations of Stanislavsky's attempt to work on the actor's concentration and attention was that he assumed the commonplace view of seeing as pictorial and the eye as perceiving "mental images." Benedetti defines the Russian *Vldenie* ("mental image") as "The picture the actor sees in his mind which relates to what he is saying or hearing" (in *An Actor's Work* 684).

Noë observes how, if we are looking at any object, whether a cup sitting on a table, a chair across the room, or a fan to the right over one's shoulder and above one, part of the object is hidden to view or absent, and yet it is "there." Contrary to the commonplace understanding of visual perception as pictorial, visual perception is always partial and fractal; in other words, in a certain sense what we see is only what is available to us from where we are located. Had I turned my head further "to see" the fan, it would have appeared to me from the position in which I was sitting in the room. But only the bottom of the fan blades would be visible to me, and that part of the motor casing available to view from my position in the room.

My interest here is in moving beyond accounts of objects in visual perception to the complex territory of what Merleau-Ponty identified as "the power to reckon with the possible," (*Phenomenology of Perception* 125) in other words, how we can utilize both motor as well as perceptual skills to encounter, experience, and generate what is not literally present to us as objects within our immediate environment by deploying of our active imagination. The actor's work with visual perception is not limited to the realm of what is encountered with objects or the environment within the immediate visual field of performance, but also *incorporates embodied acts of visualization and/or the imagination*—two realms of "the possible" that often constitute an essential part of an actor's performance score.

In *Mindsight* philosopher Colin McGinn sets out to provide a comprehensive investigation of the subject of the imagination. McGinn begins his study by differentiating between seeing something and actively imagining (or visualizing) it. McGinn points out that unlike percepts or what we perceive as we "see," "images can be willed but percepts cannot" (McGinn 12).[4] Following

Wittengenstein's observation that "imaging is [...] doing [...] [rather] than receiving," McGinn reminds us that "'visualize' is a verb of action while 'see' is not [...]. Forming an image is something I *do*, while seeing is something that happens to me [...]" (12–13).

Although McGinn is certainly correct that percepts per se cannot be willed, from the enactive perspective discussed above, his account of seeing is *far too passive*. To specifically "see" or "hear" what is available at the horizon of consciousness within the sensory/phenomenal fields available at any moment, is *to be active in relation to what we attend to*. What is important about McGinn's perspective is how in contrast to the physical constitution of our visual field for enactive encounter, when we actively visualize and utilize our "inner eye" ("mind's eye" or active imagination) *we are no longer bound by the constraints of the visual field of sight per se*. Visualization as a way of working with the active imagination can be described as a voluntary psychophysical act in which one sustains one's attention (and the ancillary awareness that arises from attending to) over time—such as the example of following one's breath described in detail below.

PERCEPTUAL/SENSORY SKILL ACQUISITION AND ACTING

An enactive approach to both perception and acting is counterintuitive in that it rejects the overly simplistic view of an input/output model where "perception is input from the world to mind, action is output from mind to world, thought is the mediating process" (Noë, *Action in Perception* 3). This overly simplistic input/output model is too often assumed in some American versions of Stanislavskian, conventional, textually based acting where the actor is taught to analyse and score a script (input), and then acts the score (output). Rather than the computer model of perception and the mind assumed when scoring a text, the actor, like other skilled practitioners, should understand how they engage the entire world of performance from a phenomenological perspective—as embodying and inhabiting a particular world of the "I can" through the development of specific modes of perceptual awareness-in-action developed through psychophysical training and/or experience. The actor's score should be viewed as one part of the actor's "I can" to be inhabited and embodied in the moment of performance.

Therefore, actor training might productively be viewed as a specific form of "perceptual apprenticeship" (Downey) through which the actor learns increasingly subtle and complex modes of directing one's attention and opening one's sensory awareness in/to/through the specific tasks, actions, and qualities that constitute the horizon of a performance score actualized in a specific theatrical environment. How might training in perceptual skills such as directing attention and/or opening a specific sensory awareness be taught to actors as a way of enhancing the actor's ability to more fully engage/embody/experience each task/action of a performance score?

AN EXAMPLE OF "PERCEPTUAL APPRENTICESHIP" AND "SKILL ACQUISITION": LEARNING TO "ATTEND TO"

> Yes it *is* hard to shift from distracting circumstances, slow down, and train oneself to attend [...] Becoming fully aware of something relatively simple—this inbreath, this outbreath—is a good place to start.
> (Austin, *Zen-Brain Reflections* 29)

At this point, I want to introduce a practical example of perceptual training and skill acquisition—how the actor can begin to quiet what Zeami described as the squirrel-like "busy" mind of the actor,[5] and become more attentive by learning to "attend to" the in-breath/out-breath.[6] The example I provide is of attention and awareness training that is part of the preliminary psychophysical training process for actors I have developed over the past thirty plus years (Zarrilli, *Psychophysical Acting*). I provide a description of the set of breath control exercises that introduce practitioners to a complete system of pre-performative training. I then provide a phenomenological description and analysis of how over time and with repetition one directs one's attention and simultaneously learns to open one's awareness while attending to.

Preliminary breath-control exercises.[7]

EXERCISE 1

Stand with the feet at shoulder-width, knees unlocked, hands at your sides. Keep the external eye/gaze focused straight ahead at eye level, but focused through the point ahead. Keeping your feet firmly rooted to the ground through the soles of the feet, sense down through the soles of the feet. Keeping the external eye/gaze focused straight ahead, allow your "inner eye" to focus on the in-breath. Keeping the mouth closed, follow the path of the breath on the inhalation, tracking its path through the nose, and down to the region about two to three inches below the navel—*dantian* (in Chinese; *nabhi mula* in Malayalam). As the breath "arrives" in this region, let it fill out, slightly expanding the lower abdomen. Attend to the in-breath as it comes to completion. Sense the slight space between this conclusion of the in-breath, and the initiation/impulse for the beginning of the out-breath. Keeping the inner eye focused on the breath, follow the exhalation from below the lower abdomen up through the torso, out through the nose, all the time keeping the sense of the breath's connection to the navel region as the diaphragm flattens out slightly. Sense the moment of completion of the out-breath, and the space before the impulse for the beginning of the next in-breath.

Repeat this pattern of in-breath (initiation ... sustain ... completion) and out-breath (initiation ... sustain ... completion) tracking the in-breath down, and the out-breath back up and out. If there is any type of distraction, acknowledge it, then bring your attention and focus back to following the in-breath or the out-breath. Sense the moment of initiation of the in-breath, its continuation as it is drawn in and down, and each moment of its completion. Sense the space between this moment of completion of the in-breath and the moment of initiation of the out-breath. This space between is that place where the potential for impulse and action reside; therefore, *it is the space where acting begins.*

After a few repetitions of this first breath control exercise, I also ask participants to imagine that their eyes are no longer located in their head, but rather, that their eyes are located at *dantian* in the lower abdomen. One should now be "looking" with both the external and inner eyes from the abdomen.

EXERCISES 2, 3, AND 4

While in Exercise 1 the body remains overtly still, in the next three exercises simple movements of the arms/hands are coordinated with each inhalation/exhalation—all the while keeping the external focus fixed on a specific point through which one looks ahead, and keeping the inner eye focused on tracking each inhalation/exhalation to and from the region below the navel. In Exercise 2 the hands/arms are extended but the elbows are not locked. Initially, the extended hands/arms ride an exhalation up to shoulder height. On the ensuing inhalation, the hands/arms open to the outside, coming to a momentary pause point on the completion of the inhalation, and then close back to center or the beginning point on the exhalation. In Exercises 3 and 4 different positions of the arms/hands are coordinated with each inhalation/exhalation.

This same pattern of utilizing the "inner eye" to follow the breath on each inhalation down, and each exhalation back up and out is practiced through a complete repertoire of preliminary yoga-stretching exercises that take approximately 20–30 minutes to complete. These preliminary exercises are followed by practice of *taiqiquan* (short-form of Wu style) for approximately 20–25 minutes. Altogether these sustained, attentive breathing exercises last 40–50 minutes.

DISCUSSION AND ANALYSIS

Visualization and use of the active imagination are "attention-dependent" (McGinn 27); in other words, one directs one's attention in a specific manner. As exemplified in the above exercises, one activates the "active" imagination at the same time one maintains an open perceptual awareness (McGinn 32–33). For instance, one remains simultaneously attentive to following the "inner eye" *while remaining open* to the visual field through the external eye as the gaze remains focused through a point ahead, *and* while keeping an open peripheral awareness. The active use of the "inner eye" in following the breath, and the imaginative re-location of the outer and inner eyes from the head to *dantian* are "'non-occlusive,' i.e., they do not block my sensory systems or cause them to malfunction or even distort the phenomenal character of my percept; image and percept happily coexist" (McGinn 33). The practitioner is able to "attend to" following the breath, the inner eye, *and* to the point directly ahead, while simultaneously sustaining an open awareness of the periphery of the visual field.

McGinn argues that "the mind's eye does afford a kind of seeing, that the experiences it delivers are straightforwardly visual, and that the phrase 'the mind's eye' is not metaphorical. It is literally true that we see with our mind; 'mindsight' is not an oxymoron (unlike 'blindsight')" (McGinn 42). For McGinn "The mind's eye [...] is an active organ" (46). Importantly, *for the actor this active mode of visualization or embodied activation of the imagination can be trained and developed. It is a perceptual skill to be acquired through assiduous practice.*

As a mode of pre-performative training of the actor's bodymind, keeping one's external eye focused through a point ahead, and simultaneously keeping the inner eye focused on tracking inhalations/exhalations to and from the region below the navel is a way of "deconditioning" our busy, analytical, squirrel-like minds. It is simultaneously a way of gaining access to both specificity of "attending to," as well as a fuller, felt sensory awareness of the bodymind as a gestalt. All kinds of potential traps await the practitioner when first encountering this type of psychophysical training of attention.

In the type of mindful breathing described above, with assiduous daily practice each breath eventually occupies "the foreground of the mental field" so that attention is loosened from any/all other thoughts, and one opens one's awareness to the physical/felt sensations that are available in the act of attending to—the "in" and "out" movements of the lower abdomen, the wide open periphery of the visual field, and so on. Austin offers a scientific explanation for why following the breath to/from the *dantian* and being attentive to the abdominal region is not easy:

> Our brain circuits already pay more attention to sensations arising from the head than they do from the chest, and pay still less attention to sensations from the abdomen. This normal phenomenon is termed "rostral dominance."
>
> (Austin, *Zen-Brain Reflections* 477)

Attentive, lower-abdominal breathing allows one to become attuned to an awareness of the bodymind that is *removed from head/chest areas*. This type of subtle perceptual awareness is invited as the practitioner is instructed to open one's awareness through the breath as one visualizes the breath reaching *dantian* and passing into/through the lower body—right down to/through the soles of the feet.

In further opening one's awareness to the lower body, the practitioner begins a process of exploring the subtleties of the relationship between the physical and mental/cognitive/perceptual elements interwoven at the horizon of consciousness. Japanese philosopher Yuasa Yasuo describes this process of perceptual skill development as "cultivation" (18); in other words, one is cultivating an ever subtler type of attention and embodied/sensory awareness.

The process is not necessarily easy. The beginner often struggles to direct attention to "follow" the breath. When teaching the first exercise, I ask practitioners to use the tip of their right finger to represent the breath, and then to track the finger as it follows the breath on its journey in through the nose, and down ... down ... down to *dantian*. This usually helps the individual begin to track the breath in and down, and then back up. For some participants, there can either be far too much *intention and effort* so that one self-consciously "pushes," *or* there is too little intentionality or specificity so that virtually "nothing" is happening; for instance, the neophyte is not yet utilizing the kind/quality of attentiveness necessary to sustain following the breath with one's "inner eye."

By assiduously performing this series of exercises, with guidance *over time* both attention and perceptual/sensory awareness are subtly attuned and cultivated as "complex psychophysiological changes" occur.[8]

- As one gives up "trying" or "pushing," the sense of intentionality at first necessary in learning the exercise ideally disappears to a point where there is no intentionality at all in the relationship to each in-breath, out-breath. Rather than being contained by the instruction to follow the breath, the "fields" of attention to and awareness of gradually open out, expanding and deepening.
- Associated with the initial effort and intentionality, the (will-full/autobiographical) self gradually recedes and/or drops out completely. This self could be said to "let go" as it (ego/will) recedes into the background.
- McGinn calls our attention to "the sensory character of the image," in other words, the "something it is like to have a visual image" (37), or in this example the use of the active imagination engaged with the inner eye. The "felt-sense" of the quality and relationship that is undeniably "my experience" (*ipseity*) to the embodiment of directing the active imagination is a crucial part of experiencing the phenomenon per se. This is the felt-sense that breath/energy (*qi/ki*) is circulating/moving within as one follows the breath, thereby animating the entire body-mind. This felt-sense is enhanced through a process of sedimentation, for instance, one gradually becomes a "*ki*-sensitive" person. One senses the "breath" moving through the feet, the top of the head, radiating out through the peripheral awareness, and behind. The "intensity" and "properties" of one's embodied awareness change—for example, there is greater openness, a "heightened" quality of attentiveness, and also greater specificity of attention per se as well as the sensory awareness that accompanies being attentive.

- There is an increasing proprioceptive sense of the bodymind as a gestalt in practice of these exercises.[9]
- As one gradually quietens the mind and intentionality, one achieves what is sometimes described in Zen Buddhist practice as no-mind (*mushin*) or "beginner's mind" (*shoshin*)—a mind "ready for anything [... and] open to everything" (Claxton 198). "No-mind does not mean coma. It means that no self-centered thoughts interrupt the flow. Similarly, 'non-action,' implies that your old *I-Me-Mine* isn't intervening. It does not mean that all motor behaviour stops" (Austin, *Zen-Brain Reflections* 38). In a state of no-mind, one does "*not have to think to be conscious* ... consciousness starts with *being aware*" (Austin, *Zen-Brain Reflections* 296).
- Ideally one inhabits a heightened, constant state of attentive readiness as well as an open awareness—a state where there is constant inner motion (Austin, *Zen-Brain Reflections* 297).
- Perceiving and doing are integrally interwoven—doing is perceiving, and one perceives in/through the doing.
- Equally one is being active/passive within immediate repetition of the structure of the exercise, responding to/acting/enacting in the moment to what arises in the horizon of phenomenal consciousness.

Given the dominance of the visual in the Western/cosmopolitan context, these initial psychophysical exercises initially work with/through the visual as the first point of departure; however, the repertory of phenomenal/sensory fields explored in the psychophysical training I have developed expands to incorporate heightening of sensory and auditory awareness—processes of tactile awareness and deep listening.[10] As one becomes attuned to the nuances of a heightened mode of attending to and simultaneously is able to open to deeper/fuller modes of sensory awareness, there develops what could be described as a feedback loop between where one directs one's attention and the opening of awareness to what is being done, i.e., the felt quality or resonance of how the bodymind is being engaged in that process of doing.

Two aspects of the experience of practicing these exercises stand out. In being attentive with the inner eye, in being attentive through the point ahead with the external gaze, and by opening one's sensory awareness both outward and inward, one is stretching both attention and awareness *toward* something. Attention reaches out into the environment as well as "out" within one's own bodymind. We attend *to* things, orient toward them, face them (Austin, *Zen-Brain Reflections* 38), while simultaneously sustaining an awareness of *the from,* in other words, keeping open to the subtler modes of awareness available to us from which the "to" emerges. As Thompson explains, one gradually suspends "one's inattentive immersion in experience" and develops "meta-awareness"—an "awareness of awareness" (*Mind in Life* 19). What develops is one's ability to constantly "reinhabit" the flow of experience "in a fresh way, namely, with heightened awareness and attunement" (Thompson, *Mind in Life* 19). Secondly, there is an integrated, inter-sensory relationship between, and engagement with our other senses, including proprioception, *as a gestalt*. The bodymind ideally operates as an integrated whole as one dialectically engages attending to and awareness of what one is doing as it is done. In achieving heightened attention there is equally an "attending with" and "attending to" the body in the act of its deployment of attention and awareness. Over time this heightened mode of somatic inhabitation can become a form of tacit, practical knowledge informing how one utilizes attention and awareness in performance.

As suggested above, and as described in the detailed example that follows, when enacting a performance score the actor is a perceptual being responding in the moment to her environment with an embodied consciousness that has been attuned through the rehearsal process to the sensory potential available in her score, i.e., the actor opens herself to the "feeling" of the form when moving, or to the "saidness" of the words in the act of speaking, or the echo in the sonority of the heard in attentive listening. Merleau-Ponty observes how, "Like crystal, like metal and many other substances, I am a sonorous being, but I hear my own vibration from within […]" (*The Visible and the Invisible* 144–45). One of the most nuanced discussions of this specific optimal state of consciousness in performance is that articulated by Zeami within the Japanese *noh* tradition where the performer's ideal state of consciousness is a fully embodied state of non-dual awareness/consciousness. To attain this state, "the actor must train until he reaches a level at which his innermost intent is beyond his own discriminating consciousness"—an active state of *mushin* ("no-mind") that lies beyond active intellectualization and where the effects of a performance "are not the result of the actor's conscious intention" (Quinn 226, 229).

APPLICATION TO PERFORMANCE: THE ECHO CHAMBER

What are the implications of this description and analysis for the actor's work in actual performance? I conclude with a discussion how the type perceptual attention and awareness discussed above, and developed through long-term psychophysical training, were deployed when performing *The Echo Chamber*—a production of The Llanarth Group.[11] *The Echo Chamber* was co-created by Kaite O'Reilly (with text by O'Reilly), Peader Kirk, Ian Morgan, and Phillip Zarrilli. It premiered at Chapter Arts Centre (Cardiff) 27 January–February 4, 2012, with Ian Morgan and Phillip Zarrilli performing and with lighting by Ace McCarron. Along with *Told by the Wind* (2010), *The Echo Chamber* is the second part of a projected trilogy created between East Asian aesthetic principles, contemporary physics, cosmology, and astrophysics.

Lasting approximately fifty-five minutes, the performance score consisted of fourteen "structures" of varying lengths interweaving text (mostly authored or adapted by O'Reilly) and psychophysical movement/imagery scores co-created during the development period and performed within a shifting soundscape (by Kirk). The two performers are on-stage throughout, composed and/or juxtaposed in relation to one another. As defined by McCarron's evocative and precise lighting, in some structures the two men inhabit specific sections of the performance space in parallel—sometimes completely in their own worlds (for example, Zarrilli stage right; Morgan stage left). In other structures, they seem to enter another's space. And in yet other structures they are actively aware of the presence of an Other—even if who this Other might be is not specified. In a few structures, they enter a common space where there are traces of a relationship and interaction—although this is usually indirect. One example of this subtle interaction is in Kaite O'Reilly's text for the concluding structure, *Outside Palindrome*. In delivering the following text, each performer is seated in a dim pool of light—they are separate and apart, yet inextricably linked as each voice is an echo of the other.

OUTSIDE PALINDROME BY KAITE O'REILLY

Ian Morgan	Phillip Zarrilli
Outside, in the dark.	Alone
	In the dark
In the dark of the lane and no light,	in the matter of night in that lane,
except the distant speck of the stars,	jots of light,
no moon, no	bright stabs,
no light but the speckling overhead,	no light but the promise of the infinite
the galaxy or milky way	in the dark
and the depth of the night as if	
he could fall	
upwards and into it,	the possibilities there,
yes,	giddy with the constellation
	overhead,
a headlong flight into the infinite,	leaning back,
the vast.	raised upwards,
But no such luck.	anchored to the earth
No.	feet planted side by side in the lane,
No fall into the infinitely vast,	two feet in the sensible walking
	boots anchored,
but a standing, no,	head raised upwards as if ready
	to fall,
a slouching,	slouching outside in the dark,
slouching outside in the dark,	slouching, no standing
head raised upwards as if ready to	
fall but anchored	ready for the fall into the infinitely
	vast
two feet in the sensible walking boots,	such luck

feet planted side by side in the lane, anchored to the earth as the head swam,	the vast
raised upwards,	a headlong flight into the infinite yes,
giddy with the constellation overhead, the possibilities there,	falling upwards and into it, the depth of the night
in the dark,	the galaxy or milky way
no light but the promise of the infinite,	the speckling overhead
the jots of light, bright stabs in the matter of night in that lane,	light
alone,	moon the distant speck of the stars
in the dark.	light in the lane outside in the light.

In performing this specific text-based structure, as one of the performers my attention and awareness were dialectically deployed between/among five closely related modes of engaging attention and/or sensory awareness:

1. *"tasting" the words*—in delivering text I open my awareness to the shape and feel of the words in my mouth as they are said;
2. *deep listening*—I attend to and open my auditory awareness to the text spoken by Morgan, as well as to the text I speak—absorbing hearing in saying;
3. *tempo-rhythm*—I attend to the inherent tempo-rhythm in O'Reilly text, allowing that to guide the impulse to speak, and auditorially absorb the tempo-rhythm of Morgan's speaking, as he in turn is responsive to my delivery;
4. *active resonance*—in my vocal delivery I embody, *in the moment,* what is evoked by O'Reilly's rich imagery in capturing the awe of the vast universe we inhabit.

To take a second example of the deployment of directing attention and opening awareness in *The Echo Chamber*, I will briefly describe my phenomenal engagement in the two closely related structures immediately prior to *Outside Palindrome*. Structure 12 is a very short transitional structure, *Still and White*, with the following text by O'Reilly:

ZARRILLI: Snow …
      Night frost …
      Crackling cold …
      Beneath my feet … ice crystals form …
MORGAN: Still. And white. Obeying mathematical laws of surprising subtlety. Crystals and polycrystals. Needles and dendrites splintering through. A fragment of the original broken symmetry at the beginning of time.

My four lines of poetic, fragmentary text consist of a series of images relating to winter—snow, frost, cold, ice. Seated just prior to the delivery of the first word, "Snow ...," using my peripheral awareness, I sense a shift in the environment I am inhabiting in this moment which is different from what I had been attending to in the prior structure/scene. There is "something" there in the environment, but what is it? At this point I do not know. Similar to my noticing the air moving in the room while writing this essay in Singapore, what is it that is hovering on the horizon of my phenomenal/sensory awareness? I take the time to attend to *what might be present* and allow this possibility/question to "fill" my awareness ... but *what it might be is still unknown* to me. It remains a question. But gradually, sensing that what is "there" is in the space above me and somewhat in the distance, I slowly look up. "It" is there. "It" is snow falling from the sky. Looking up and seeing, I then simply observe, speaking:

"Snow"

Using the type of psychophysical awareness that is developed when following my breath with my "inner eye," I look up from *dantian* with my "inner eye" and using my active imagination, I see, watch, and track a snowflake as it "appears" and continues "falling." I move toward it, and it "lands" in my right palm, melting.

On the horizon of my consciousness, another "something" is there, but I do not yet know what it is. With my external focus still on my palm where the snowflake has melted, my visual gaze and attention shifts to the visual horizon at just above my eye-level. There ... scanning the visual horizon before me ... "night frost" appears in my active imagination. I speak again:

"Night frost ..."

I sense the space around me ... along my skin and in the air to my right, dropping my visual focus down right so that I heighten both my attention and open my sensory awareness through my skin and ears ...

"Crackling cold ..."

Another 'something' at the horizon of my consciousness ... my feet (which are bare) ... the soles of my feet . ...Sensing them, I attend to the soles of my feet ... sensing that something is happening beneath my feet where they touch the floor ...

"Beneath my feet ... ice crystals form ..."

And now ... something else again ... sounds at first from a distance ... capturing my auditory awareness. Even as Morgan delivers his lines from

Structure 12 (above), a sound-mix (recorded music) physically draws me downstage into a shaft of space running through the centre of the playing space from downstage to upstage. There, on the visual horizon, and in the midst of the impulses of sound beginning to move me, I look ahead and scan the horizon, speaking:

"Over the fields of last night's snow … ice …
Over the fields of last night's snow … ice …"

In Structure 13, "Willow dance," Morgan and I "dance" out this semi-improvised structure as the music moves each of us. Following a relatively set choreographic pattern in terms of our use of space and timing off of one another, my primary task is to allow what I sense as ice-like/electric impulses (driven by the music) originating in the soles of my feet to pulse into and through my entire body. I no longer have an external point of visual attention; rather, my "gaze" is indirect, and I have opened my attention and awareness through my ears, and inside my body down to my feet as they encounter the floor. Although as a performer I remain "centered" and balanced, I work against this centeredness as the pulses of the music drive through me. From the audience's perspective I move erratically, responding to electrifying impulses that I cannot/do not seem to control. My eyes and visual attention are directed not outward into the environment, but continue throughout the "dance" to be directed back *inside of me*. My external eye never focuses on any point external to me as *I am moved* by/with/through the pulses of the music during this eleven-plus-minute structure.

CONCLUDING DISCUSSION

The specific examples from *The Echo Chamber* offered above provide examples of how the horizon of the actor's phenomenal/sensory field in performance consists of the "actual" phenomenon offered by precepts within the environment, such as the actual presence of Morgan as the other actor in the theatrical space, the "actual" sensory stimuli offered by engaging the text per se, as well as the "actual" presence of what is enacted/brought into the environment by engaging my active imagination and my heightened and open awareness. Just as visual percepts are not static pictures at which we look, use of the active imagination does not produce *pictures that I look at or see*. Rather when engaging the active imagination, each specific "image" is emergent in the moment of its embodied appearance—like "seeing" "snow" or "feeling through the skin" the "crackling cold." In an enactive view of acting, each active image materializes or "shows up" in the moment of its appearance. The phenomenal/sensory field of the actor is constituted at the horizon of consciousness by the actor's "actual" bodymind and by the aesthetic and fictive (but nevertheless actual) images which have been actively generated and developed as part of the performance score.

NOTES

1. For example, see Stewart, John, Olivier Gapenne, and Ezequiel A. Di Paolo, eds. *Enaction: Toward a New Paradigm for Cognitive Science*. Cambridge: MIT P, 2010.
2. See Depraz, Natalie, Francisco J. Varela, and Pierre Vermersch, *On Becoming Aware: A Pragmatics of Experiencing*. Advanced in Consciousness Research Book 43. Amsterdam: John Benjamins Publishing Company, 2003; and Evan Thompson, *Mind in Life: Biology, Phenomenology, and the Sciences of Mind*. Cambridge: The Belknap Press of Harvard UP, 2007.
3. It is important to note that the focus on the nature of subjective experience in phenomenology is never reduced to an ego-driven, narcissistic sense of self-absorption, but rather focuses on the "feel of what happens" to or for "me" within an experience.
4. McGinn provides an incisive discussion of the difference between the "inner eye" and percepts: "There is no boundary to the image imposed by the constraints of optics and retinal anatomy, so we do not have the experience of taking in new imaged objects as we shift the orientation of the inner eye: we do not *point* the inner eye in a new direction when we form a new image [...] There is no blind spot, caused by the origin of the optic nerve from the retina to the brain. The imagined object is not presented as in some definite spatial relation to the perceiver—that is, typically, in front of him [...] The visual field of the body's eye is deeply connected to the facts of sensory anatomy and physics, but the image is under no such constraints. This is why we can imagine what has no privileged spatial relation to the body. The intuitive manifestation of this is that perceived objects are felt to be in a definite relation to the bodily eyes—they are arranged before them in a spatial manifold—but the inner eye does not present its objects in any such relation to the body" (22–23).
5. Cognitive scientist James Austin recently asked essentially the same question Zeami posed long ago: "How can one escape from that restless 'monkey-mind,' let go of discursive thoughts, settle down into clear, bare awareness?" (*Zen-Brain Reflections* 33).
6. All modes of embodied, skillful, virtuosic practice require the development of heightened modes of attention and the opening of one's awareness appropriate to that specific type of practice whether football, carpentry, meditation, or acting. The type of attentive breathing described here is utilized to train the martial artist as well as for meditation. Depending on the context, purpose, and mode of instruction, the same exercises can be used to open awareness and attention outward into the environment, inward in specific ways, or to balance attending to and awareness of that is simultaneously outward *and* inward.
7. These breath exercises were taught to me by Sakhav P. V. Mohamedunni Gurukkal of the Navajeevan Kalari Sangham in 1983. In Kerala, one simply does the exercise, imitating the master. There is little if any explanation. As a consequence, it takes years to achieve an optimal state of practice. The

instructions and explanation of the inner and outer eye are my own. The instructions help create a bridge that allows the actor to access the potential benefit of the exercises sooner than later.
8. Austin, *Zen-Brain Reflections* xxv. At a basic physiological level, Austin explains that these changes operate through "excitation, inhibition, and disinhibition. The words describe the way impulses from one neuronal module go on to increase or decrease the firing rates of other cell assemblies. Few of the resulting configurations actually filter up into consciousness, let alone into accurate first-person reports" (*Zen-Brain Reflections* 3). Austin tracks changes to the "*field, intensity, structure, properties,* and *flow*" of the extraordinary state (*Zen-Brain Reflections* 296). I utilize and expand on his four categories.
9. Austin explains how "When proprioceptive is used in the neurosciences, it refers to vital internal sensory signals, the ones that help establish our *physical* sense of self. These signals arise chiefly from special receptors in our muscles, joints, and tendons. When stretched, these receptors help us generate a sense of our body's position and movement within external space. Proprioceptive impulses join other somatosensory messages up in the parietal cortex" (*Zen-Brain Reflections* 11).
10. See Zarrilli, *Altered Consciousness*; Ansuman Biswas, and Zarrilli, *Psychophysical Acting* on tactile and other modes of awareness.
11. For a video trailer of *The Echo Chamber* visit www.youtube.com/watch?v=fpSoq-qPvnI. The text in the trailer is "Outside Palindrome," and there are excerpts of "Dance the Willow Dance." Founded in 2000, the Llanarth Group is an association of theatre/performance artists dedicated to producing international theatre of the highest quality through in-depth psychophysical training of actors from all cultures. *The Echo Chamber* was funded, in part, by the Arts Council of Wales.

WORKS CITED

Austin, James H. *Selfless Insight: Zen and the Meditative Transformations of Consciousness*. Cambridge: MIT P, 2009.
———. *Zen-Brain Reflections*. Cambridge: MIT Press, 2006.
Biswas, Ansuman. "The Music of What Happens: Mind, Meditation, and Music as Movement." *Music and Consciousness*. Eds. David Clarke and Eric Clarke. Oxford: Oxford UP, 2011. 95–110.
Cardena, Etzel and Michael Winkelman, eds. *Altering Consciousness: Multidisciplinary Perspectives Volume 1: History, Culture and the Humanities; Volume 2: Biological and Psychological Perspectives*. Santa Barbara: Praeger, 2011.
Clarke, David and Eric Clarke, eds. *Music and Consciousness: Philosophical, Psychological, and Cultural Perspectives*. Oxford: Oxford UP, 2011.
Claxton, Guy. *Hare Brain and Tortoise Mind*. London: Fourth Estate, 1998.
Csordas, Thomas J. "Somatic Modes of Attention." *Cultural Anthropology* 8.2 (1993): 135–156.
Downey, Greg. "Educating the Eyes: Bio-Cultural Anthropology and Physical Education," *Anthropology in Action: Journal for Applied Anthropology in Policy and Practice,* 12.2 (2005): 56–71.
Gallagher, Shaun. "Phenomenological Approaches to Consciousness." *The Blackwell Companion to Consciousness*. Eds. Max Velmans and Susan Schneider. Malden, MA: Blackwell Publishing, 2007. 686–696.

Hare, Tom. Trans. *Zeami: Performance Notes.* N.Y.: Columbia UP, 2008.
Ingold, Tim. *The Perception of the Environment.* London: Routledge, 2000.
James, William. *The Principles of Psychology.* Cambridge: Cambridge UP, 1890/91.
McGinn, Colin. *Mindsight: Image, Dream, Meaning.* Cambridge: Harvard UP, 2004.
Merleau-Ponty, Maurice. *The Visible and the Invisible.* Trans. Alphonso Lingis. Evanston: Northwestern UP, 1968.
———. *Phenomenology of Perception.* Trans. C. Smith. London: Routledge, 1962.
Nearman, Mark. "Zeami's *Kyūi*: A Pedagogical Guide for Teachers of Acting." *Monumenta Nipponica,* 33.3 (1978): 299–332.
Noë, Alva. *Varieties of Presence.* Cambridge: Harvard UP, 2012.
———. *Action in Perception.* Cambridge: MIT P, 2004.
Quinn, Shelley Fenno. *Developing Zeami: The Noh Actor's Attunement in Practice.* Honolulu: U of Hawaii P, 2005.
Romdenh-Romluc, Komarine. *Merleau-Ponty and Phenomenology of Perception.* London: Routledge, 2011.
Seager, William. "A Brief History of the Philosophical Problem of Consciousness." *The Cambridge Handbook of Consciousness.* Eds. Philip David Zelazo, Morris Moscovitch, and Evan Thompson. Cambridge: Cambridge UP, 2007. 9–33.
Stanislavsky, Konstantin. *An Actor's Work.* Trans. Jean Benedetti. London: Routledge, 2008.
———. *An Actor Prepares.* Trans. Elizabeth Reynolds Hapgood. New York: Theatre Arts Books, 1980 [1936].
Taylor, Carman. "Foreword." *Phenomenology of Perception.* Maurice Merleau-Ponty. London: Routledge, 2012.
Thompson, Evan. *Mind in life: Biology, Phenomenology, and the Sciences of Mind.* Cambridge: The Belknap Press of Harvard UP, 2007a.
Thompson, Evan and Dan Zahavi. "Philosophical Issues: Phenomenology." *The Cambridge Handbook of Consciousness.* Eds. Zelazo, Philip David, Morris Moscovitch, Evan Thompson. Cambridge: Cambridge UP, 2007. 67–87.
Varela, Francisco, J. Evan Thompson and Eleanor Rosch. *The Embodied Mind: Cognitive Science and Human Experience.* Cambridge: MIT P, 1991.
Whyman, R. *The Stanislavsky System of Acting: Legacy and Influence in Modern Performance.* Cambridge: Cambridge UP, 2008.
Yuasa Yasuo. *The Body.* Albany: State U of New York P, 1987.
Zarrilli, Phillip. "'…' presence …' as a question and emergent possibility: a case study from the performer's perspective." *Archeologies of Presence.* Eds. Gabriella Giannachi and Nick Kay. London: Routledge, 2012. 119–152.
———. "Altered Consciousness in Performance: West and East." *Altering Consciouosness, Multidisciplinary Perspectives, Vol. I.* Eds. Etzel Cardena and Michael Winkelman. Santa Barbara: Praeger, 2011: 301–326.
———. *Psychophysical Acting: An Intercultural Approach after Stanislavski.* London: Routledge, 2009.
Zeami, Motokiyo. *The Flowering Spirit: Classic Teachings on the Art of No.* Trans. William Scott Wilson. Tokyo: Kodansha International, 2006.
Zelazo, Philip David, Morris Moscovitch, Evan Thompson, eds. *The Cambridge Handbook of Consciousness.* Cambridge: Cambridge UP, 2007.

5 Playing the Subject Card
Strategies of the Subjective
Philipa Rothfield

> *I love him who lives for knowledge and who writes to know that one day the Overman may live. And thus he wills his own downfall.*
> (Nietzsche qtd. in Deleuze, *Nietzsche and Philosophy* 174)
>
> *Prevent the things you have been doing and you are half way home.*
> (Alexander 6)

INTRODUCTION

Postmodern choreographer Russell Dumas is reluctant to leave his dancers to rehearse on their own. Why? Because they will only practice their "bad habits." How could they do otherwise? If we are our habits, as Dumas often claims, then there is very little we can do to overcome them. *Or is there?* Alexander technique represents an attempt to overcome habit. Predicated upon its own diagnosis of what is bad about habit (its tendency to contract into action), Alexander technique offers a strategic response, one which aims to inhibit habit so as to make way for something else: the possibility of moving otherwise. Alexander spoke of non-doing in relation to his technique, the aim being to subtract "the doer" from "the deed."[1] Although non-doing appears to lack subjective agency, the technique actually calls for a very specific mode of engagement on the part of its subject. There are two trajectories implicit within Alexander work: one, a certain way of dealing with subjectivity (*qua* habit), and two, the generation of movement beyond the habitual everyday. The first trajectory (subjective engagement) is a condition of possibility for the second (creating difference beyond the habitual body). Rebecca Nettl-Fiol writes that, "Non-doing [in Alexander technique] allows the space for something different to occur" (105). I am interested in the creation of this space. What does it mean to make space for something new to occur in the body—beyond habit—and how might this be conceived in philosophical terms?

The following discussion will draw upon and bring into relation two distinct philosophical approaches towards the body. One integrates the body with subjectivity; the other keeps them apart. Maurice Merleau-Ponty's phenomenological account of perception resists mind/body dualism by pursuing a fully corporeal sense of the subjective. His notion of the lived body brings subjectivity and the body together, focusing on what a body does within the subject's existential milieu. Friedrich Nietzsche also looks at what a body does, but he attempts to *extract* the body from subjectivity. Nietzsche appeals to relations between underlying forces as the basis for the subjective realm. The key difference between these two approaches lies in their attitude towards subjectivity. While Merleau-Ponty is interested in following subjectivity through the variety of its lived incarnations, Nietzsche takes a dim view of the subject-position and all that it entails. For Merleau-Ponty then, the philosophical (and existential) value of subjectivity is given, while the thrust of Nietzschean philosophy is to move *beyond* subjectivity. Nietzsche thus inserts a philosophical wedge between subjectivity and the body.[2] Pierre Klossowski and Gilles Deleuze both work this gap between subjectivity and the body.[3] Building on Klossowski's distinction between (subjective) understanding and a much broader corporeal intelligence, Deleuze pursues the trajectory of Nietzsche's movement beyond the human. His interpretation of Nietzsche's philosophy examines the means whereby subjectivity can become something other than itself. By positing a horizon of overcoming, he explores the possible emergence of an outside or beyond subjectivity, not for the sake of mere destruction—nihilism—but in order to crack open new territory, beyond the confines of "all known values" (Deleuze, *Nietzsche and Philosophy* 177). In the context of movement discourse, one might interpret Deleuze's pathway as the pursuit of difference in the body, beyond the forces established by and associated with training, technique and habit.

I want to use both philosophical approaches—phenomenology and Nietzschean philosophy—to describe what goes on in practices like the Alexander technique, which aim to displace subjectivity so as to enable the body to perform beyond its habitual repertoire. While Alexander technique will ultimately be construed in terms of Nietzschean overcoming, it also operates on the subjective side of the philosophical divide: Alexander technique requires a nuanced pragmatism on the part of the dancer-subject in order to succeed. In what follows, I claim that there are a variety of ways to perform subjectivity, that subjectivity is itself liable to strategic deployment. The reference to strategy is two-fold: first, that subjectivity can be regarded in strategic terms, as something that can be "played" within movement practices, and second, that phenomenology can itself be treated strategically, that is, "tactically used without necessarily retaining general commitment" to all its presumptions (Gross 193).[4] I draw on Merleau-Ponty's phenomenological account of the lived body in order to determine the manner in which subjectivity is strategically deployed within Alexander technique. I have argued elsewhere that Merleau-Ponty's existential phenomenology paves the way for a focus on the different ways in which the body is lived.[5] Rather than expound a common modality of embodiment, I look to the vicissitudes of practice and situation as differentiating factors that impact upon the nuances of the lived body. In this context, the notion of the lived body is invoked as a means to discern what goes on in techniques, like Alexander, which employ subjectivity so as to defuse it, and which acknowledge habit in order to overcome it. The common feature of these strategies is their element of *undoing* understood in terms of overcoming.

My proposition is that there are times when we can view subjectivity as giving way to a kind of corporeal takeover, whereby subjectivity plays itself in the mode of its own overcoming, so that the body can extend itself: beyond the givens of habit, towards new corporeal terrain. I will argue that these two moments—subjective overcoming and corporeal becoming—are present in practices that, like Alexander, target the downside of habit.[6] My argument will be that the student of Alexander technique aims towards an active destruction of subjectivity, articulated in terms of inhibition and non-doing, towards a horizon of new corporeal value. In so doing, practices such as the Alexander technique straddle the Nietzschean divide between the lived body (the domain of subjectivity) and that which lies beyond (corporeal becoming).

ALEXANDER TECHNIQUE

Alexander technique is predicated upon a critique of everyday human movement, specifically its tendency to contract into action.[7] Contraction (foreshortening) is a consequence of the common tendency to fixate upon the ends of action rather than their means of achievement. Alexander technique analyzes movement in directional terms, that is, as a set of movement trajectories (directions) expressed in the body. Alexander's depiction of contraction is therefore framed in terms of direction: that most people foreshorten their bodies by allowing their head to move down and back relative to the spine, a widespread pattern (or direction) that is both habitual and unconscious. Alexander also noted the effect of these habits on perception, which tends to normalize the body's habitual posture.[8] Thus a person used to stooping may feel erect when they are not. Similarly, the attempt to "stand straight" can be interpreted in all sorts of ways because the effort itself is mediated by a distorted perceptual compass.[9]

By way of response, Alexander proposed a two-fold strategy—*inhibition* plus *the Alexander directions*. Inhibition is very important for Alexander, who sees it as the only way to resist the subconscious habits of everyday life (15). According to Alexander, inhibition is the gateway for the introduction of new kinaesthetic experiences. The task of inhibition is to defuse habit, making room for a different kind of agency in the body, hopefully prompted by the Alexander directions. The Alexander directions are a set of trajectories or vectors articulated in thought (and in action) to counteract the widespread predisposition towards contraction. Their aim is towards expansion in movement. For example: *free the neck to allow the head to move forwards and up, so that the back can lengthen and widen*. They are meant to be a practical antidote to contraction.

Activation of the Alexander directions is easier said than done because the directions represent a *modus operandi* foreign to habitual subjectivity. The notion of inhibition is a start, but how to make the next move? This is where the Alexander teacher comes into play, as the facilitator of new modes of thought in the body.[10] The role of the teacher is to make change possible, in the form of new movement possibilities. Alexander teachers work through the dynamics of touch. On the one hand, touch is a kind of diagnostic tool, an opportunity to feel what a body is doing, but it is also an avenue of introduction. Touch is the means by which new modes of corporeal thought pass through the hands into another body. Through touch, teachers make new corporeal forces *available* to the body of the other. Eva Karczag writes, "My Alexander hands-on knowledge allows me to impart to students a subtle, energetic quality of touch, and the concept of non-doing, the kind of touch where thinking translates though the hands into one's partner" ("Explorations within the New Dance Aesthetic" 45).

The quality and character of the Alexander teacher's touch depends upon the porosity of corporeal boundaries, and aspires towards a flow of insight from one body to another. Elizabeth Dempster writes of the flow of insight through touch as the "transmission of precise kinaesthetic experience" ("Some Notes on the Staging of Ideokinesis" 38). Touch enlivens the connection between bodies, whereby thought in one body can provoke new thoughts in the body of the other. Its proximity encourages the passage of new information, new corporeal possibilities. Kinaesthetic experience is made available to the body of the student. Whether and how that experience is taken up is a question of learning or change. Inhibition of old habits is no easy task. As John Dewey, a long-time student of the technique, writes: "The hardest thing to attend to is that which is closest to ourselves, that which is most constant and familiar. And this closest 'something' is precisely, ourselves, our own habits and ways of doing things" (qtd. in Alexander 178). Alexander was of the view that the body will revert to its ingrained habits if the subject attempts to act, that agency is itself 'tainted' by the habitual. Hence the need for *inhibition*.

The introduction of the directions—which Alexander calls "the means whereby"—aims to supplant habit with another set of possibilities.[11] Perhaps thinking the Alexander directions neutralizes the tendencies of habitual subjectivity. The Alexander technique specifically asks the subject to stop before embarking upon any action. Stopping could be seen as the means to create a gap between intention and action. The subsequent thought of the directions insinuates itself into that gap, keeping habit at bay through their expansive remit. Students are asked to renew the directions time and again, to repeatedly think them in the body. If the directions represent a mode of expansion in the body—contra contraction—their ongoing renewal aims to resist lapsing into end-oriented movement. It is as if the directions keep the body in a state of dynamic readiness, towards a wide spectrum of possibility at each and every moment of renewal. If habit contracts into goal-directed action, then the Alexander directions keep the body alive to the wider possibilities that inhabit the moment. The Alexander body is not committed to the performance of any particular act but is *a body available to movement*.[12] The notion of availability signals the activity of the directions, Alexander's "means whereby" bodies might sustain openness (resistance to closure). In light of the above, it could be suggested that the practice of expansion is a means to keep alive the virtual (and shifting) field of possibility underlying the dynamic body. Once an action takes on a goal-directed character, the virtual field of possibility is liable to shrink towards the subject's habitual means of movement and the teleological ends of motor intentionality. Hence, Alexander's emphasis on the "means whereby" and its several strategies aimed to cultivate expansion in the body.

It is no easy matter to resist the habits of a lifetime. The tendency to contract into action is well ensconced and clearly embedded within action *per se*. This means that any deliberate attempt to act is doomed right from the start. It is also where the subtlety of the practice lies—in the requirement to stop, that is, to inhibit one's normal way of doing things and to somehow think the directions but not "do" them. The technique thereby cultivates a distinction between "end gaining" (habitual motor intentionality) and "the means whereby" (activation of the Alexander directions in action) (Alexander 14). The aim is to give up end gaining in favor of the means whereby. Inhibition on the one hand, directional thought as a mode of non-doing on the other. How might this be understood in phenomenological terms?

PHENOMENOLOGICAL NON-DOING

Merleau-Ponty's depiction of our usual movement subjectivity is quite similar to Alexander's notion of end gaining, that is, the tendency to focus on the intended ends of action. In *Phenomenology of Perception*, Merleau-Ponty writes of a subject typically oriented towards the object. He also uses terms such as "bodily purpose" (Merleau-Ponty 99) and "motor intentionality" (137–8) in order to describe the sense in which the body comprises "an attitude directed towards a certain existing or possible task" (Merleau-Ponty 100). Hubert Dreyfus defines motor intentionality as "the way the body tends towards an optimal grip on its object," an exhibition of what he terms "absorbed coping" (63). The general point is that our everyday movement habits serve our purposes well, so well that they merge with our very projects. Many phenomenologists give expression to the seamless immersion of the lived body in its situation, and indeed, Alexander would probably agree with all that they would say. The difference lies in Alexander's critical diagnosis of immersion (absorbed coping) and the pragmatic implications of his response. The Alexander technique aims to resist immersion. Alexander is more interested in loosening than maintaining grip. The technique aims to convert the subject's immersion in the perceptual scene into another *modus operandi* altogether, namely the means whereby. According to the technique, the means whereby lies beyond habit (requiring inhibition instead), comprising a mode of activity distinct from the intentional moment of movement (since it calls for non-doing). In a sense, the focus on "the means whereby" rather than "end gaining" takes the teleology out of action.

A key question for phenomenologists of the Alexander technique is whether inhibition can be accommodated within motor intentionality at all. Merleau-Ponty's attitude towards movement subjectivity is broader than his depiction of the typical perceptual attitude. His investigation of the brain-damaged Schneider not only clarifies the flexibility of "normal" facility, but it also acknowledges that there is a variety of (non-normative) movement possibilities.[13] The notion of inhibition and non-doing could be construed as one of these modes of possibility. Their attempt to displace the habitual suggests a deconstructive attitude directed towards the typical tendencies of perceptual life, a kind of transformation aimed to extract the intentional moment from the subject's everyday milieu. Non-doing is not a kind of doing, however. Rather, it represents the attempt to "cancel out" habitual subjectivity.

THE BODY IN NIETZSCHE

The invocation of the Alexander directions does not work on the plane of subjectivity because subjectivity is for Alexander inherently limited. The directions represent a movement beyond subjective agency. It is at this point that I want to venture another way of thinking about the body in movement, one which sharply distinguishes between subjectivity and the body. I want to contrast the phenomenological view with what I shall call the Nietzschean body. Although Nietzsche does not theorize the body as such, he often appeals to the superior values inherent in corporeal becoming. In *Daybreak*, he effectively displaces the subject-position in favor of a corporeal account which appeals to the workings of underlying drives. According to Nietzsche, the self is an end-point, the manifestation and symptom of the transitory dominance of one drive over the others. The "function" of the self is to interpret these relations of dominance, an interpretation which is itself bound to the vicissitudes of the drives. The body in Nietzsche is thus conceived as a momentary formation, a relation between drives (or forces) whose dynamic becoming arises from their embedded will to power. Nietzsche's will to power is a principle of becoming. It is the driving force behind the creation of events, the generative principle that inheres in all that which occurs, in all becomings. The will to power is neither an act of human will nor a scientific form of (efficient) causality. Rather it is embedded within events. It is a mutable, organizing principle that momentarily shapes the chaotic forces of the world.

The Nietzschean departure from phenomenology arises both in its scepticism towards subjectivity as well as its appeal to dynamic relations between forces. Although life is refracted through a sense of personal identity (*qua* experience), for Nietzsche, this perspective is inherently distorted. Subjectivity is in short a mode of misrecognition: "What gives us the extraordinary strength of our belief in causality is *not* the great habit of the succession of occurrences but our *incapacity* to *interpret* what happens other than as happening out of *intentions* (Nietzsche, Late Notebooks 74).

Hence the lure of the phenomenological project is testimony to our incapacity to experience the world beyond the gamut of our own subjectivity. Nietzsche would not deny the *appearance* of phenomenological subjectivity (the subject as phenomenon), but he would question its veracity (the subject as causal agent). His denial that there is a doer behind the deed is thus not a dispute with appearances. Like the anti-humanist and the poststructuralist, he acknowledges the force of subjectivity while attributing its source to forces beyond the subject-position (Nietzsche, Late Notebooks 60). The subject is therefore an end-point and not the source of human agency:

> Everything which enters consciousness is the last link in a chain, a closure. It is just an illusion that one thought is the immediate cause of another thought. The events which are *actually* connected are played out below our consciousness: the series and sequences of feelings, thoughts, etc., that appear as symptoms of what actually happens!
> (Nietzsche 60, my emphasis)

Nietzsche thus runs a different line to Merleau-Ponty's notion of the lived body as that which integrates subjectivity with corporeality. Although Merleau-Ponty fully recognized that often it is the body which acts (especially according to habit), the subject for Merleau-Ponty is entitled to claim the body's agency as its own. By contrast, Nietzsche treats subjectivity as a symptomatic formation masking an underlying corporeal reality. The Nietzschean body consists of multiple forces in contest with one another. Nietzsche thereby distinguishes between what the body does (by virtue of the drives) and the subject's access to, and experience of, what the body does. We imagine ourselves as the authors of our actions. This is the façade of human agency, the tendency to posit oneself at the centre of thought and action. It is the drive to subjectivity, manifest writ large and represented in the phenomenological project.

INTERPRETING NIETZSCHE

Nietzschean philosophy forces a split between subjectivity and the body, between the perspective of subjectivity and that of corporeal becoming. Nietzsche's interpreters, particularly Deleuze and Klossowski, take up this difference in Nietzsche. Klossowski addresses the way in which the subject appropriates the body's changing states as its own. For Klossowski, this amounts to a hermeneutic problem: how am I able to make sense of my body's fluctuations as expressions of a singular, sovereign self? The point is that the work of constructing an ongoing identity out of fluctuating corporeal states pursues a different interest from the plane of corporeal activity as such. Klossowski writes that "the body provided Nietzsche with a completely different perspective, namely, the perspective of active forces" (19).

Deleuze's trajectory is slightly different. While he equally distinguishes between subjectivity and the body, he sets out to follow through the transformative potential of Nietzschean philosophy, moving beyond subjectivity towards another kind of becoming. For Deleuze, the difference between subjectivity and a non-subjective order of becoming can be clarified through Nietzsche's distinction between master and slave morality.[14] According to Nietzsche, slave morality is the means by which the powerless (slaves) reframe the actions and achievements of the powerful (masters). The slave re-values the positive achievements of the masters by deeming their activity evil. Slave morality derives (and applies to itself) the virtue of goodness by negating the value of the other's achievements. It does not depend upon the slave's *actions* so much as a *reaction* to the other, along with a re-evaluation of the other's moral worth. Nietzsche makes the point that the slave's re-evaluation occurs in the realm of the imaginary. The slave doesn't *do* anything apart from reverse the values associated with action. Action is no longer good because it is affirmed, it is judged according to this newly minted scale of moral virtue.

Deleuze draws upon Nietzsche's distinction between master and slave morality in order to distinguish between two very different realms: the world of action and the domain of reaction. He makes a great deal of the fact that the "work" of the slave is all about re-valuing what the master does. The slave doesn't "do"; rather, she/he reacts, re-values, and feels. Reaction is a key element in the characterization of human experience. It is not where things get done but is rather the site of reinterpretation and appropriation, the means by which the doer is (re)constructed out of the deed. Deleuze develops a framework for distinguishing between these two very different types—action and experience— which he utilizes to show how the one type can *become* the other.[15] Firstly, becoming-reactive represents the turnaround of active force into the "spider web" of experience.[16] And conversely, becoming-active represents the conversion of experience or consciousness into something else. Deleuze extends this categorization of becoming through a discussion of the two kinds of quality that characterize the will to power. In brief, these are affirmative and negative. In this scheme of things, not only is reactive force able to become active, it can be linked to a change of quality in the will to power from negative to affirmative. In order for this to occur, *something must happen* to subjectivity which is typically associated with a negative will to power. Deleuze discusses this moment and manner of transformation where subjectivity gives over to the emergence of another type. He calls it active destruction (Deleuze, *Nietzsche and Philosophy* 174).[17] Active destruction is the means by which subjectivity, as a type, is overcome. Likewise, the "man of active destruction" is the one who wants to be overcome (Deleuze, *Nietzsche and Philosophy* 174). Deleuze writes, "Zarathustra praises the man of active destruction 'I love him who lives for knowledge and who wishes to know that one day the Overman may live. *And thus he wills his own downfall*'" (*Nietzsche and Philosophy* 174). Active destruction enables Deleuze to follow the overcoming of subjectivity into new, affirmative territory, beyond the reactive domain.

UNDOING AS OVERCOMING

It has been suggested that, from a phenomenological point of view, inhibition takes the teleology out of action, and the intentionality out of motor intentionality. Inhibition and non-action seem to take the puff out of subjectivity. But not so for the body. Viewed through Nietzschean critique, the story continues in a different vein. First of all, undoing can be seen as a means to overcome subjectivity. Nietzschean philosophy suggests that subjectivity can give way to the body through staging its overcoming. In *Daybreak*, Nietzsche poses a range of explorations, aimed towards the creation of new corporeal values. Many of these hint at overcoming subjectivity. Nietzsche writes of the need to "lose oneself", of the attempt to think and feel differently, of the need to conduct a campaign "against yourself", "to construct anew the laws of life and action" (*Daybreak* 103, 305, 373, 451).

Overcoming in Nietzsche is a prelude to the creation of new forms of value, new modes of corporeal creation. It is as this point that Alexander's focus on inhibition and non-doing enters the picture. Alexander technique exemplifies Nietzsche's domain of experimentation in the name of overcoming. Its wager is that subjectivity can be deployed, defused and demoted in order to facilitate the enhancement of corporeal capacity towards what Deleuze calls the moment of transmutation, according to which the constraints of subjectivity give way to an affirmative manner of creation. The decisive moment for Deleuze hovers between the demise of subjectivity and the creation of value, where "difference begins its play" (*Nietzsche and Philosophy* 190). Active destruction represents the movement from the human to a new way of thinking, "other than the human type" (Deleuze, *Nietzsche and Philosophy* 163). Active destruction represents the shift from the domain of the subjective to the sphere of corporeal creation. Its overcoming of subjectivity is an antidote to the forces of reaction (subjectivity). From the point of view of the subject, active destruction is the prospect of annihilation, but from the point of view of the body, of the dance of becoming, active destruction enables the "joy of becoming," manifest in the arts of "dance, play, and laughter" (Deleuze, *Nietzsche and Philosophy* 174, 176).

The purpose of this discussion is to position Alexander technique in relation to the notion of overcoming. The two moments of Alexander technique—inhibition and the directions—could be posed in Deleuzian terms as the active destruction of subjectivity towards a new mode of corporeal becoming. The movement from subjectivity towards corporeal difference is a transition between 'types' according to which the reactive apparatus (the self) sheds its own skin.[18] Thought within the terms of this discussion, inhibition could be posed as the work of the one who "wants to be overcome" (Deleuze, *Nietzsche and Philosophy* 174). In phenomenological terms, inhibition could be seen as a refusal to adopt the typical end-orientation embedded within perceptual subjectivity, a mode of resistance to the absorption implicit in the habitual everyday. Strategically, inhibition opens the body up to difference. It takes the subject to the brink. The work of the Alexander directions is to propel the subject beyond the field of habitual motor intentionality into the domain of new corporeal possibility. One might suggest that the efficacy of inhibition extends to the brink of subjective agency but no further, while the directions take up where inhibition leaves off.

According to Deleuze, active destruction is a prelude to affirmative change. It is a necessary part of the process by which the human is able to move on. This process enables the emergence of a new power, "the conversion of heavy into light," a kind of expansion in the body (*Nietzsche and Philosophy* 176). If this is the work of the negative, its role is to pave the way for something new, fresh and unknown. The work of active destruction deconstructs epistemological conceptions of the knowing subject for a new mode of thinking. Deleuze describes thought in Nietzsche as a journey made by an arrow. The arrow is not a property of the thinker but a projectile: "He [Nietzsche] compares the thinker to an arrow shot by Nature that *another thinker* picks up where it has fallen so that he can shoot it somewhere else" (Deleuze, *Nietzsche and Philosophy ix*, my emphasis). Transposing somewhat, we could trace a similar transition within the terms of Alexander technique. The journey may begin with inhibition but continues with the directions, a projectile movement of thought away from the one who knows towards a horizon of new possibility.

CONCLUSION

While phenomenology will likely construe undoing as yet another card up the subject's sleeve, Nietzschean philosophy focuses on the creation of corporeal value. Spinoza's remark that we do not know what a body can do is often cited within corporeal philosophy (Part III). There are two ways of approaching this claim, one, from the point of view of the subject, and two, from the point of view of the body. For Spinoza, the ethical domain is concerned with the enhancement of a body's capacity, with its becoming otherwise. A body that becomes more powerful becomes better in an ethical sense.[19] Deleuze has a distinctive way of reading Spinoza's corporeal ethics, beyond the compass of subjectivity.[20] The thought is that a body becomes more powerful by way of its own activity, through what a body does or rather becomes. Subjects come for the ride in this process, less as sovereign pilots of the ship than as finite beings with a finite perspective that develops along with the body. Alexander technique can be situated within this philosophical milieu, as a trajectory of thought, beginning with subjectivity, then moving towards an expression of greater corporeal power. It is an ethical pursuit, a projectile of thought, transitioning from one domain to another. To that extent, it is the creation of difference in the body beyond the tried and true.

This collection proceeds from an inquiry into the relation between performance and phenomenology. Philosophers sometimes query the Nietzschean (and anti-humanist) critique of subjectivity, asking what motivates such a critique from *inside* the subject-position? This is where I believe certain movement practices have something to offer. Not only does the body take the lead here, leaving subjectivity behind, these modes of approach aim to enhance the body's capacities. Insofar as they do this, they "play" subjectivity in the mode of (its own) active destruction. To what extent this can be generalised and/or adapted is an open question, one which depends upon the vicissitudes of practice, their relation to habit (formation and overcoming), and finally, their specific kinaesthetic and performance values. It is also moot whether subjectivity can actually be overcome or whether these strategies merely work towards overcoming. This is because playing the subject card belongs to *another* game. If this card is played well, the game changes, like Nietzsche's arrow shot by one thinker and picked up by another. Such that finally, as Nietzsche notes:

> So it is that, according to our taste and talent, we live an existence which is either a *prelude* or a *postlude*, and the best we can do in the *interregnum* is to be as far as possible our own *reges* and found little *experimental states*. We are experiments: let us also want to be them!
>
> (*Daybreak* 457)

ACKNOWLEDGEMENTS

The discussion of movement practices in this paper is informed by the understanding and generosity of those artists and practitioners with whom I have worked over many years. This is difficult to make visible according to the conventions of academic acknowledgement but is key to my having anything to say about dance. In the context of this discussion, I would therefore like to acknowledge Margaret Lasica, Russell Dumas, Sally Gardner, Julia Scoglio and Anneke Hansen; also Eva Karczag, Pam Matt, Lisa Nelson, Deborah Hay and Joan Skinner. I would in particular like to thank my Alexander teacher, Shona Innes and David Moore for his very hands on Alexander Yoga classes, also to Shelley Senter for introducing me to the technique.

NOTES

1. The distinction between the doer and the deed was made by Nietzsche in *On the Genealogy of Morality*: "... there is no 'being' behind the deed, its effect and what comes after it; 'the doer' is invented as an after-thought—the doing is everything" (28).
2. This manner of distinction between the body and subjectivity is not a form of dualism. For Descartes, the mind is the locus of subjectivity and the basis of a subjective agency, which exerts itself upon the body. Nietzsche's position has to do with the formation and value of the subjective point of view posed against the difference of an underlying corporeal reality. All activity for Nietzsche is in a sense corporeal (the work of forces) rather than the result of a sovereign agent controlling a mindless body.
3. See Deleuze, *Nietzsche and Philosophy*, and Klossowski.
4. In "What Is Feminist Theory?," Elizabeth Gross (later Grosz) looks at the ways in which feminist theory can subversively engage patriarchal texts without needing to subscribe to all their presuppositions. Were this not possible, feminism would be doomed to a theoretical separatism which would need to keep a proper distance from patriarchal thought or risk contamination. The effect of Gross's argument is to open up a space of strategic engagement.
5. See Rothfield, "Differentiating Phenomenology and Dance" and "Living Well and Health Studies."
6. Habits are not always problematic. Habits allow for the performance of complex tasks, and indeed, habit-formation plays a key role in dance training. But habits can also stand in the way of change precisely because of their potency. For further discussion on habit formation in relation to movement, see Rothfield, "Beyond Habit."
7. The following discussion of the Alexander Technique arises from my own encounter with the technique through the corporeal generosity of its teachers as well as the writings of its practitioners. Like the American pragmatist John Dewey, who wrote about the technique, my own perspective combines the experience of the student with speculations of the philosopher.
8. Alexander writes: "Almost all civilized human creatures have developed a condition in which the sensory appreciation (feeling) is more or less imperfect and deceptive. [...] The connexion between psycho-physical defects and incorrect sensory guidance must therefore be recognized by the teacher in the practical work of re-education" (13). Alexander's point is that there is no Archimedean reference point to be found inside the field of experience that can guarantee an accurate sense of posture.
9. Alexander notes: "He gets what he feels is the right position, but when he has an imperfect co-ordination, he is only getting a position which fits with his defective co-ordination" (11). Rebecca Nettl-Fiol writes of the gap between what we are doing and what we think we are doing ("First it was dancing" 122).
10. Alexander writes that it is the role of the teacher to introduce "new sensory experiences" (14).
11. Alexander writes; "[...] in the application of my technique the process of inhibition, that is, *the act of refusing to respond* to the primary desire to gain an 'end' *becomes the act of responding* (volitionary act) to the conscious reasoned desire to employ the *means whereby* that "end" may be gained" (58).

12. This turn of phrase is often cited by the choreographer Russell Dumas to signify a body unbound by or exceeding classical (fixed modes of) movement vocabulary. For Dumas, a body available to movement is open to adapt itself to new choreographic material (personal communication). The phrase is also used by Alexander teacher Shona Innes to describe the sense in which a body can be open to a range of movement possibilities in the moment. It is a way of capturing the role of the virtual within the Alexander technique (personal communication). Eva Karçzag speaks of the body as constantly in motion, "a finely-tuned instrument always available to change" ("Moving the Moving" 33).
13. See Merleau-Ponty esp. Part One, Ch. 3, and Rothfield, "Living well and health studies" on the importance and legitimacy of non-normative styles of movement.
14. See Nietzsche, *On the Genealogy of Morality*, esp. Essay One.
15. See Deleuze, *Nietzsche and Philosophy*, esp. Chapters 2 and 4.
16. Nietzsche writes: "The habits of our senses have woven us into lies and deception of sensation: these again are the basis of all our judgements and 'knowledge'—there is absolutely no escape, no backway or bypath into the *real world!* We sit within our net, we spiders, and whatever we may catch in it, we can catch nothing at all except that which allows itself to be caught precisely in *our* net" (*Daybreak* 117). See also Nietzsche, *On the Genealogy of Morality*, Essay Two.
17. See Deleuze, *Nietzsche and Philosophy*, Chapter 4.
18. Deleuze writes "it is a question of an ethic and a typology—a type of force, an ethic of the corresponding ways of being" (*Nietzsche and Philosophy* 120).
19. See Rothfield, "Embracing the Unknown, Ethics and Dance" and Deleuze, *Practical Philosophy* esp. Chapter 2.
20. For Deleuze, "In short, the model of the body, according to Spinoza, does not imply any devaluation of thought in relation to extension, but, much more important, a devaluation of consciousness in relation to thought: a discovery of the unconscious, of an *unconscious of thought* just as profound as *the unknown of the body*," *Practical Philosophy* 19.

WORKS CITED

Alexander, F. Matthias. *The Essential Writings of F. Matthias Alexander, The Alexander Technique*. Ed. Edward Maisel. New York: University Books, 1989.

Deleuze, Gilles. *Nietzsche and Philosophy*. Trans. Hugh Tomlinson. New York: Columbia UP, 1983.

———. *Practical Philosophy*. 1970. Trans. Robert Hurley. San Francisco: City Light Books, 1988.

Dempster, Elizabeth. "Some Notes on the Staging of Ideokinesis." *Writings on Dance* 22 (2003/2004): 37–48.

———. "A Conversation with Shona Innes." *Writings on Dance* 22 (2003/2004): 49–56.

Dreyfus, Hubert. "Reply to Romdenh-Romluc." *Reading Merleau-Ponty On Phenomenology of Perception*. Ed. Thomas Baldwin. London and New York: Routledge, 2007. 59–69.

Dumas, Russell. "Dance for the Time Being." *Dancehouse Diary* 1 (2012): 10.

———. Personal Communication. 11 Feb. 2010.

Gross, Elizabeth. "What Is Feminist Theory?" *Feminist Challenges, Social and Political Theory*. Eds. Carole Pateman and E. Gross. Sydney: Allen and Unwin, 1986. 190–204.

Innes, Shona. Personal Communication. 21 Apr. 2012.

Karçzag, Eva. "Explorations within the New Dance Aesthetic." *Writings on Dance* 14 (1995/1996): 39–52.

———. "Moving the Moving." *Writings on Dance*, 14 (1995/1996): 33–8.

Klossowski, Pierre. *Nietzsche and the Vicious Circle*. Trans. Daniel Smith. London: Continuum, 2005.

Merleau-Ponty, Maurice. *Phenomenology of Perception*. 1945. Trans. Colin Smith. London: Routledge and Kegan Paul, 1962.

Nettl-Fiol, Rebecca. "First It Was Dancing." Eds. Melanie Bales and Rebecca Nettl-Fiol. *The Body Eclectic, Evolving Practices in Dance Training*. Urbana and Chicago: U of Illinois P, 2008. 101–125.

Nietzsche, Friedrich. *Daybreak, Thoughts on the Prejudices of Morality*. 1881. Eds. Maudemarie Clark and Brian Leiter. Trans. R.J. Hollingdale. Cambridge: Cambridge UP, 1997.

———. *On the Genealogy of Morality*. Ed Keith Ansell-Pearson. Trans. Carol Diethe. Cambridge: Cambridge UP, 1994.

———. *Writings from the Late Notebooks*. Ed. Rüdiger Bittner. Trans. Kate Sturge. Cambridge: Cambridge UP, 2003.

Rothfield, Philipa. "Differentiating Phenomenology and Dance." *The Routledge Dance Studies Reader*, Eds. Alexandra Carter and Janet O'Shea. London and New York: Routledge, 1998. 303–318.

———. "Embracing the Unknown, Ethics and Dance." *Art and Ethics*. Ed. Paul Macneill. Dordrecht: Springer Publishing. (2014).

———. "Living Well and Health Studies." *Merleau-Ponty, Key Concepts*. Eds. Ros Diprose and Jack Reynolds. Stocksfield, UK: Acumen Publishing, 2008. 218–227.

———. "Beyond Habit, The Cultivation of Corproreal Difference." *Parrhesia* 18 (2013): 100–112. Web. 10 April 2014. <http://www.parrhesiajournal.org/parrhesia18/parrhesia18_rothfield.pdf>.

Spinoza, Benedictus de. *Ethics and on the Improvement of the Understanding*. Trans. R. H. M. Elwes. The Barnes & Noble Library of Essential Reading. New York: Barnes & Noble Books, 2005.

6 Fleshing Dead Animals
Sensory Body Phenomenology in Performance

Peta Tait

This chapter uses performances by Jill Orr and Nikki Heywood to consider the perceptual disordering provoked by the presence of dead animals in live performance. The contrasts between liveness and deadness and between the human and the nonhuman threaten to conceal the political implications of privileging human experience. A phenomenological approach to the problem of the dead onstage will contribute to understanding the ethical crises borne of these performances. It will do so by challenging the idea that deadness is stillness.

CARCASS SMELLS

Years after the event, I am haunted by the impact of the bloodied bones and pieces of flesh, the remnants of dead animal carcasses, in a 2003 performance created by Jill Orr and called *The Sleep of Reason Produces Monsters—Goya*.[1] Orr is renowned in the visual arts for her body-based performance art (Marsh, *Body and Self* 121–33; Goldberg, Marsh, *Performance, Ritual, Document*), and recently performed at Venice International Performance Art Week (Tait, *Performance Couplings*). In *The Sleep of Reason*, Orr utilized the remains of domesticated farm animals from an abattoir in a durational nine-hour performance. During this endurance event, the dead animal bones were manipulated by a silent human figure in an ambiguous white costume working knee-deep among the bloodied remains. A multi-layered significance emerged from this performance that both evoked the horror of the abattoir and at the same time suggested rituals for the dead, the performance of a type of afterlife remembrance ceremony. Orr's performance made clear how sensory body perception influences performance reception and spectatorship.

Indeed, the impact of Orr's performance was much more than the visual impact of mounds of raw meat, fat, and bone. The initial impact of this performance was not through sight, but through an overpowering smell as spectators walked into the performance space.

A total bodily sensation of repulsion had me stop and turn around to leave immediately. The smell assaulted my body and produced an involuntary response. But I wrestled with this overwhelming reaction, and it subsided. All of this was before I saw pieces of dead animal on the far side of a large transformed gallery space. As I became accustomed to the smell of dead animal in the space, I began to see that there were bones and body pieces suspended from the ceiling and lying in uneven piles on the ground. Before any thought concerning the ethics of using dead remains occurred to me, my first experience of Orr's performance required me to physically override a sensory imperative to flee; these moments continue to be restaged in body memory.

There were structured interludes in the performance when Orr moved to the back of the gallery and stood posed, motionless against the wall—her body still, like a hunted animal in a spotlight. After several minutes, the performer moved away, leaving an imprint of a silhouette of her own shape on the wall. This remained in place for some minutes after she moved away, before fading, and was made possible by a particular paint on the surface of the wall under special light. The human form was frozen in shadow. The ghost of a human form remained on stage for some time before it faded away; this suggested a *spectre* that haunted animal death in a paradoxical reversal of the title's reference to Goya's picture.

The stark aftermath of death in Orr's work forced itself onto the spectators through the multi-sensory engagement with what Jane Desmond terms the "'yuck' factor" in biological decay (371). These responses to the performance in turn transformed under the pressure of a semiotic reading that confronted the ambiguity of Orr's performing persona. Was Orr's human figure in a kitchen, a slaughterhouse, or a temple shrine? Her white costume suggested a cook or a factory meat worker, but her slow action suggested a nurse or a mortuary attendant or even a leader of a ritual. But there was a further possibility: was the figure operating in a more inconceivable location, such as in a death camp? This multiplicity remained throughout the performance as Orr handled and manipulated the pieces of dead carcass and bone into piles or hanging sculptures. That is to say, in addition to whatever role she was "playing," she was also acting like an artist.

A well-known international precedent was artist Marina Abramovic in her infamous piece, *Balkan Baroque* (1997). Both Abramovic's and Orr's performances transgressed the social adherence to spatial compartmentalization that reaches from abattoir killing floor to supermarket freezer tray. The use of abattoir remains (bones and offal) in a gallery space pointed to the wholesale usage of animals in human society outside of proscribed spaces. Human carnivorous appetites, the mutilation of flesh, and the consumption of animals intersected with the circumstances of abject substances in a gallery space. Both pieces relied on their titles to convey significance, just as both pieces relied upon the "live" interaction of a living human with the remains of animals to experience the impact and consider the scale and costs of slaughtering living beings.

Orr's performance alludes to human-animal relations and, through the title, to depictions of animals historically in the visual arts and how they haunt the human psyche. A preponderance of animal bodies in the history of European visual art (Donald) gave way to their absence within modernism that was noted by John Burger, and subsequently followed by a renewed focus on animals in recent visual art (Baker, *The Postmodern Animal*). As Steve Baker has shown, there has been an effort by visual artists to represent living animals in accordance with contemporary values and arguments in animal studies,[2] and he lucidly analyzes this innovative arts practice in relation to postmodernism and the politics of animal rights. Damien Hirst's dead, bloodied animal head with flies being hatched and killed has recently been restaged at Tate Modern, and the controversy surrounding it revealed the mores attached to the presence of animals in art.[3] An objectified dead animal part as the substance of art in a gallery sits uneasily alongside pro-animal-focused art works created by artists who travel to where animals live in their habitats to make art (Baker, *The Postmodern Animal*).[4] These latter visual arts practices happen at the intersection of live bodies, habitat, and representation and seek to reconfigure the visibility and invisibility of the nonhuman animal in aesthetic culture. Other artists work polemically as they seek to graphically present the brutal social treatment of animals in industrialized farming and to politicize animal death rather than aestheticize interspecies spaces. Such artwork bears witness to practices pursued out of sight of most people living in industrialized areas.

In her commentary on Chinese artists who illuminate human animalness and comment on culture through the integration of live animals into art installations, Meiling Cheng suggests that the complexity of the cultural and socio-political background in China means that paradoxically, her analysis may "succeed and fail" at the same time (71). The rural and urban divide might be a given, but so too is the centrality of Chinese food culture and public market stalls and restaurants that kill small animals during the process of cooking and serving. In addition, Cheng contrasts Wang Jin's *To Marry a Mule*, which cleverly juxtaposes ideas of animal husbandry and beasts of burden with a human social framework of Western marriage (72–3), with more provocative art that uses dead animal bodies. Cheng outlines how some artists will go to extremes with their use of the bodies of living animals and kill a cat or a pig for a filmed performance, which leaves her with unresolved questions about the efficacy of any artistic statement that involves the artist's undertaking painful and violent acts with animal bodies (79).

The time of death seems crucial to a consideration of the ethics of Orr's artwork with carcasses. A presumption of the pre-existing circumstances of death in another context underlay Orr's art installation, so that the actual issue of ethical practice became one of how *remains* should be contained or treated with respect and whether the utility for performance is disrespectable of the animal life since passed. The possibility of a sacrifice for the larger meaning was compromised by omnipresent human decision making unless the central point is to challenge the potency of human control over animals even in death. Orr's performances open out this possibility within the sensory rejection of decay.

A POLITICS OF SENSORY SHOCK

The ways in which an encounter with other species relies on sensory body responses need to be emphasised within twenty-first-century ethical challenges to human denial of the exploitation of animal bodies. But sensory experience should be explicated rather than assumed because it underpins all encounters with other species, live or dead.

In her critique of taxidermy, as "theaters of the dead," Desmond writes that "[i]t is not unusual to see dead animal bodies on display" because stuffed animals have been a longstanding part of social entertainment (347). As Desmond explains about taxidermy technologies: they originated in straw-stuffed skins but had evolved into "life-like" dramatic dioramas with natural settings and family groupings for the turn-of-the-twentieth-century museum display. An "illusion of realism" created by the taxidermy remains the primary intention of taxidermists entering competition championships in the twenty-first century (354). Spectators are culturally accustomed to viewing dead nonhuman bodies arranged in life-like stasis, and these practices are not widely questioned. But such scenes promote sentimentality as they eschew the sensory realism of death.

The interspecies values behind taxidermy display for human entertainment require that the animal's death be sidelined (Desmond 348). Desmond argues that for "the fiction of realism" to work, the killing must be camouflaged in an "ironic epistemological structure" (354). A visual perception of an animal fur skin in a life-like pose allows human curiosity to be satisfied, and in close proximity, the living animal would take fright and flee. But stillness is ambiguous in an encounter with taxidermy; a spectator's deliberation on the death of the other can be diverted with a body pose set in narrative framing so that an animal appears static *in situ*. Instead, the animal might seem to be in a pose of alertness and watchfulness in the proximity of other species. Even though the posed animal body is completely immobile, it is not meant to be perceived by spectators as a dead body.

In contrast, with Orr's *The Sleep of Reason* the overpowering smell of the carcasses produced a visceral shock. My own sensory shock initially preceded all semiotic readings of Orr's performance and required a mind–body struggle simply to continue on to the installation. The smell and subsequent sight of raw bones and bloodied flesh was the central point of the encounter in which Orr constantly touched and moved them. The visceral shock of the smell was followed by the sight of touched and handled carcass remains as sensory responses converged. Spread across the space, the remains appeared chaotic and out of control and abject.

If one intention of the performed action was to increase awareness of the compartmentalized treatment of animals, then a physical impact this powerful might prefigure political intervention. The human habit of obscuring the exploitation of the nonhuman body's materiality finds a challenge in an encounter with other species' bodies so grounded in sensory responses. Extreme sensory repulsion may upset how the world is bodily perceived and potentially cut through patterns of social avoidance. Visible difference in a body shape and texture, including species, however, might cause a hesitation in sensory engagement that makes someone suddenly aware of an unfolding sensory process in relation to other bodies and the world around. The interruption of continuous, seamless sensory engagement offers the potential to expose the function of implicit socio-political influences in a sensory encounter with animal bodies in the world.

Regardless of the political uses to which it may be put, Orr's handling of animal carcasses in live performance provided a potent depiction of animal deadness. Unlike the stuffed and stilled animals in taxidermy displays, these guts reeked of decay. Orr's performance delivered a heightened somatic confrontation with exposed innards for human spectators in a scene of death. But what happens when a sensory body encounters a decaying dead body or body part? To answer this question, we must consider the ways accounts of embodied perception presume an involvement with the living. In other words, the encounter with death-ness, the phenomena that are of death, will depend first on how we make things live.

FLESHING LIVE

The importance of visuality in performance is accepted (Bleeker), as are the ways in which multi-sensory effects are staged and received by "sensing bodies" (Di Benedetto). Yet the sensory reception of performance is contingent on embodied attunement disturbed by the use of dead remains. The perception of the lived body actively engages with the world around and other bodies and objects through the senses; Merleau-Ponty (*Phenomenology of Perception*) describes a process of subjective experience that reaches outward and through unfolding action that folds back into itself. And yet Merleau-Ponty's "philosophy of the sensible" requires a human body attuned to *moving* phenomena in the world (252). It can be pointed out that humans are sensorily attuned to the motion of other bodies and over time this orientation is socially influenced as a seamless, uninterrupted, almost physiological habit.

Physical action and the choreographed and athletic movement of other bodies attract sensory focus, especially framed by performance. Attentiveness to other bodies and their aliveness typifies body-based performance; bodily responses to movement are part of reception. Performance can come "alive" to the viewer where a quality of action is made visible by a different body and/or the spatial context (Heathfield 8). In a way, the self's awareness of bodily sensations in response to performance is akin to a process of feeling alive. This bodily attunement to action is likely to encompass the actions of nonhuman animal performers, although trained animal performance suggests that to sustain audience attention over time animals need to also perform human-like action (Tait, *Wild and Dangerous*). The bodily attunement to movement of a living entity also seems indicative of a perceptual condition of liveness. As film and electronic arts in recent years have expanded concepts of live and interactivity, felt responses in the moment contribute to the reception of all types of movement in performance, whether delivered live or recorded, and by moving or inert bodies. The embodied self that can be understood to be in a process of sensorily reaching outward can also be said to bring acculturated experience of liveness to the reception of performance.

Merleau-Ponty (*Phenomenology of Perception*) proposes that an embodied sensing self is engaged in outward movement towards the "flesh" of the world, a flesh that is not in itself experienced as sentient but as an enfolding of the visible into the invisible and which supposes comparable existences in the surrounding world. Where seeing, hearing, and smelling happen simultaneously, the unfolding and enfolding bodily processes in the seer might be considered to be "fleshing" the performance. This process presumes, yet again, that the performance is in movement, is of movement. And yet, this is not to say that movement constitutes the live. Not everything moving is living.

SKIN CRAWLS

Relic #5 (2011), created by performer Nikki Heywood with musician Sam Pettigrew, presented segments in which Heywood juxtaposed her naked body with an old, tattered fur coat and then worked with the head of an animal, seemingly a deer head without antlers.[5] The patchy, aging fur lay discarded on the floor of the pre-performance space as an object prop, an amorphous shape beneath it. Heywood's limbs slowly became visible from underneath the fur in a butoh-like, slow crawling action, and the fur was no longer inanimate. A visual impression of disturbance was reinforced aurally with loud, nonmelodic sound played live on an electrified double bass. The second and third parts of this performance involved moving with and among inanimate objects and in ritualistic celebratory ways so that these objects and animal body parts and the female body became interchangeable. These movements were underpinned by Biblical and Shakespearean references and included segments in which the animal head, which was fake, was displayed, held, and worn or carried like a trophy or a pet. A loud sound score reinforced an impression of disorder and disharmony, so that *Relic #5* generated sensory discomfort and unease and made the "skin crawl."

A naked female body shedding a skin in real time clearly intersects with discourses on gendered violence, bodily repression, and transformation. The effect of the older naked female body doubled back on the discarded fur with loaded significance, decentering any erotic implications. Animal fur has traditionally provided a second fake skin for body-to-body encounters, and its use in *Relic #5* also alluded to notions of furs as female fashion and the wearing of differentiated species fur to signal social status.

Above all, *Relic #5*'s pervasive blending of human movement and animal remnant/animal representation obstructed human attunement to species identification, beginning with the remade fur shape that could not be identified. Merleau-Ponty's lecture "Animal Life" outlines the longstanding philosophical denial of the lived experience of other animals. He contrasts this "classical" view to the "modern" approach to science and the arts, which allows us to perceive movement in the divergence of two lines projected on a screen (Merleau-Ponty, *The World of Perception* 57). He writes: "The person watching this 'crawling' will think they see a virtual substance, a sort of fictitious protoplasm, flow from the center of the 'body' to the mobile extremities which it projects ahead of itself" (Merleau-Ponty, *The World of Perception* 58). For Merleau-Ponty, human perception of the world lodges itself in the "perception of life" that we can, though often fail to, recognize within the surrounding world. In the viewing of Heywood's crawling movement, a crawling flow seemed to double back on the spectator. The reaching-out that Merleau-Ponty describes as the nature of perception does not have to rely on species body recognition, but can, and in his view should, be disjointed. *Relic #5*'s transactions provided the opportunity for this disordering.

Later the head of a dead animal and the live performer became interchangeable, offering a response to the question posed by Una Chaudhuri about how to perform the animal out of othered facelessness. A taxidermied mounted stag or other animal head might be a commonplace hunting trophy as a mounted wall display, but when moved around and held and transposed onto the moving human body, the animal head took on an uncanny dimension that further frustrated the assignment of subjecthood to Heywood and her props.

Perhaps most disarmingly, these representations and remains of animals troubled not only boundaries between human and animal, but between the live and the dead. From time to time, the animal head appeared momentarily alive in a fleeting conjoining of body parts in performance; the represented animal was subjectively fleshed as human and a deer face substituted for a human face. But this was a combination of a mask and mover. Even more disturbing was Heywood's movement beneath the tattered fur. The slow-moving, live body emerging out from under a dead fur blurred a sensory impression of liveness and deadness. As the live body emerged from under the fur skin, the sensory encounter repeatedly oscillated between seeing live action and fleshing dead animal. Here, movement did not register as liveness. Instead, it amplified the deadness, the no-longer-living-ness, of the fur.

A fur might be imagined to have less sensory impact in comparison with bloodied raw fat, muscle, and bone. And yet the sensation of movement within or under the animal remains proved to this viewer to be similarly provocative. In Heywood's performance, the cloak of dead animal remains had dried and aged, its link to the living obscured. Her movement animated the pelt, but far from investing it with life, the movement invested it with the qualities of death. Because death may be an end, but *the dead* persist(s). *Sleep of Reason* brought this home through its overwhelming sensory assault. What reached the spectators of Orr's piece was not simply an idea of animals whose lives had ended, but it was the experience of decay. Decay is active. It contains movement. The rotting flesh and offal from an animal reach out differently than the animal head or dried animal fur hung on a wall. The taxidermied animal has had its movement stilled, even in poses of movement. The decaying animal, however, still moves, still transforms. This is the movement of deadness that keeps death from being the opposite of life. Both Orr and Heywood's performances upended any presumed dichotomy between death and movement by locating movement in the condition of death, in deadness. What remains after death still moves if it was ever living, and only the stilling of that movement in our minds or our ideologies prevents us from knowing our responsibilities to the dead.

In his *Corporal Compassion: Animal Ethics and Philosophy of Body,* Ralph Acampora compares a "transhuman ethos" of "moral phenomenology" with "Continental European thought" and rejects the ways in which "bodily presence and exchange" between species are taken for granted (128). He argues that the sensate body is foundational to experience and thus ethical values in human-animal relations. In proposing an idea of "bodiment," Acampora argues that the "intersomatic domain" can manifest "our bodily participation as animals ourselves operating on a zoomorphic register" to challenge interspecies values and behavior (30, 130–1). In his investigation of an ethical philosophy of human-animal relations, he asks how a controlling gaze can be displaced so that it might bodily see what it is imposing on other bodies. In Acampora, these seeing and seen phenomenological bodies are living entities; that is, they are alive.

Orr and Heywood's performances, however, propose that our embodied perception links humans not so much to the living as it does to movement, and movement can be found in death. *Sleep of Reason* and *Relic #5* invite philosophical reflection about disturbance in sensory body engagement in the fleshed space of live performance and as a process of fleshing. The smell and sight of handled skinless, bloodied, bone and fat and the sight of, and sound accompanying, the bearing of fur and wearing of an animal head produced disorder and disturbance. These in turn point to a moral phenomenology that is transhuman in the way Acampora and Merleau-Ponty sought while also going much further: these performances open the way to forging responsibility not simply to other living animals, but also to animals in all states of life and death.

The use of dead animals in live performance can compel the spectator's sensory engagement not simply owing to any imagined species barrier or anthropomorphism, but because it can stage movement common to the dead material and the spectators. Sensations ranging from visceral shock to aural discomfort may offer a body-based driver that cuts through pre-existing patterns conditioned by socio-political frameworks. Our own connection to death is not through our mortality but through our investment in the movement of life, a movement that death continues and does not end.

NOTES

1. I viewed this performance at 45 Downstairs, Melbourne, Australia, on 21 June 2003. A media controversy focused on a $10,000 arts grants towards this performance.
2. See also Sunstein and Nussbaum, Armstrong and Botzier.
3. I viewed this exhibition, "Damien Hirst," at Tate Modern on 12 July 2012.
4. The ethics of biological art and with transgenetic tissue cultures is a separate discussion because it involves growing living tissue for human purposes and making cell life rather than working with the remains of an autonomous species after death.
5. This performance had three parts and was a commissioned performance work for the 2011 Global Animal conference, and the author viewed it 7 July 2011, U of Wollongong. It is part of a series of performances in *Museum of the Sublime* by Heywood, who is well known for contemporary performance works over three decades.

WORKS CITED

Acampora, Ralph R. *Corporal Compassion: Animal Ethics and Philosophy of Body.* Pittsburgh: U of Pittsburgh P, 2006.
Armstrong, Susan and Richard Botzier, eds. *The Animal Ethics Reader*, London: Routledge, 2008.
Baker, Steve. *The Postmodern Animal.* London: Reaktion Books, 2000.
Bleeker, Maaike. *Visuality in the Theatre.* Basingstoke: Palgrave Macmillan, 2008.
Chaudhuri, Una. "(De)Facing the Animals." *The Drama Review* 51:1 (2007): 8–20.
Cheng, Meiling. "Animal Works in China." *TDR: The Drama Review* 51:1 (2007): 63–91.
Desmond, Jane. "Postmortem Exhibitions." *Configurations* 16:3 (2008): 347–78.
Di Benedetto, Stephen. *The Provocation of the Senses in Contemporary Theatre.* New York: Routledge, 2010.
Donald, Diana. *Picturing Animals in Britain 1750–1850.* New Haven: The Paul Mellon Centre for Studies in British Art by Yale UP, 2007.
Goldberg, RoseLee. *Performance and Live Art since the 60s.* New York: Thames and Hudson, 2004.
Heathfield, Adrian, ed. *Live: Art and Performance.* New York: Routledge, 2004.

Heywood, Nikki. "Museum of the Sublime: Relic #5: Notes Towards a Fragmented Performance." *Animal Studies Journal* 1:1 (2012). Web. Nov. 2012. <http://ro.uwa.edu.au/asj/vol1/iss1/8>.

Marsh, Anne. *Body and Self: Performance Art in Australia 1969–92*. Melbourne: Oxford UP, 1993.

———. *Performance, Ritual, Document*. Melbourne: Macmillan, 2014.

Merleau-Ponty, Maurice. *The Visible and the Invisible*. Trans. Alphonso Lingis. Evanston: Northwestern UP, 1995.

———. *Phenomenology of Perception*. Trans. Colin Smith. London: Routledge, 1996.

———. *The World of Perception*. Trans. Oliver Davis. London: Routledge, 2004.

Sunstein, Cass R, and Martha C. Nussbaum, eds. *Animal Rights: Current Debates and New Directions*. New York: Oxford UP, 2004.

Tait, Peta. *Wild and Dangerous: Animals, Emotions, Circus*. Basingstoke: Palgrave Macmillan, 2012.

———. "Performance Couplings," *Performance Research*. 18:2 (2013): 139–140.

7 Vibrant Materials
The Agency of Things in the Context of Scenography

Joslin McKinney

> *I believe that encounters with lively matter can chasten my fantasies of human mastery, highlight the common materiality of all that is, expose a wider distribution of agency, and reshape the self and its interests.*
>
> (Bennett, *Vibrant Matter* 122)

INTRODUCTION

Trends in contemporary performance and multimedia, site-specific, and immersive theatre suggest that, more than ever, the materials of scenography—space, light, sound, structures, objects, fabrics, textures, and colors—play a central role in audience experience. Nonetheless, our understanding of this role played by materials is underdeveloped. The late works of Maurice Merleau-Ponty, particularly *The Visible and the Invisible*, develop a phenomenological account of perception from a non-hierarchical relationship between subject and object. The viewer here is not a distanced observer; rather, he or she experiences the world from within "[...] the weight, the thickness, the flesh of each color, of each sound, of each tactile texture [...]" (Merleau-Ponty, *The Visible and the Invisible* 114). He describes a reversible relationship between the viewer and the thing being viewed where a kind of exchange occurs and "the things pass into us as well as we into the things" (Merleau-Ponty, *The Visible and the Invisible* 123). This reversal between the seer and the seen is "a reciprocal insertion and intertwining of one in the other" (Merleau-Ponty, *The Visible and the Invisible* 138). This points towards the possibility of a phenomenology of materiality with profound implications for understanding the role of scenography in performance.

Throughout this chapter, Merleau-Ponty's ideas of reversibility and the "flesh" underpin my thinking through the interaction and exchange between the human and nonhuman in scenography. The process of apprehending scenography is figured here as a reciprocal and ongoing process where the "force and flow" of materials (Ingold, "The Textility of Making" 91) works on the subject as much as the subject tries to apprehend the material. Whereas Merleau-Ponty starts from the point of view of the perceiving body, arriving eventually at the *chiasm*, which is a crossing over between seer and seen, Tim Ingold and others such as Jane Bennett have focused on the force of materials themselves. Pursuing the concerns of "new materialism,"[1] both Bennett and Ingold go further than Merleau-Ponty in examining the extent to which vitality, force, or power can be attributed to matter, independent of human agency. Using Merleau-Ponty, it is possible to understand how the seer and the seen are bound in a reciprocal relationship and how reversibility between subjects and objects applies to the experience of scenography. But beyond that, what is it that objects and materials themselves might be capable of?

A key focus of this chapter will be a piece of practice-based research, *Beneath the Forest Floor*, which I have been developing in order to address these issues. It is a scenographic environment designed to explore the potential of objects and materials in the context of a participatory performance. It utilizes a consensual approach to exploring and making, incorporates collaboration between human and nonhuman agents, and facilitates an improvisatory engagement with, and within, some of the stuff of scenography. But first I will present a brief review of how phenomenological thinking has informed the ways we conceptualize scenographic objects and materials so far, and I will have a look at Tadeusz Kantor and Heiner Goebbels as two theatre makers who grant objects and materials a very active role. What kind of role is this? Could we say that objects and materials in their performances have agency? What kind of agency would that be? Then I will turn to a discussion of *Beneath the Forest Floor* for a further exploration of the role of objects, materials, and things.

PHENOMENOLOGY AND SCENOGRAPHIC OBJECTS

While it is clear from research into the phenomenological dimension of theatre that scenography (as "scenery") is one of the essential materials through which theatre "makes itself" (States 1), the concentration of much theatre phenomenology has been on the human rather than the nonhuman. Meanwhile, influential accounts of scenography have tended to emphasize the artistic intention of the designer, presenting scenography as a branch of visual art (Bablet) and often using semiotic methods to decode the work (Kennedy and Fischer-Lichte). These are largely hermeneutically focused accounts of scenography, and they echo what Ingold terms a "hylomorphic" model:

> Any thing, Aristotle had reasoned, is a compound of matter (*hyle*) and form (*morphe*), which are brought together in the act of its creation. Accordingly, making begins with a form in mind and a formless lump of "raw material," and it ends when form and matter are united in the complete artifact. In the history of modern thought, this *hylomorphic* model of creation was both further entrenched and increasingly unbalanced. Form came to be seen as actively imposed, whereas

matter—thus rendered passive and inert—became that which was imposed upon.

(Ingold, "Ecology of Materials" 432)

A hylomorphic account of scenography has the scenographer as prime agent imposing form on materials and the audience then reading backwards "from a finished object to an initial intention in the mind of an agent" (Ingold, "The Textility of Making" 91).

Phenomenological approaches to theatre remind us that scenography does not operate exclusively in the scopic realm and neither is the scenography, like any work of art, simply "an index of the intentions of the artist," which can be accounted for simply by "cause and effect" (Ingold, "The Textility of Making" 99). Bert O. States goes some way towards redressing reductive views of scenography by giving equal attention to objects and actors. His account of "perceptual encounters" with the theatre (States 1) incorporates a concept of the stage "[...] as a shifting image in time and space, formed by the interplay of visual and aural events" (States 51) where literary and pictorial elements interpenetrate one another in such a way that we might say "the ear sees scenery and the eye hears it" (States 53). These striking inversions echo Merleau-Ponty's observations about synesthetic perception and the intercommunication of senses:

> One sees the hardness and brittleness of glass, and when, with a tinkling sound, it breaks, this sound is conveyed by the visible glass [...] One sees the weight of a block of cast iron which sinks in the sand, the fluidity of water, and the viscosity of syrup. In the same way, I hear the hardness and unevenness of cobbles in the rattle of a carriage, and we speak appropriately of a 'soft,' 'dull,' or 'sharp' sound.
> (*Phenomenology of Perception* 229–230)

Merleau-Ponty investigates here the way in which our visual and aural senses are part of our embodied understanding of how things feel, their weight and movement, the way one material contributes to our apprehension of another. Materials acting on each other and in combination produce a network of sensible matter of which the viewer can be part.

In theatre, we may be tempted to make distinctions between image and text, the physical space and the fictional place it refers to, but crucially States sees that the interpenetration of image and text means that "stage space and stage event are one and the same thing: They are reciprocal entities" (States 50). And from this it follows that there is a "level on which actors cannot be distinguished from furniture" (States 50). States goes further than most others in decentering the human agent. Many accounts, while acknowledging the "phenomenal instability of theatrical objects" (Garner, "Staging Things" 55), insist that the scenic space and the things within it are "objectified" in a field of vision until the actor draws them in to the corporeal field (Garner, *Bodied Spaces* 3) and suggest that "it is the actor who confers meaning upon the object" (McAuley 205).

Gay McAuley's view of the central position of the performer is reflected, she feels, in the words we use to describe stage objects. She points out that "prop" suggests the object as a support to the actor, and in a similar vein, the French word for prop—*accessoire*—implies a secondary and nonessential function. And while the term "properties" suggests that objects can convey inherent meaning by the "bodying forth" of qualities of character or place (175), for McAuley the signifying powers of objects are determined by the people who have selected them and placed them on the stage. The most striking use of objects in this regard are those which are seemingly "arbitrary" or inexplicable (in that they appear to have no physical or communicative function in the performance) but nonetheless "remain to haunt the spectator's memory" and provide troubling or poetic images (McAuley 198–9). Further, "It is the rupture with the real world, the inability to ascribe function, the realization that the object can be neither understood nor controlled that gives such surreal objects their power (McAuley 199). McAuley acknowledges that the operation of objects can be independent from performers, but she is troubled by these apparently surplus objects that threaten to "take precedence over the actors" and reduce their task to servicing the "glittering surface" of the set design (206).

In *Postdramatic Theatre*, Hans-Thies Lehmann discusses several examples of theatre makers for whom objects taking precedence over actors is not a problem but an opportunity. As an early advocate of the significance of things in performance, Kantor was motivated to "valorize the objects and materials of the scenic action in general" (Lehmann 72). Kantor often used discarded materials, such as cart wheels, old wooden planks, and furniture, that he felt were capable of transcending their former function and abject vulnerability once they were placed on the stage. Here their worthlessness in real life was inverted and they became a focus for contemplation and revelation. His "bio-objects," where performers were bound to objects worn like costumes, produced a hybrid actor-object, each constituent part affecting and affected by the other (Pleśniarowicz 181–2). In *The Dead Class* (1975), where human performers carry around life-size mannequins as memories of their past selves, a kind of exchange takes place:

> [T]hey change the stage into a landscape of death, in which there is a fluid transition between the human beings (often acting like puppets) and the dead puppets (appearing as if animated by children). One could almost say that the verbal dialogue of drama is replaced by a *dialogue between people and objects*.
>
> (Lehmann 73)

In other examples of postdramatic theatre, objects even perform without people. Goebbels' production *Stifter's Dinge* (2007) is "a composition for five pianos with no pianists, a performance without performers." The objects in it are "protagonists" interacting with other scenographic materials such as light, sounds, ice, water, and mist, to create "a play with nobody acting" (Heiner Goebbels). In conversation with Lehmann, Goebbels has said:

> I am interested in inventing a theatre where all the means that make up theatre do not just illustrate and duplicate each other but instead all maintain their own forces but act together, and where one does not rely on the conventional hierarchy of means. That means, for example, where a light can be so strong that you suddenly only watch the light and forget the text, where a costume speaks its own language or where there is a distance between speaker and text and a tension between music and text. I experience theatre as exciting whenever you can sense distances on stage that I as a spectator can cross.
>
> (Lehmann 86)

Kantor and Goebbels provide examples of the way scenographic practice utilizes a rich array of human and nonhuman objects where the usual hierarchies of the stage are reconfigured and where the intercommunication of senses that Merleau-Ponty proposed is the foundation for scenographic experience. In order to think through the relationship between subjects and objects in scenography in more detail, I will consider whether what objects are doing in these examples can be understood in terms of agency.

CAN OBJECTS BE AGENTS?

Kantor and Goebbels both deal with objects as though they have agency of their own. Yet do they? And if so, what kind of agency? Kantor takes two distinct approaches: (1) objects of "the lowest rank" are transformed through performance to become objects of truth and contemplation that activate the audiences' imagination, and (2) "bio-objects"—combinations and confrontations of performers and objects—articulate dramaturgical concepts in concrete form (Klossowicz 176–83). But are these objects operating independently or are they actually reliant on a human agent? In the first approach, it might be argued that the object's capability to engage the audience relies on theatrical framing and the selection of objects in the first place while in the second the object is made to impose a physical and palpable impact on the performer and effect some kind of agentic change. Kantor's own sensibility as an artist guiding and controlling the selection and deployment of objects[2] is, of course, significant in both of these approaches.

Ingold describes how a conventional view of objects is one in which the artist is the central figure in selecting and manipulating inert materials to create something that viewers can read back from. Thus, an object is defined as something that "however metrically close remains distant" and seemingly complete in itself (Ingold, "Toward an Ecology of Materials" 435–6). Kantor's objects appear to fit this description because his own role as artist makes him responsible for the selection of materials and the designation of objects. But this is not to say that Kantor sees materials as inert. On the contrary, he is drawn to the capacity of materials and of found objects to exert a powerful presence without the need of a performer, although it not clear whether Kantor sees this as a mystic or metaphysical power or as a material one. Goebbels describes a perceptual experience where the spectator is engaged through and between the different languages of various theatrical objects and materials—text, performer, costumes, light, and sound. He suggests this might be experienced as distance between objects and materials, but this is clearly not the distance engendered by complete objects to which Ingold refers. Goebbels emphasizes the experience of the viewer as a process of ongoing meaning making and deflects attention from himself as the initiator, even though a performance, especially one like *Stifter's Dinge,* is a carefully calibrated object-like entity.

A problem with attributing agency to objects in these examples is that the term object tends to implicate the artist-maker and lead us back to the idea of an active human agent exerting one's intention on passive materials. Therefore perhaps, rather than asking how materials have agency, we might do better to focus on their capacity to become active participants, incomplete potentialities, or as Ingold puts it, "substances-in-becoming," which together with other materials produces a "gathering of materials in movement" ("Toward an Ecology of Materials" 435). Ingold is convinced of the vitality of materials, but he eschews the idea of both material and human agency in favor of a theory of "animate life" (*Making* 96) where materials, bodies included, play an active part:

> As a bundle of potentials in an ever-unfolding field of forces and energies, the body moves and is moved not because it is driven by some internal agency wrapped up in the package, but because as fast as it is gathering or winding itself up, it is forever unravelling or unwinding, alternately breathing in and out.
>
> (*Making* 96)

Though Ingold would rather dispense with the idea of agency all together, he sees the forces and flows of materials as central to their potential to come together in active participation (*Making* 96). This active participation is ongoing and not marked by a clear beginning and end as would be the case with what he terms an "internal agency."

Bennett, similarly aiming to escape the bind of passive objects and intentional subjects, considers the "agency of assemblages" (20–26). This idea underlines the extent to which agentive capacities are distributed across "macro- and microactants" (Bennett 23) as they work together in a confederation. Bennett insists on the "distinctive capacities and efficacious powers" (ix) of materials, which give them nonintentional agentive potential and claims that anything that "has sufficient coherence to make a difference,

Vibrant Materials 127

produce effects, and alter the course of events" (x) might be considered to have agency of some kind. Her term "thing-power," which is "a vitality intrinsic to materiality" (Bennett) can be applied to all kinds *of* "nonhuman bodies, forces, and forms" and its effects can be revealed "even though it resists full translation and exceeds my comprehensive grasp" (Bennett 122).

Both Bennett and Ingold make it clear that materials include all things, human and nonhuman, and that the vitality of materials resides in how the interaction between materials may evoke a dissolving of boundaries between subjects and objects. Based on their ideas, I would like to argue for an understanding of the agentive capacity of objects, materials and things as based on the propensity of materials to operate in relation to other materials in an ongoing and inter-determined relationship. This offers a way to conceptualize a nonintentional, reciprocal exchange between bodies and materials,

Figure 7.1 Beneath the Forest Floor 2013, photo: David Shearing.

and as such, it offers a rethinking of agency that focuses on the "contingent capacities for reflexivity, creative disclosure, and transformation" (Coole 113) in line with what Merleau-Ponty describes as the flesh. Merleau-Ponty's account of the "flesh" is the implication of the subject in the object and (vice versa) in a common flesh that refuses "to submit to the exigencies of clearcut separation or logical identity" (Grosz 96). Distinctions between objects and subjects fall away, resulting in an "intercorporeal being" (Merleau-Ponty, *The Visible and the Invisible* 143). While this offers a leveling and intertwining of the human and the nonhuman, it does not address the potentiality of materials themselves. However, in establishing the inter-corporeal nature of the flesh, Merleau-Ponty has set up the possibility for inter-determined and ongoing operations of materials, which new materialist thinkers such as Bennett and Ingold now propose.

In what follows I will use an analysis of *Beneath the Forest Floor* to explore the potentiality of objects, materials, and things in a specific performance where I can identify the way various reciprocal exchanges manifest themselves and different orders of agency, distributed across a range of beings, objects, materials, and things intersect.

BENEATH THE FOREST FLOOR

Beneath the Forest Floor is a participatory performance where scenographic materials and the way human actants engage with them is the main focus. The "set" consists of three metre-long white silk strips suspended in a circle, and using a collection of objects—gloves, puppets, and materials including snow confetti, charcoal, paper, and masking tape—and three performers (me and my collaborators, Rosie Hannis and Isla Watton) we begin by demonstrating some of the things that the materials can do and instantiating a simple framing narrative based on cycles of creation and destruction. The "forest floor"[3] of the title refers to the idea of a fertile place where layers of material accrue, where unfamiliar things can emerge, shielded from the bright light of day. The lighting is focused on the centre of the suspended circle of white silk strips so that it feels a little like a clearing in the woods. We begin by pulling on white cotton gloves and making a kind of canopy by tying the silk together across the space, scribbling white paper black with charcoal, making birds that perch in the silk, and folding and tearing paper to build a structure (we think of it as a power plant). We place a small puppet on top of it, but the structure cannot hold the weight and thus collapses. Then we pull apart what we have done and push the materials into a heap in the middle burying it with more paper and handfuls of snow confetti. After the "demonstration" section, Isla hands out gloves to each member of the audience and we start a new cycle of making; we reveal more puppets, unearth things from the heap, and rearrange the space, making new structures. The gloves are intended to be an invitation for the audience to participate and start to explore the materials and make interventions of their own. The performance is brought to a close with another, heavier confetti snowfall. Then we ask the audience, sitting in the debris of the performance, to talk about and reflect on their experiences.

Figure 7.2 Beneath the Forest Floor 2013, photo: David Shearing.

From the midst of the performance my collaborators and I can observe multiple ways of responding as participants are able to discover for themselves what they can do with materials and what the materials do to them. The discussion with participants that takes place immediately afterwards is recorded, and the transcripts of those discussions adds a more conscious reflective dimension above and beyond the experience of the performance. Performance as a research strategy "encompasses intimate, playful, and even banal or ambiguous gestures as conduits for thoughts and emotions" (Hansen and Kozel 212) and, using participatory performance to investigate scenographic materials, assists in encouraging an imaginative engagement with things and attentiveness to what people do with things and a heightened awareness of how the things themselves behave. Below I reflect on and from the "thickness" (Hansen and Kozel 212) of performances of *Beneath the Forest Floor*. I draw on my experience of being part of the performances and seeing and feeling what happens around me during the performance and also on reflections from audience members communicated through post-performance discussions and questionnaires.[4]

130 *Joslin McKinney*

Figure 7.3 Beneath the Forest Floor 2013, photo: David Shearing.

MATERIALS, OBJECTS, AND THINGS

In *Beneath the Forest Floor* we could distinguish between objects, materials, and things. The objects could be said to be those entities which carry with them a sense of purposeful expression that has been inscribed by their makers; the puppets, the gloves, and the set, whereas the materials, the paper, the charcoal, and the masking tape are those that have the potential to attain multiple purposes and meanings. But as we shall see, even objects are not fixed in their meaning and they might also behave like materials, or as "things." A thing differs from an object in that it is a gathering of lively matter, involved in "ongoing formation" rather than the result of subjective intention imposed on inert materials (Ingold, "Toward an Ecology of Materials" 435–6).

The set has been determined by us, the makers, with the explicit intention of creating an artifact that performs in distinct ways. But as part of this construction it is important that inherent qualities of the materials used are apparent to participants. Some of what the set does is intended to invite interaction through touch and movement; the white silk strips are soft and light and brush delicately across arms and faces, are luminous in the light, and they float slowly back into place when moved. The design of the "forest" follows the materials that it is made from and attempts to draw attention to that; the strips hang from a large hoop, suspended from the lighting rig so that it can be pulled to make the movement of the silk more pronounced, creating more shadows and disturbing

Vibrant Materials 131

Figure 7.4 Beneath the Forest Floor 2013, photo: David Shearing.

Figure 7.5 Beneath the Forest Floor 2013, photo: David Shearing.

the air. The set is an object in so far as particular intentions on the part of the makers have informed its realization; however, it is also a "thing." In *Beneath the Forest Floor* designed objects can become things when the intention of the maker-performers recedes and the interaction of participants with the materials follows a trajectory that is informed by the vitality of the materials themselves.

Charcoal, paper, and masking tape appear inert until they are taken up and used by someone. Once there is physical contact, the latent qualities of the materials invite and condition interaction in different ways. Some participants enjoy the soft scribbly noise that the charcoal makes. Others are drawn by the way charcoal changes white paper to black and makes clean things dirty (one participant tried to make white gloves black on the inside). The construction paper is stiff enough to be folded and rolled so that structures can be created, although for some participants it is uncompromising and unforgiving. The masking tape creates a strident but satisfying tearing noise as it is pulled off the roll and it sticks to other materials. Each of these materials has its own "language," as Goebbels might say, and participants are differently drawn to them. The snow confetti—small squares of white tissue—is soft and dense. It falls in small twirling arcs, pattering on the floor and patterning it. Several participants remark that they find it more inviting and interesting than the paper to work with because its yielding nature is more immediately responsive to human touch. Ingold points out that "following materials" ("The Textility of Making" 93), rather than exerting our will upon them, occurs widely in practices of art, craft, and design: "As practitioners, the builder, the gardener, the cook, the alchemist, and the painter are not so much imposing form on matter as bringing together diverse materials and combining or redirecting their flow in the anticipation of what might emerge" (94).

Following materials and redirecting their flow becomes a possibility once we acknowledge the reversibility of the seer and the seen, the toucher and the things being touched, which Merleau-Ponty describes. Hands are incorporated into the "universe" they interrogate through a "crisscrossing" process between the touching and the tangible (Merleau-Ponty, *The Visible and the Invisible* 133) that is founded on a propagation of exchanges between "bodies of the same type" (143). This seems to be borne out by the way the little squares of delicate tissue which tend to stick together invite a particular kind of touch and movement of the fingers. This in turn allows the white flakes to separate and fall gently. The stiff paper seems to require firmer and more decisive handling. Ingold's account of the making process indicates how Merleau-Ponty's conception of phenomenological perception might be actively incorporated in the pursuit of an aesthetic experience. Indeed, the overarching purpose of *Beneath the Forest Floor* is to instigate a process of following materials; however, this is complicated by the particular participants, each of which responds to this invitation in different ways. Their previous experience of and confidence in handling materials along with their preferences and affinities with certain material qualities is a contributing factor to the particular trajectory of each performance.

Figure 7.6 Beneath the Forest Floor 2013, photo: David Shearing.

Participants, not surprisingly, differ with regard to the extent that they are engaged or motivated by the open-ended nature of *Beneath the Forest Floor* and our pursuit of the potentiality of materials, above and beyond more conventional performance methods. The objects that attract the most attention are the puppets; perhaps the most clearly defined theatrical objects in the performance. They are most obviously objects in the sense that they are designed artifacts; small bean-bags which can sit in the palm of a hand with simple arms and legs which are attached loosely to the bodies and heads marked just with small shiny buttons for eyes. However, the design of the puppets aims to imbue them with performative potential that is as much based on their material properties as it is on their resemblance to human beings; as objects, therefore, they are deliberately incomplete. Attached to their sack-like bodies, weighted with rice, their rudimentary limbs which dangle from their bodies and the heads settle at unpredictable angles. Some participants are made uneasy by this limp, broken quality. Others are interested in the challenge of finding ways to animate them or simply to be with them. They are not easy to control because they have their own material being. Like the snow confetti, they condition the way they can be handled and this in turn influences the way the handler needs to adapt to them.

The introduction of the puppets tends to throw other materials into dramaturgical relief; for example, when in the demonstration phase a puppet is balanced on the paper structure, an abstract construction suddenly becomes a vivid and particular landscape "like a filmic image or a painting" (Leeds participant). In this way, the potential of the other scenic materials becomes fixed, and in a few cases even limited by the objectness of the puppets. They can detract from open explorations of the other materials insofar as, in the presence of the puppets, they may become merely their accessories. One reflection was that the puppets assumed a "privileged" status over the other materials and "possibilities became less open" (Stanford participant) as soon as they were brought on. In contrast to this, other participants have found that the puppets fulfil a role as "entrees to materials" (Stanford participant) and they provide a motivation or cue for participants to engage with all the other materials. However, it seems from what we have observed that this route (via puppets) to experiencing all the other materials is propelled by the human agency of the participants being transferred to the puppets and can restrict the ways that the other materials are used; that is mainly in the service of the puppets. The puppets, then, are objects with thing potential, but the more they are treated as objects, the less they reveal their thing-power. Thingliness in the context of this performance resides not only in the way each object or material behaves separately but in the way they operate in combination.

The white gloves in our performance operate somewhere between the categories of materials and objects. Wearing them seems to make our hands into objects; at a remove from us. The gloves are a device through which we invite participation and a means by which we draw attention to the handling of materials; the gloves resemble those used for handling precious objects. In other words, the gloves alter the semiotic and the experiential qualities of the participants' interaction with the other materials. They impose their own structure and qualities on the nature of the action; the masking tape sticks to them and tugs at them, they attract charcoal dust; they make hands sticky and clumsy. If a participant has an intention to make a particular intervention, wearing gloves can be frustrating because they make it difficult to impose pre-determined form on to the other materials. However, if we think of the hands, the gloves, and the other material that they come into contact with as components of a larger whole—the sensible world of the performance—where all bodies and all materials communicate with one another through reciprocal insertion and intertwining, intention might be said to limit perception. From Ingold's perspective it is clear that hylomorphic intention shuts down the possibility of a more emergent and intertwined experience of the materiality of scenography on the part of each participant. Further, this materiality is constituted within the context of a collection of agencies of different kinds that might be seen to be competing; the intentions of designers, performers, and participants rub up against the agentive capacity of materials. Intention on the part of the human agents in the performance impedes the possibility of a more broadly distributed agency where materials operate in relation to other entities in an open-ended and ongoing relationship.

The interactions of thing-power in *Beneath the Forest Floor* occasionally result in something that approaches the condition of an object; an image or an action that fleetingly attains the status of a shared proposition amongst participants. Across all the performances a variety of social narratives have been played out: the response of societies within a hostile environment; the evolution of hierarchical societies with elaborate paraphernalia, such as headdresses, chariots, and thrones; the domination of one society or environment over another. When Merleau-Ponty says that we are "condemned to meaning" (*Phenomenology of Perception* xix), he is recognizing that "inner" perception is inextricably linked to "outer" consciousness: "The phenomenological world is not pure being, but the sense which is revealed where the paths of my various experiences intersect, and also where my own and other people's intersect and engage each other like gears" (xvii, xx).

It is not just the puppets that evoke these existential forces. The circle of silk strips tends to encourage participants to place themselves in the space in ways which facilitate cooperation and sharing, reflecting as it does a long-established spatial principle of communal activity and storytelling. And the fact that the set has been designed in this way, or that some participants want to resist the logic of the circle by working across it or moving outside it, does not diminish its thing-power; along with the other materials, the circle is still making an active contribution to the wider operation of the scenography in the performance. Even materials and energies that are not designed but are nonetheless part of conditions of each performance are contributing: the shadowy dimensions of the studio, the temperature in the room, and dust caught in the light influence to some degree the way each performance develops. Here Bennett's use of the "assemblage" helps define how a "vibrant materials of all sorts" (23) can operate. An assemblage, such as an electrical power grid, is a cluster of materials, energies, and beings that can produce effects which are distinct from the individual materials from which it is constituted. At the same time, it is not a "stolid block but an open-ended collective" (Bennett 24). Applying this idea to *Beneath the Forest Floor* it is possible to see how images cluster and cohere temporarily across the performance amid a host of other interactions which are local to particular bodies or materials.

CONCLUSION

The vitality of materials in *Beneath the Forest Floor* is seen in their interaction rather than in their singular entities. This interactive assemblage becomes a thing in itself where various energies work together through the trajectory of the assemblage in an open-ended way where images and ideas cluster but do not achieve a totality or completion. Scenography actively engages the vibrancy of materials and in so doing reflects a redistribution of agency in performance. This is not an even redistribution because different materials have different capacities, intensities, propensities, and potentialities, but it is a redistribution that does not privilege the human.

A phenomenological approach to scenography may reveal such vitality of objects, materials, and things and show how this vitality does not depend on human agency. This is not only the case with immersive, participatory performance such as the one discussed here, but it applies to more conventional performances, too. Encountering a scenographic thing involves the process as Ingold describes when viewing a "living" work of art; that is, being able to "look *with* it as it unfolds in the world, rather than *behind* it to an originating intention" (*Making* 96). To look with or to follow materials is a strategy of viewing as well as making, and if we are to fully explore the range of ways that scenography operates, we need to rethink some assumptions about the ways audiences are engaged. Similarly, Merleau-Ponty observes that art, especially painting, allows ways of seeing the world that other modes of expression do not. Between the painter, the paints, and the scene and between the painting and the viewer a "kind of crossover occurs, when the spark of the sensing/sensible is lit" (Merleau-Ponty, "Eye and Mind" 125). This happens because of a fundamental recognition between our bodies and the things we perceive, which is necessary for perception to occur at all: "Quality, light, color, depth, which are there before us, are there only because they awaken an echo in our bodies and because the body welcomes them" (Merleau-Ponty, "Eye and Mind" 125).

This places the viewer as well as the artist within the thickness of materials as part of an ongoing process. Here, Ingold's concept of the textility of making complements and extends Merleau-Ponty's idea of the flesh by insisting on the active participation of materials in processes of making and viewing art. For Ingold it is not recognition in our bodies that initiates the process of perception, but the contrapositioning of "mindful or attentive" bodies and "flows and resistances of the material," which comprises our encounters with the material world (*Making* 101).

Both Merleau-Ponty and Ingold stop short of claiming agency for materials. Merleau-Ponty is cautious about the idea of power of things themselves to exert agency and doubts whether things have any "inner power" of their own (*The Visible and the Invisible* 162). And although Ingold sees materials as fully part of the process of making and experiencing artworks, he too questions the need to ascribe agency to objects. We only need a notion of material agency because things are too often reduced to objects and thus cut off from the "flux of vital materials;" we need a theory, not of agency, but of life, he says (*Making* 95–97). Nonetheless I find it useful to think about the agentive capacity of materials in the particular context of scenography, which in most cases arises from a clear intention. As we have seen with my particular example, the intersecting intentions of the scenographer and of the participants come into contact with the capacities of the materials themselves. A phenomenology of materiality draws attention to how intentions can be thwarted, diverted, or transformed from within the performance, through the way the materials themselves behave. In turn, these materials, "saturated with agentic capacity" (Coole 92) influence and shape the performance as it unfolds. Part of the delight of this performance, and of scenography in general, is to be found in the process of relinquishing mastery as the materials begin to work on the viewer.

Bennett's notion of "thing-power" goes further than either Merleau-Ponty or Ingold and holds out the possibility of a vitality that is intrinsic to materials themselves. Bennett herself is aware of a potential problem with the term in that it tends to "overstate the thinginess or fixed stability of materiality" (20). However, the substantive point about thing-power, especially as far as scenography is concerned, is that it always operates in relation to other sources of thing-power; it is always part of an assemblage where each "member-actant" maintains its own flow of energy or "pulse" (Bennett 24). The materials from which scenographies are constructed consist of vibrant potentialities, which can be active as part of the assemblage, which is a performance. In scenography bodies, materials and objects are, within the thickness of performance, all capable of becoming things that contribute to the assemblage.

ACKNOWLEDGEMENTS

Heartfelt thanks to:
Rosie Hannis and Isla Watton, my research collaborators and technical staff at the University of Leeds and Stanford University.

All the participants in the *Beneath the Forest Floor* performances at the University of Leeds, UK (May 2013), at the Performance Studies international conference at Stanford University, USA (June 2013) and at Light Night, Leeds, UK (October 2013).

Minty Donald for pointing me to Jane Bennett.

NOTES

1. New materialism is a response to ethical and political challenges of 21st century, which involves addressing "questions about the nature of matter and the place of embodied humans within a material world" (Coole and Frost 3).
2. Tadeusz Kantor's performances, especially the later work, often dealt with events from his own life where he played himself, sitting at the side of the stage watching his own attempts to stage memory and sometimes intervening.
3. The title *Beneath the Forest Floor* refers to development of an earlier piece of practice-based research into audience experience of scenography called *Forest Floor* (see McKinney, "Empathy and Exchange").
4. There have been six performances of *Beneath the Forest Floor*, two in May 2013 at the University of Leeds, UK, two at Stanford University, USA, in June 2013 as part of the Performance Research international conference, and two more

as part of Light Night in Leeds, UK, an annual multi-artform festival aimed at growing new and more diverse audiences and developing new work, in October 2013. Each time there have been between 10 and 15 participants, and the comments reproduced here are drawn from recordings at all six performances.

WORKS CITED

Bablet, Denis. *The Revolutions of Stage Design in the 20th Century.* Paris: L. Amiel, 1977.
Bennett, Jane. *Vibrant Matter: A Political Ecology of Things*, London: Duke UP, 2010.
Coole, Diana and Samantha Frost, eds. *New Materialisms: Ontology, Agency, and Politics,* London: Duke UP, 2010.
Coole, Diana. "The Inertia of Matter and the Generativity of Flesh." *New Materialisms: Ontology, Agency, and Politics.* Eds. Diana H. Coole and Samantha Frost. London: Duke UP, 2010. 92–115.
Fischer-Lichte, Erika. *The Semiotics of Theater.* Trans. Jeremy Gaines and Doris L. Jones. Bloomington: Indiana UP, 1992.
Garner, Stanton B. Jr. *Bodied Spaces: Phenomenology and Performance in Contemporary Drama.* Ithaca: Cornell UP, 1994.
———. "Staging 'Things': Realism and the Theatrical Object in Shepard's Theatre." *Contemporary Theatre Review* 8.3 (1998): 55–66.
Grosz, Elizabeth. *Volatile Bodies: Towards a Corporeal Feminism.* Bloomington: Indiana UP, 1994.
Hansen, Lone Koefoed, and Susan Kozel. "Embodied Imagination: A Hybrid Method of Designing for Intimacy." *Digital Creativity* 18.4 (2007): 207–220. Web. 1 January 2014.
Heiner Goebbels, *Stifter's Dinge.* Brochure. London: Artangel, 2012.
Ingold, Tim. "The Textility of Making." *Cambridge Journal of Economics* 34.1 (2010): 91–102. Web. 1 Jan. 2014.
———. "Toward an Ecology of Materials." *Annual Review of Anthropology* 41 (2012): 427–42. Web. 1 Jan. 2014.
———. *Making: Anthropology, Archaeology, Art and Architecture*, London: Routledge, 2013.
Kennedy, Dennis. *Looking at Shakespeare: A Visual History of Twentieth Century Performance.* Cambridge: Cambridge UP, 1993.
Klossowicz, Jan. "Tadeusz Kantor's Journey." *The Drama Review* 30:3 (1986): 176–83.
Lehmann, Hans-Thies. *Postdramatic Theatre.* Trans. Karen Jürs-Munby. London: Routledge, 2006.
McAuley, Gay. *Space in Performance: Making Meaning the Theatre.* Ann Arbor: U of Michigan P, 1999.
McKinney, Joslin. "Empathy and Exchange: Audience Experience of Scenography." *Kinesthetic Empathy in Creative and Cultural Practices.* Eds. Dee Reynolds and Matthew Reason. Bristol: Intellect, 2012. 219–235.
Merleau-Ponty, Maurice. *Phenomenology of Perception.* Trans. Colin Smith. 1962. London: Routledge, 2001.

———. *The Visible and the Invisible*. Trans. Alphonso Lingis. Evanston: Northwestern UP, 1968.

———. (1993) "Eye and Mind." Trans. Michael. B. Smith. *The Merleau-Ponty Aesthetics Reader: Philosophy and Painting*. Ed. Galen. A. Johnson. Evanston: Northwestern University, 1993. 121–149.

Pleśniarowicz, Krzysztof. *The Dead Memory Machine: Taduesz Kantor's Theatre of Death*. Trans. William Brand. Aberystwyth: Black Mountain P, 2001.

States, Bert O. *Great Reckonings in Little Rooms*. Berkeley; Los Angeles; London: U of California P, 1985.

8 Doing Time with the Neo-Futurists

Jon Foley Sherman

This is an idea of time:

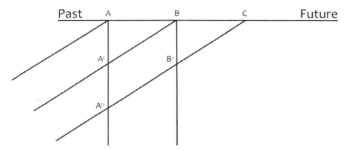

Figure 8.1 From Maurice Merleau-Ponty, *Phenomenology of Perception* (London: Routledge, 2012), 400.

We identify a moment, A. That moment transforms into something else, B. When we carve B out from the world, it does not simply bring the remnants of A with it, but it establishes a relation in which A transforms into B but also into A^I. A splits up, carried with us and left past us. When we carry another moment from B, the process repeats and extends with the arrival of C, but also of B^I and the transformation of A^I into A^{II}. Naming these moments, the telling of them as moments, requires a language that allows them to exist simultaneously in more than one tense.

In his analysis of what this image describes, Merleau-Ponty writes in *Phenomenology of Perception*, "Time is the unique movement that harmonizes with itself in all of its parts, just as a gesture envelops all of the muscular contractions that are necessary for producing it" (2012 442). For example, and to take the image of the contracting muscle into a spatial metaphor, a step forward transforms the arrangement of a body into a new location while still remaining a step with, as it were, one foot in the past. We simply cannot find ourselves in "the" present without also touching the past and transforming into the future. "Since being and passing by are synonymous within time, the event does not cease to exist by becoming past" (*PP* 2012 443).[1] Each moment we perceive arrives while also veining into other moments that constitute a relationship to what followed and preceded. They are, and cannot help but be, in concert. A note might be discerned, cherished, savored, or regretted, but it only exists as an element in a milieu. Merleau-Ponty continues, "A, A^I, and A^{II} [...] and B and B^I [...] are not linked together through a synthesis of identification that would congeal them to a point in time, but rather through a synthesis of *transition*" (*PP* 2012 442–43).[2]

Time in this description escapes assignment as a whole through its continual opening, revealed most plainly in the experience of "the present," a mode of time that "is not locked within itself, but transcends itself toward a future and toward a past" (*PP* 2012 444). This means that we never experience the present as an entirety because in the so-called present, we are constantly pulled towards the future and drawn from the past. "I am not, for myself, directed toward the present time; I am just as much directed toward this morning or toward the night that is about to arrive, and although my present is surely this present instant, it is also just as much today, this year, or even my entire life" (*PP* 2012 444). Time is transition. Moments are not moments but movements that adhere to the movers. The different tenses of time work in relation to each other and bear within and between the roots of the others: "When I say that I see an object at a distance, I mean that I already hold it or that I still hold it, the object is in the future or the past" (*PP* 2012 277). In other words, we cannot perceive in one tense.

The shortcomings of this graph, adapted by Merleau-Ponty from Husserl (*PP* 2012 440), are many. To begin with, a *line* represents the lived experience of a person in two dimensions, and, despite Merleau-Ponty's insistence on the importance of transitions, this image does not itself move. But beyond the constraints common to all still representation, this graph falls short in a way that Merleau-Ponty alluded to but did not explicitly address. Namely, this image fails because it addresses a single subject; it describes time but only as one person lives it.

This particular failing comes into sharp relief when we put time on stage, or, more particularly, when we stage time. "Staging time" refers in this case to the explicit performance of temporal consciousness, that is, of our perception of time. In this chapter I undertake a phenomenological analysis of time in the work of the Neo-Futurists in order to consider the plural perception of time. Merleau-Ponty's reflections on time provide a starting point for considering the Neo-Futurists' work, which in turn can be understood to push past Merleau-Ponty's return to a single subject. Through an analysis of how our desires shape time and how time can be performed for others, I propose that our own temporal transitions gain *sense* (as in direction, as in meaning) through the witness of others, real and/or imagined.

NEO-FUTURIST TIMES

The Neo-Futurists are a 25-year-old ensemble that produces original work in a small theater located above a funeral home in Chicago's Andersonville neighborhood, once a Swedish, then a lesbian, then a gay area, and now home to more and more moneyed heterosexual couples and families, most of them white. In 2004 a branch opened in New York, and they now perform weekly at the Kraine Theatre in the East Village. The Neos, as they are called locally, maintain a roughly 12-person ensemble that each week writes and performs *Too Much Light Makes the Baby Go Blind* (*TML*), an event that consists of 30 plays in 60 minutes. *TML* is performed at 11:30 on Friday and Saturday nights and 7:00 on Sundays (10:30 Friday and Saturday in New York), and each week an audience member rolls a die to determine how many new pieces must be written for the next week. At the beginning of each performance, a cast member introduces the concept of the show to the audience. The plays are listed as numbered menu items with corresponding numbers clipped to a clothesline over the stage. Once a play has been performed, audience members call out which play they want next and the first Neo to grab a number announces what the play will be. Before the performance starts, a Neo sets a dark room timer hanging on the wall to 60 minutes; the show ends either when all the plays are performed or when the timer goes off, whichever comes first.

Both the Chicago and New York companies produce "primetime" shows; these are original plays written by company members and performed by casts that include local actors. No matter what their subject matter (from penal systems, such as *Crime & Punishment: A (mis)Guided Environmental Tour With Literary Pretensions* [1998] to Vermeer [*Curious Beautiful* (2000)] to a train collision between an army transport and a circus train [*Roustabout: The Great Circus Train Wreck* (2007)]), the plays are performed in a style that seeks to bluntly present the performers and their means of production. The Neos are dedicated to "non-illusory, interactive performance that conveys our experiences and ideas as directly and honestly as possible," and it is not uncommon for actors, even those performing characters, to refer to each other by their first names (Neo-Futurists, 2008).[3]

Naturally, the Neos tell a lot of stories about themselves. Many of them are true. "[C]onveying our experiences and ideas as directly and honestly as possible" leaves a lot of leeway, they take full advantage of it, and reframing is their specialty. These plays function simultaneously as confessional, memorial, and science lecture. Old slights, prides, lovers, mistakes, embarrassments, problems, triumphs, meals, and lessons are assembled. Reenacted often. Relived but this time better: things unsaid said, undone done, done undone, said said louder. Interactive storytelling based on personal experience—known here as Neo-Futurism—does more than present intervening presents; it stages how these interventions take place now, then, and everywhere in between. The plays range from dramatizing an encounter at a chain restaurant while on vacation as a child to gender bending the horrific misogyny of the children's classic "The Giving Tree" to a primetime show about that trip to Lake Powell Sharon Greene took at the age of 25 in the company of virtual strangers. The Neos work what Merleau-Ponty identified as "the initial ambiguity of memory: to retain is to hold onto, but at a distance" (*PP* 2012 446). They hold onto those stories but also maintain distance so that they may share them with attendants. This distance they often compromise by literally approaching attendants, by baring intimate details of their lives, and often by baring more than that. Indeed, on-stage nakedness offers a useful starting point for thinking about time and performance.

NEO NAKEDNESS, TIME, AND DESIRE

> We're fucking late-80s performance artists, what do you want? As soon as I was cast I knew it was inevitable, even though I had only seen *TML* once at that point. It's like a *TML* play genre: the shorty, the line-play, personal monologue with a task, the down-spot play, the first naked play I wrote for *Too Much Light* play.
>
> (Reid, Interview)

No matter how particular in any play, Neo nakedness can be understood to pose a question common to all on-stage nakedness: is there a way to arrive beyond the vast expanse of uneasiness accompanying a moment when *all you're thinking about is the naked body of a person you don't know right there in front of you?* In one primetime show, the New York Neos addressed this question head on with a show performed almost entirely in the nude. *The Soup Show*—the 2010 show that inspired Young Jean Lee's *Untitled Feminist Show*—began each night with Cara Francis, Erica Livingston, and Desiree Burch each separately spotlit and naked, posing in a different "classical" posture.[4] A voice came over the speakers and asked the attendants to spend the next three minutes using the pencils in their programs to sketch one of the women. This gave the attendants several things: (1) The freedom to look at the bodies of the women. To *inspect* them. "You kind of need to check out the bits," Livingston said. "If you try to act like you don't want to do that, then that's distracting" (Interview). So look. And make a record of that looking. Externalize it. Also, the pencil is yours. (2) The time to adjust to the nakedness of the women. To *get over it*. In early twenty-first century USA, most people aren't naked in front of anyone other than a lover or teammate or a stranger at the Y. So these women were. And the voice said it was okay and the time attendants took to look made it so. (3) The consequent freedom to *listen*. So this nakedness meant something, means something, will mean something. So what it meant/means/will mean won't be clear until the attendants are ready to think about something other than, "these three naked women and they're naked." Following the different waves of feminism through an episodic format during which naked women bathe and perform in a tub before offering vials of bath water to the audience requires more than an interest in naked bodies. But that interest, Francis recalled, was allowed (Interview). The women accepted it and gambled that it could transform into something else *given enough time*.

These three minutes of time are only a fraction of the performance. Three minutes is a *long* play in *TML*. The writer performers and the audience members don't have the time for adjustment. Chicago Artistic Director Jay Torrence notes about nakedness in *TML*, "a delicate aggression that occurs in the room. It's almost painful for the audience to endure. [...] There's nothing casual about the response" (Interview). Torrence, in alignment with comments made by Livingston, Francis, and Reid, identifies here a compression of affect related to the compression of time. Torrence notes how difficult it can be to establish much of anything beyond the initial shock, for example, in his "Ass-a-oke," which is exactly what you think it is, or Eliza Burmester's "The Tackle," which consists of an innocent ice cream cone eater tackled three times in a row by a naked person.

It goes without saying that few things quite focus our attention like that moment in a play where a naked person appears quite close to us. This provokes different desires for time. A desire for it to pass quickly or slowly, to change its aspect for us. To move faster so that we don't have to look anymore or to move slower so that we can look longer. The actor's naked body disrupts the experience of time by directing our attention to time, especially in the frame of a play that cannot last too long and may not last long at all. Which is to say that in *TML* plays with nudity, the compressed relationship to the exposed human form rearranges our experience of time; the actor's naked body can remind us that we can only experience time through our relationship to it. Or, more precisely, Neo nakedness throws our experience of time into a crisis in which we want that relationship to be something other than what it is. And to want something is to believe in its ability to change, or at least to change its relationship to you. When we want something of time, we glimpse how much it depends on us.

In English we say that a clock "tells" time and a working clock is supposed to talk to us in numbers about when now is. A broken clock, other than the two times a day it is "correct," is either an historian or a prognosticator. But the seconds and minutes on a clock tell time in a language we sometimes forget, a language that is in any event learned and not inherent. Anyone apart from a loved one or stuffed next to an unpleasant one on a long trip knows this. The language of time I speak most fluently tells of the time I spend with and away from my son. It's not simply that time is relative, it's that our emergence into the world through embodied relationships with others finds expression, too, in our relationship to time.

Of course, long before people were getting naked in small theaters above funeral homes on Chicago's Northside, physicists had understood that time can be bent by the speed at which its observer travels, just as space can be bent by gravity. Furthermore, these performances are not proof of anything, they are simply opportunities to reflect on what it means that time can be bent by desire, aversion, curiosity, and anxiety. Time means nothing free from our embodiment, a state of being that involves our bodies but does not originate from them alone. Merleau-Ponty wrote about the misleading image of time as a river and noted that it attempts to describe time as both that which flows *and* the movement of the thing that flows (*PP* 2012 434). In addition, the image only works if we "surreptitiously place in the river a witness to its flowing" and for whom the flow will be quite confusing: The water passed by flows not to the future but towards the past, while the "still-to-come is on the side of the source" (*PP* 2012 434). His principal point, however, is that even this metaphorical flow requires a vantage point to even perceive it as a flow, a look *from someone* that goes upstream or down or across. This vantage point constitutes an involvement with the flow, the flow's dependence on a vantage point to be understood as a flow at all. But this does not go far enough, does not even extend past his subsequent claim that two different experiences of time can meet in their projection into the present (*PP* 2012 457). To trace out the phenomenological consequences of embodied time, we need to wait. Three minutes can suffice.

"NOW I ASK YOU"

The premise: acting out the stage directions and only the stage directions of notoriously fussy stage direction writer Eugene O'Neill would be hilarious. Example stage direction:

> LUCY appears on the left. She is slender, dark, beautiful, with large eyes which she attempts to keep always mysterious and brooding, smiling lips which she resolutely uses to express melancholy determination, a healthy complexion subdued by powder to a proper prison pallor and a vigorous, lithe body which frets restlessly beneath the restriction of studied, artificial movements (414).

The experiment: a *Too Much Light* play of Act 2, Scene 1 of *Long Day's Journey Into Night* in which a narrator reads stage directions that the cast enact with exaggeratedly affectless precision. The result: much laughter. The conclusion: a full-length, "primetime" production of seven non-copyright-protected plays of O'Neill, *The Complete & Condensed Stage Directions of Eugene O'Neill, Volume 1: Early/Lost Plays* (*TC&C*).[5]

Each play began with its title announced by narrator Jacquelyn Landgraf, a swift arrangement of props and furniture, and then a cast member setting one of six clocks to the (approximate) beginning time of the action, followed by the narration and enactment.

Many moments in the production provide rich opportunities for thinking about time, starting with those clocks. Although obviously nonfunctional, the clocks offer, at the least, a nod to the visibility of the darkroom timer used in *Too Much Light*, a breezy reference to the staging's simultaneous acknowledgment and disregard for detail, and a desultory index of each play's difference from the others, their shared deadpan performance style notwithstanding. Another way of thinking about time would be to consider how the radical compression of the play's length accounted for its comic aspect. The efficient yet manic embodiment of the stage directions seemed to demonstrate the absurdity both of O'Neill's precision and of any actor trying too literally to make good on O'Neill's promises. With no time for relationships to develop or change the space, the actors' movements gave us Henri Bergson's "dancing jack" at work: people submitting themselves to the automation of fulfilling outside dictates.

Of all these moments and many others, one stands out. Towards the end of the last play in the evening, *Now I Ask You* (1916), Landgraf reads this stage direction:

> LUCY snatches the revolver from the table. The noise of the motor increases in volume. Closing her eyes tightly, LUCY lifts the revolver to her temple. There is the sound of a shot. An interval of three minutes during which the theater remains darkened.
> (Neo-Futurists, *TC&C* 30)[6]

This being the United States of Litigation, Exit lights remained illuminated and the theater was not pitched into utter darkness. But dark enough it was and there we sat. Charles Isherwood complained, "This dictate is followed precisely by the Neo-Futurists, and you become quickly aware of how long three minutes of darkened silence can seem, and why it is sometimes wiser to honor the spirit of a stage direction rather than the letter" (Review).

But of course it is precisely *because* we are thinking about how long three minutes can seem that this stage direction deserved the literal enactment it got. At the New York production I attended, the beginning of the darkness was met with scattered laughter as the crowd realized that yes, we were going to wait for three minutes. But of course we weren't waiting. We were counting, we were listening, and some of us were figuring that this play had asked for three minutes of darkness and nothing else approximately 36 years before John Cage's *4'33"* premiered. But the theater very quickly filled with the attention of the attendants who responded with cheers and laughter to every noise that arose from within their ranks. A cough. "Ha!" A sniffle. "Heehee!" That titter. "Heh." The laughter was nervous, easy, very Freudian Relief Theory. What *were* we doing? When *would* these three minutes end? After three minutes, of course.

Pace Isherwood, because time can *only* seem and is not *is*, this moment does important work for the attendants. In Merleau-Ponty's evocative words: "I do not think the passage from the present to another present, I am not the spectator of this passage, I accomplish it" (*PP* 2012 444). In those three minutes everything we did could be resolved into the *accomplishment of those three minutes*. Part of what made them so exciting was that throughout the entire performance up to that point, when or as Landgraf read a direction, an actor undertook it in a literal—and often as a consequence screwball—way. They moved and spoke as if under the compulsion to enact the directions they were given. And then all of a sudden so were we. Told that the next three minutes would pass as an interval in darkness, it was left to the audience members to accomplish these stage directions. Which is to say, it fell to us to accomplish this time. As the laughter demonstrates, we were also capable of doing other things with this time, such as listening for and reacting to any signs of action. Nonetheless, in the frame of this performance, once Landgraf told us that the next three minutes would be an interval in darkness, we all became the performers of that moment of the play. Its goal could not be achieved without us. Staying meant not only that we were "accomplish[ing]" time, but that doing so made us part of the performance.

The whiff of compulsion—the only way to *not* do the time would have been to leave—can be seized upon in order to consider both the performance and the performativity of time. We might find tensions between the latter, time's enactment within and as prolongation of subject formation through discourse, and the former, the *doing* of time with others, that can tell us something further about time. In fact, Merleau-Ponty's words above pose this very question, or rather the fact that those are not his words so much as they are those of his most recent English translator, Donald A. Landes. It turns out that attempting to move Merleau-Ponty's French text to English generates a semantic thicket whose clearing might reveal much about what it means to do time in public.

The original text reads: "Le passage du présent à un autre présent, je ne le pense pas, je n'en suis pas le spectateur, je l'effectue" (*PP* 2006 483). Much rests on the meaning of, "l'effectue." A literal translation would read, "The passage of the present to another present, I do not think it, I am not its spectator, I carry it out." In contrast with Landes' translation of the last phrase that reads, "I accomplish it," the first translation by Colin Smith reads, "I perform it" (*PP* 1962 421). Now, Smith was of course translating before theorists corralled "to perform" within the work of discursive subject formation and affirmation. In terms of excavating Smith's and Merleau-Ponty's intentions, "perform" remains unproblematic so long as we maintain its pre-performance studies meaning. It means, "to do," which also seems to me to be an accurate translation of "effectuer:" "I do not think the passage of one present to another present, I am not its spectator, I do it."

The *doing* of time need hardly earn exemption from the societal constraints of performativity; it can take on repetitive, regulatory functions in a wide variety of settings, from the academic to the corporate to the carceral. Consider, for example, the context of idiomatic speech in the USA, where "doing time" refers to serving a sentence in prison. Not only is their punishment described in terms of time, for prisoners stripped of the freedoms of movement and association, there is little else to do *but* the time they are assigned to spend behind bars. All projects and remediating work become ways of "doing" the time assigned behind bars. When we do time, we can (almost) always find ourselves involved in a discursive project not of our own making.

And yet Smith's translation, when taken together with these three minutes in *TC&C*, pushes us towards an understanding of time that goes beyond performativity *per se* and elaborates Merleau-Ponty's claim that each of us accomplishes time through embodied existence. We are always doing time, and in the theater we do multiple times, as those phony clocks remind us. But for those three minutes we had the opportunity to experience the unraveling of that doing. We listened for the actors and heard ourselves become actors. We strained for a point outside ourselves and found ourselves there, outside ourselves, doing time. Time becomes more than transition, it becomes plural.

TELLING TIME

It may be that,

> The past, then, *is not* past, nor is the future future. It only exists when a subjectivity comes to shatter the plenitude of being in itself, to sketch out a perspective there, and to introduce non-being into it [...] the temporal dimensions—insofar as they perpetually fit together—affirm each other, never do more than make explicit what was implied in each one, and each express a single rupture or a single thrust that is subjectivity itself. Time must be understood as a subject, and the subject must be understood as time.
>
> (*PP* 2012 444–45)

Time may be the becoming of subjectivity that brings with it a perspective and the capacity to install nonbeing (abstraction) into the world. This is the standard phenomenological account in which "consciousness always finds itself already at work in the world" (*PP* 2012 456) and thus inseparable from worldly phenomena. In this formulation, the transitions of time come into being through our own embodiment of each temporal tense.

However, embodied existence refers not simply to the fact that we have bodies through which the world takes flesh; it refers to the irreducible binding of our own experiences to those of others. To have a body is to have a relation with other bodies. Performativity teaches us that these relations belong to the world of discourse and power. Beyond this, performance suggests that these relations not only gain their meaning, but they come into being through the attendance of other people. The subjectivity that breaks apart the plenitude of being requires a living perspective on *it*, a perspective associated not with an abstract arrangement of power, but with the unreliable, inconsistent, and breathing situations of other people. These perspectives belong to others who themselves are not outside of time and observing it in us, but whose own embodiment of time involves perceiving it through others.

Those three minutes of *TC&C* can be understood to propose that each of us works as Merleau-Ponty described the different tenses: we affirm each other and make explicit what our own doings of time implies. This can only be implied by each of us and requires the recognition of others. We tell time together. Rather than time as "the" subject, time is our performance of subjecthood for and with others. No one is strictly a spectator of time, and yet our own doing of time requires the existence of others who can witness our doing. We might find them assembled in the dark of a small New York performance space, or we might find them in our memories as we walk alone along a mountain ridge. But they are there while there is time.

While a subject might attempt to differentiate time, doing so has no *meaning* without other people. In order for time to have a sense, it must involve acts of transformation. And these acts can only be understood from a situated relation with each act. Which is to say, time isn't in our minds or outside of us—the intellectualist and empiricist fallacies. It exists through our relations with others, through our embodied transitions that record and manifest time as a phenomenon. These transitions are not entirely idiosyncratic; they demand the experience of others in order to register. For *our own* transitions to register as such, they require *another* point of view. We must perceive or remember *or at least imagine* another subject attending to us in order for us to experience time.

This is why performance can tell us so much about time. When people assemble before each other to tell time differently, strangely, they foreground questions about to whom the transitions that constitute time belong. "Live" performances (are supposed to) tell us that the time is now, whether or not anyone is broadcast from far away. But performance is not a clock, and during performance odd things happen to time. A comprehensive theory of time in performance is neither possible nor desirable. And yet we can enrich the senses of what it means to live with others by reflecting on how (some) performances tell (us about) time. The performances under consideration here were devised by a collective whose practices and very name gesture towards the constraints and possibilities of temporal awareness. Their obsessively self-referential and time-aware work provide a rich terrain for thinking about how every gathering, no matter how small, makes clear something that the graph above cannot: we never tell time alone.

NOTES

1. Because of its repeated use in the chapter, *Phenomenology of Perception* will be referred to as *PP*, followed by the publication year of the edition cited.
2. My emphasis.
3. This description of their work has been taken down. The current "About Neo-Futurism" page on their website contains a brief manifesto written by

founder Greg Allen: "Neo-Futurism is a new [sic] approach to performance that advocates the complete awareness and inclusion of the actual world within the theater in order to achieve a goal: to bring people to a greater understanding of themselves and each other. Rather than upholding contemporary theatrical conventions of character, setting, plot, and the separation of audience and performer, Neo-Futurism aims to present actual life on stage by creating a world in the theater which has no pretense or illusion. [...]The bottom line is that Neo-Futurism does not buy into 'the suspension of disbelief'—it does not attempt to take the audience anywhere else at any other time with any other people. The idea is to deal with what is going on right here and now. These guidelines are not set forth as "rules and regulations" but more as a jumping off point with which, it is hoped, people can find a greater meaning in their everyday lives. The aim is to empower and affirm, not just the lives of the performers, but the lives of the audience members as well." Greg Allen, *About Neo-Futurism*, 2014 http://neofuturists.org/about-neo-futurism/, accessed 25 Apr. 2014.
4. *The Soup Show* was directed by Lauren Sharpe and premiered in March 2010.
5. The original *TML* play was called *The Complete and Condensed Stage Directions of Eugene O'Neill, Volume 1: Act 2 Scene 1 of Long Day's Journey Into Night*. It was written by Christopher Loar and premiered in New York in 2009. Loar then assembled seven writer-performers who created the staging for the seven plays whose stage directions Loar had edited, and that play premiered in 2011. The cast: Danny Burnam, Brandon Donaldson, Cara Francis, Connor Kalista, Jacquelyn Landgraf, Erica Livingston, and Lauren Sharpe. The O'Neill plays: *A Wife for a Life* (1913); *The Web* (1913); *Thirst* (1913); *Bound East for Cardiff* (1914); *Servitude* (1914); *Before Breakfast* (1916); *Now I Ask You* (1916). After a run at two theaters in New York, the show toured to the O'Neill festival at Arena Stage in 2012.
6. Also, O'Neill, *Complete Plays*, 466–67.

WORKS CITED

Allen, Greg. "About Neo-Futurism." (2014) Web. 25 Apr. 2014. <http://neofuturists.org/about-neo-futurism/%3E>.
Francis, Cara. "Interview." Personal Interview. 20 May 2013.
Isherwood, Charles. "Long Day's Journey into Laughter." Review. *New York Times* (12 Sep. 2011) Web. 10 May 2013.
Livingston, Erica. Personal Interview. 13 May 2013.
Merleau-Ponty, Maurice. *Phénoménologie De La Perception*. 1945. Paris: Gallimard, 2006.
———. *Phenomenology of Perception*. 1945. Trans. Donald A. Landes. London: Routledge, 2012.
———. *Phenomenology of Perception*. 1945. Trans. Colin Smith. International Library of Philosophy and Scientific Method. 4th ed. London: Routledge & Kegan Paul, 1962.
Neo-Futurists, The. "The Complete & Condensed Stage Directions of Eugene O'Neill, Volume One: Early/Lost Plays." (2011).

———. "Homepage." (2008) Web. 20 Dec. <2008. http://www.neofuturists.org/index%3E>.

O'Neill, Eugene. *Complete Plays*. The Library of America. Vol. 1. 3 vols. New York: The Library of America, 1988.

Reid, Tim. Personal Communication. 25 Mar. 2013.

Torrence, Jay. Personal Communication. 23 May 2013.

9 The In-Common of Phenomenology
Performing KMA's *Congregation*

Eirini Nedelkopoulou

This chapter approaches the relationship between the individual and the group by considering the experience of solitude in the context of the interactive public performance, *Congregation* by KMA. I start this discussion with the suggestion that performance concerns a spatial embodied reality of exposure between singularity and plurality. This reality resonates the phenomenological claim that "our individuality is inherently social in the way that it is experienced" (Ingram and Protevi 574). In the current context of "socially turned"[1] art that positions the participant in the place of the performer, it is worth foregrounding phenomenology's approaches to social mechanisms in order to comprehend the dynamics of the audience's performance.

The chapter forms a phenomenological analysis of the modes of participation in *Congregation* through the perspective of Jean-Luc Nancy's sociopolitical negotiation of "in-common." Nancy's "being-in-common" expresses both "the desire of the effectuation or formation of 'community' (as communion) through myth and the impossibility of any effective myth" (Morin 92). Therefore, on one hand, Nancy's philosophical scope identifies with the Derridean skepticism towards institutional frameworks and a rejection of common values and substance amongst the members of a community. On the other hand, Nancy's thought demonstrates strong phenomenological qualities and investigates structures that make the world possible. Drawing on this ambiguous dynamic of "being-in-common," which enhances and contradicts phenomenology's foregrounding of relationality, I explore the tensions that define contemporary understandings of social relations on the basis of interaction, exposure, and difference. *Congregation* engages playfully with these tensions, inviting a different understanding of participation as performance of solitude; that is, participation which is *not* performed alone.

Congregation follows a decentered structure, which rethematizes the notion of community shifting from identity to difference, from proximity to isolation, and from disjunction to connection. The chapter rethinks participation not as a product or work of plurality but as a space of assemblage of solitaries, where participants are alone while together. The phenomenology of in-common in *Congregation* emerges as praxis of sense that defines

The In-Common of Phenomenology 153

audience's engagement/disengagement and lies in the *limitation* of their contact.

KMA'S CONGREGATION

According to their website, KMA is a "collaboration between UK media artists Kit Monkman and Tom Wexler. Their work is primarily focused on illuminating, encouraging, and developing interactions between people in public spaces using digitally controlled projections."[2] KMA creates projects for theater, film, and television. *Congregation* is an interactive kinetic light installation that takes place within a public space, a space that people often go past on their way back to and from work, while walking their dogs, jogging, or picking up their children from school.

Figure 9.1 *Congregation*, Rockbund Art Museum, Shanghai, 2010. Photo: Sun Zhongqin.

The project was designed for accidental pedestrian-performers: joggers, families, friends, and strangers, which is to say anyone who happened to go past urban landmarks and city squares, such as Market Square in Pittsburgh, Rockbund Art Museum in Shanghai, Bournemouth Square, Tate Britain in London, Tapseac Square in Macau, Bury Light Night. The setup of the installation is simple and straightforward: a 50-foot-wide screen and a light projection on a 25-minute loop of different shapes and patterns are projected within a circular space on the ground accompanied by Peter Broderick's musical score. A thermal camera at the top of a 125-foot crane picks up on the participants' presence. Then the network that the camera is connected to generates a loop of light projections, which spotlight, map, and connect the participants to and separate them from each other.

Figure 9.2 Congregation, Tapseac Square, Macau, 2012. Photo: Kit Monkman.

The In-Common of Phenomenology 155

Figure 9.3 Congregation, Market Square, Pittsburgh, 2014. Photo: Kit Monkman.

The screen is a relay and offers a bird's-eye view of the space, turning the participants into digital blobs. Striking imagery of participants' dispersal into a human-atom map is projected on the ground with light lines connecting and separating the individual circular areas and the participants within them. In the first half, participants are invited to explore an unfamiliar environment led by a projected human silhouette that appears on the ground at the center of it all. The human outline draws attention, and people position themselves in relation to this virtual presence. In the second half of the work, the human silhouette disappears and the focus shifts to the (literal and emotional) connections developed amongst the passers-by who become the project's participants. The audience responds to the visual and kinetic technology with their presence, their impromptu choreographies and their encounters with a group of strangers into the open air. Even without any verbal or textual input, the participants pick up the structure of the artwork quickly. Although the audiences' actions and reactions vary, several similar responses can be observed almost every night.[3]

For example, very often participants hold hands, creating the outline contour of the human figure; they observe the screen trying to track themselves down and wave at their virtual selves on the screen; they move playfully within the space, activating different visual effects that generate organic patterns. Some participants take initiative and group together, set up simple tasks, or organize their co-participants into different groups without

Figure 9.4 Congregation, Rockbund Art Museum, Shanghai, 2010. Photo: Tom Wexler.

necessarily talking but instead holding hands. At times, people stand still and alone within the boundaries of their circular projection. They do not hesitate to lie on the top of their projected silhouettes or the central human figure; they look up to the screen or down on the patterns and lights, to each other, or just the lit sky of the urban landscape. And indeed there are times that they drift away to get back in to the circular space, or not. More often than not, the random unpredictable reactions, initiatives, and behaviors of individuals, pairs or even groups disrupt and challenge their neighbor participants' activity, as I describe later on in the chapter.

CONGREGATION AND PARTICIPATION

Before I move to my analysis of *Congregation* as a space of "being-in-common," I would like to provide a brief discussion of the project's relevance to the current context of *participatory*, (or) *social*, (or) *interactive* art and performance. All these concepts could be used to describe *Congregation*. In the last decade or so, many pixels have lit up in the exploration of audience experience, "the hells and heavens"[4] of participatory performance. The political, economic, and psychological framework of social relations has been extensively discussed, questioned, and challenged.[5] The aesthetics and politics of participation have become a field of productive academic debate and incessant quest for artists, cultural organizations, and funding bodies.

The search for how the "we" performs, interacts, and collaborates within a context, which is more than "just art," characterizes an event-based culture that is keen to experience new conditions of togetherness, community, and belonging. For Nicholas Bourriaud in *Relational Aesthetics* (2002), participatory art and performance love to think about the making and rising of communities, the sustainability of "models of sociability," and the production of human relations (70). Routinely, participatory and socially turned performance attempts to inspire positive social contacts that are defined by "neighborliness" and by "harmony and cohabitation" (Bourriaud 47, 53). Nevertheless, this view and practice has been strongly criticized for being naïve and unrealistic by critical thinkers and for echoing in its "reversibility [...] the commodified friendship of customer services" (Martin qtd. in Ridout 13).

Congregation is part of this event-based culture, which primarily focuses on the audience's interaction and experience in public spaces. KMA is keen to test and encourage new modes of participation between members of the public. Robert Klanten, Sven Ehmann, and Verena Hanschke consider *Congregation* a "social play" and suggest that it creates "a networked 'digital playground'" where

> [t]he resulting social engagements reaffirm the urban community through embodied, rather than verbal, discourse [...]. The participants are able to take ownership of the work and the environment in which it is staged, creating a sense of occasion that informs and illuminates the public space (240).

Indeed, *Congregation* could be identified as *participatory* or *socially turned* work in the sense that both concepts aim "to restore and realize a communal, collective space of shared social engagement" (Bishop, *Artificial Hells* 275). These types of practices actively engage "others who are not the artists (so principally, but not always, audiences)" and enhance "their social engagement" (Harvie 5). Unlike *Congregation*, the popular conceptualization of participatory performance and socially turned art rarely invites either "silent solitude" (Harvie 5) or "one-to-one relationship of 'interactivity'" (Bishop, *Artificial Hells* 1). KMA's project is undoubtedly structured as an interactive practice that "places the action of the recipient at the heart of its aesthetics" (Kwastek xvii), and yet it does provide the space and the time for one to feel at peace in one's own company.

At this point, drawing on Dan Graham's opening citation of Claire Bishop's latest book, I would like to reflect on the "realness" of the audience's experience within KMA's interactive public frame. Graham claims that all artists "dream of doing something that's more social, more collaborative, and more real than art" (qtd. in Bishop, *Artificial Hells* 1). What is more real than human beings' tendency to socially co-exist, collaborate, or often isolate from their cohabitants, disrupt their peers' efforts, and even abandon the community to move on alone or with other cohabitants?

SO WHAT IS THE *IN-COMMON*?

Nancy has discussed extensively the ontology of in-common "where being is *in* common, without ever being common" ("Of Being-in-Common" 8, emphasis in original). In his *The Inoperative Community* and *Being Singular Plural*, amongst other works, Nancy rethinks community on the basis of being-in-common. In his "ontological and existential recasting" of community, Nancy refers to the latter as "a structure of a shared existence," rather than "a specific social formation or mode of organization" (James 176). In a more recent publication co-authored with Laurens ten Kate, Nancy identifies being-in-common as a topological condition where I/other, disjunction/conjunction, singularity/plurality, aloneness/togetherness coexist (40). In-common does not refer to mutual, similar, or even equal qualities between people constituting an assemblage. It refers to a liminal space "between those communicating, between the I and its other, between you and me, and between us" (ten Kate and Nancy 40). The writers underline that "anything can happen, can take place in this strange place [...] peace and violence, order and disorder, cohesion and destruction" (37). Hence, the concept of in-common offers a philosophical framework to think participation in interactive art and performance without presupposing an idealistic structure in which participants coexist.

Nancy's formulation of being-in-common is indebted to the "withness" of being-in-the-world in Martin Heidegger's *Being and Time* and particularly Heidegger's concepts *Mitdasein/Mitsein*. Both thinkers relate being-in-common with a type of making (and in Nancy's case breaking) of community. The difference between the two philosophers lies in their distinct approach to witness as being-in-common (Nancy) and common being (Heidegger). Nancy's thought regarding witness diverges from Heidegger's slide back to subjectivity. Nancy's major objection lies in the belief that Heidegger's later phenomenology "thinks access in terms of appropriation" (Morin 45). According to Nancy's alternative approach to coexistence, community needs to maintain its "common." Otherwise, it becomes a single thing (body, mind, fatherland, Leader ...)" (Nancy, *The Inoperative Community* xxxix). By losing its "common," community becomes a "work" that participants need to produce rather than experience. This is always the risk (and the trap) with participatory forms of social interaction. Community could be easily transformed into a project predicated on communal goals, eliminating difference and investing in the group's "unicity and substanciality" (Nancy, *The Inoperative Community* xxxxix).

In this respect, being-in-common has to deal with the strident and pressurized realities of participatory frameworks. These realities concern, according to Jen Harvie, "models of social relation and community that either fetishize a myth of a unified singularity and thereby obliterate difference or propose an unresolved multitude" (10). The longing for the creation of an original aesthetic community that can be sustained and regrouped and stay in contact after each event, apart from the obvious marketing and financial pressures linked to collective presence, echoes a purported premodern harmonious community. This is what Nancy would identify as a mythical picture that asks for a long-lost "familiarity, fraternity, and conviviality" (*The Inoperative Community* 10). Inspired by Nancy, Bishop argues that these communities imagined by Bourriard's relational aesthetics "require a unified subject as a prerequisite for community-as-togetherness" ("Antagonism and Relational Aesthetics" 79). These are "microtopian" communities of "immanent togetherness" (Bishop, "Antagonism and Relational Aesthetics" 67). Nevertheless, participation cannot be based on the utopia of intimate and operative communities simply because these communities have never existed in order to be longed for. On the contrary, community can only be possible on the basis of its "désœuvrement,"[6] "inoperativeness," which is constitutive of its communication and of being-in-common. Community is "what happens to us" (Nancy, *The Inoperative Community* 11).

CONGREGATION AND IN-COMMON

Commentators on *Congregation* have predictably focused on the group dynamics and the spatiality engendered by the piece. Klanten et al. observe "a large assembled group of participants learns the piece together, acting as a coincidental community, attempting to comprehend their environment in a new way" (243). Tom Wexler emphasizes the spatiality of temporary solitude and togetherness of the experience when he argues that KMA's work "causes people to stop for a moment and to reconsider their place in that space, and also their relationship to other people in that space" (in Crawley, 2014).[7] What is of particular interest in the above sentiments is Klanten's remark on a sense of belonging and Wexler's reference to a spatial experience of a collective, a congregation of singularities. Both claims refer to an open-ended spatiality that lies at the intersection of the communal, unfamiliar, personal, and public space.

This position needs to be considered in relation to the social as an ontological condition in which random passers-by find themselves in contact with one another. In *Congregation* the space and "spacing" of the relational being of (being-) in-common, (being-) with-the-others tests and challenges the social encounter within the public environment. This is not Bourriaud's affirmative relational aesthetics, a "place that produces a specific sociability" and "tightens the space of relations" (15–16). In *Congregation*, the being-with is not "presupposed," but only "exposed" through the participants' lived experiences.[8] KMA's interactive project balances between disruption and coordination; neither does "dissensus" become the objective of the practice, nor audience coordination "rests too comfortably within an ideal of subjectivity as whole" (Bishop, "Antagonism and Relational Aesthetics" 67).[9] In this instance, participants are not invited to form a mythical condition of "neighborliness" based on its members' common qualities. And yet, *Congregation* does not stage the failure of community either. Rather, it allows participants to be in-common.

In *Congregation*, random pedestrians are invited into an open-air event that is not rehearsed or dependent on any verbal or textual input. In principle, there is no particular expectation of the performers apart from making an appearance, even if this is a brief crossing of the space. In-common is created through the planned and performed hindrances to community and communication. The performance operates as an interval to the local community by inviting them to engage in a particular task with strangers. Participants act upon the conventions and stimuli available, while their immediate contribution reveals and establishes their understanding to the open work. Their impromptu choreographies are almost always incomplete, even if some of them try desperately to complete a task; for instance, to circle the projected silhouette holding hands or to create a group heart shape.

The nostalgic idea of creating a feel-good community is not completely eliminated in KMA's piece. People still try to reach a specific goal or task by interacting with audiovisual stimuli and each other. However, the interactive structure of the installation, its public character, and the passers'-by (in)activity constantly interrupts this mythical ideal of community. *Congregation* introduces a stylized framework in public that disrupts the urban community. The community within the community is consecutively interrupted and offers a type of "inoperativeness," which has no longer "to do with production or with completion" (Nancy, *The Inoperative Community* 31). According to Nancy, "incompletion" is an active process "of sharing," a "communication of finitude" that is hardly ever completed (*The Inoperative Community* 35). Although interruption is not a type of participation that *Congregation* necessarily invites, the piece interjects idealistic and purposeful modes of participation. In the absence of interruption and separation, participants cannot expose themselves to each other, as they become assimilated into the group commonality. Therefore, there is no in-common, no community.

Monkman, the creative director, admits that KMA did not plan for the audience members to connect, engage, or interact in a particular way (Personal Interview). The participants hardly ever speak to each other. They hold hands when they function in pairs or groups instead. I would argue that this form of contact is very much interlinked with a condition of in-common, being-with, not in a metaphorical or idealist context, but a materialist one. Nancy proclaims that

> The ontology of being-with can only be "materialist," in the sense that "matter" does not designate a substance or a subject [...]. The ontology

of being-with is an ontology of bodies, of every body, whether they are inanimate, animate, sentient, speaking, thinking, having weight, and so on. Above all else, "body" really means what is outside, insofar as it is outside, next to, against, nearby, with a(n) (other) body, from body to body, in dis-position.

(*Being Singular Plural* 83–4)

Being-in common as a social structure both exceeds and returns to its phenomenological dimension. According to Nancy, the "world invites us to no longer think on the level of the phenomenon, however, it may be understood (as surging forth, appearing, becoming visible, brilliance, occurrence, event), but on the level [...] of disposition (spacing, touching, contact, crossing)" (*The Sense of the World* 176). In similar terms, I focus on the "with" rather than on "being."

Figure 9.5 Congregation, 2010, Tate Britain. Photo: Kit Monkman.

In *Congregation*, technology oscillates between visibility and invisibility. The sensor thermal mechanism that activates the event can be considered as a type of panoptic technology, responsible for appropriating and surveilling human experience. However, in this particular context the network system responds to the "with" of the in-common, of you and me and others and us. Technology is not the authority that changes and defines the audiences' encounter with oneself or others; "with" is. Nancy discussing the "with" of being-with or being-in-common, writes:

> we do nothing but appear together with one another, co-appearing before no other authority than this "with" itself, the meaning of which

seems to us to instantly dissolve into insignificance, into exteriority, into the inorganic, empirical, and randomly contingent inconsistency of the pure and simple "with."

(*Being Singular Plural* 63)

The network system appears to simply indicate the potentiality of the participants' withness to soon escape their attention and interest and "dissolve into insignificance." What comes to the foreground is participants' experience of *being singular plural*.

For the first part of the performance, soon after the music starts and the digital human contour appears, people start grouping together into a circular shape framing the human silhouette. Why are random strangers repeatedly drawn to hold hands as part of the different sections in *Congregation*? This is an opportunity to think about touch as a spontaneous reaction to the artistic frame set up by KMA and also as an expression of a sense of "realness" and belonging. Touching can be risky and ambiguous in the sense that it opens one participant to another. This opening demonstrates the paradox of being incomplete, limited by the singularity of each human body, while also highlights each participant's dependency on others. Nancy writes, "Touching one another with their mutual weights, bodies do not become undone, nor do they dissolve into other bodies, nor do they fuse with a spirit—this is what makes them, properly speaking, bodies" (*The Birth to Presence* 203). *Congregation*'s "exposers" consent to their performance and participation, to this in-common convention that has an absolute limit in the contact of skin with skin. A sense of community and belonging emerges when strangers reach out their hands to touch their co-participants, whose bodies are "absolutely separated and shared" (Nancy, *The Birth to Presence* 204). Touch marks this limit between separation and sharing where singularity and plurality co-exist.

The experience of *Congregation* in Bournemouth offers an example of a clear celebration of togetherness in the name of community when a group of twenty-five participants—university students, elderly people, the homeless, and families amongst others—hold hands. This disparate community, brought together by *Congregation*, in a euphoric and gregarious atmosphere makes a circular shape with its bodies, some of them lunging with one foot towards the middle and others lying on the ground. In this overtly affirmative experience, Monkman identifies a paradox: "The more they participate, the more they become a part of a collective body (and the more the collective body borrows from, and expands on, their participation). The more they become part of a collective body, the less significant their contributions become" (KMA, "Blog").[10] As Nancy would say on this occasion:

> The community that becomes *a single thing* [...] necessarily [...] loses the *with* or the *together* that defines it. It yields its being-together to a being *of* togetherness.
>
> (*The Inoperative Community* xxxix)

Hence, participants cannot maintain themselves within the intimacy of a group; any attempt to maintain this intimacy leads to appropriation of communication and propriety of a group. Binding all participants into an idealist basis of a hypothetical shared identity suppresses and ultimately sabotages community. In this case, the welcoming of a sense of belonging is confronted with the realization of the impossibility of the group insularity.

There is a political quality to touching as an act of participation in the open air, amongst strangers and random pedestrians. While each singularity opens itself and remains open and incomplete expecting to receive from and share with the others, there are examples where participants were left out of a group or refused to hold hands with strangers. In these cases, the opening and *inclination toward*[11] others' difference is restricted as it is filtered through what Rosalyn Diprose identifies as "the meanings that provide the horizon of my sense of belonging" (126). Touching as a mode of "co-appearing"[12] brings to surface the sensitive balance between inclusion and exclusion; the artists try to obtain the former (inclusion) and avoid the latter (exclusion). Of course, one is nested into the other, as one's inclusion will always result in somebody else's exclusion. This happens because inclusion defines a border. Even if the group is welcoming, the definition of this individual group identifies a distinction that excludes those who are not part of the group.

Indeed, feel-good moments follow through the imposition of social meanings, which inevitably include exceeding the limit of one's body by touch. And these moments seem essential, as this touching and being-touched facilitate participation in interactive performance. So, while affirmative moments of acting together include assimilation of difference, they can also easily exclude difference either intentionally or inadvertently. For instance, a university student moves to the other side of the circle when a homeless man attempts to take her hand in the group's circular formation. This rapid reaction to his touch signifies the establishment and rejection of otherness through the withdrawal from the limit of another's touch. We can decide to find this proposition as an event of *othering*, and even vilification, when one is deprived of the ability to establish his uniqueness on the basis of his presupposed difference. According to Monkman, the life duration of similar moments of euphoric gatherings do not last longer than a few minutes, when a participant decides (or is made) to break from the group and devise one's own solitary space of *Congregation* (Personal Interview).

In his recently published book *Passionate Amateurs: Theatre, Communism, and Love*, Nicholas Ridout reminds us of the necessity of distance "across which one encounters someone else that permits or even produces relations" in theater audiences (148). There is an "apparent confusion between relation and unrelation," which echoes the theatrical dimension in Nancy's conception of "compearance" (Ridout 147). "We" expresses *there* and *then*, how passers-by inhabit their space inside and outside *Congregation* by being exposed simultaneously to relationship and its lack thereof.

It is useful to recall here Nancy when he presents us with the challenge to "disidentify ourselves from every sort of 'we' that would be the subject of its own representation, and we have to do this insofar as 'we' coappear" (*Being Singular Plural* 71). The "we" of the participants and passers-by is that of their exposure to each other and the world they constitute. There is, as mentioned above, a temporal and spatial specificity to the "we." Indeed, people who happen to cross a particular square or go past a specific venue during evening times comprise the performers of *Congregation*.

The "realness" of the audience's responses to *Congregation*, from their welcoming holding hands, to their irritability and finally to their withdrawal, constitutes "a relation without relation" (Nancy, "Of Being-in-Common" 7). This is exactly the paradox of community: it cannot "control its in-common," it cannot "control 'itself'" (Nancy and ten Kate 39). Therefore, as soon as participants coappear to each other in the space, "there is community," and participants are "inadvertently in common" (Nancy and ten Kate 37). Anything can happen. What audiences do not fully grasp is that the moment they try to control their in-common and engage in a particular type of operation or communal task, they stop being a community. That is, the idea of community (in an *operative* sense) fails them.

SOLITUDE/LONELINESS

Congregation neither promises nor realizes community per se. While there are moments when participants find themselves working towards a common goal and sharing the same task, there is always the possibility of somebody dropping out, being forgotten by the group, not keeping up with the task. The question is: what happens to the participant who is momentarily excluded? Or to any potential participants whose limit has been exceeded to the extent that they are rejected from a temporary community for being foreign, strange, and other? In this context, engagement between random pedestrians reveals a social and embodied vulnerability that is anchored to the sensitive negotiation between inclusion and exclusion.

Surely the homeless participant rejected by the university student in the example given above is set apart from the particular encounter for being different and unfamiliar. And yet, whether or not he accepts this rejection and departs, his reaction to the incident affects the unified presence of the circle; that is, his co-participants' response to the structure of their performance as well as the thermal sensory system of the installation, and vice versa. A participant's imposed withdrawal from a particular task (or *Congregation* overall) offers an opportunity to consider aloneness as a mode of participatory and social encounter. In particular, a potential exclusion of a participant not only identifies the failure of a harmonious coexistence of a cohesive community but it also raises a paradox. On one hand, exclusion strips a member of his or her exposure towards other participants. Aloneness occurs due to the interruption of inclination towards the other and puts the "excluded" member into a position of, as Diprose would identify it, "losing sense" (126). That is, the participant is left alone and momentarily (at least) deprived of the ability to signify his uniqueness within the context of the specific task. On the other hand, this exclusion causes the rearrangement of the circle and therefore the members' contribution becomes more significant to the system that picks up different types of activity, other than the homogeneous movement of a collective presence. The myth of togetherness is interrupted, reinstigating its in-common condition. The above incident of exclusion, as much unfortunate and troubling it proves to be, also functions as a reminder of the impossibility of community as an *operative* totality, or a *work* of careful planning. Thus, community needs to be *unworked* (*désoeuvré*); and "this is the only possible community" (Morin 76).

However, not all types of aloneness within social environments signify individuals' forced withdrawal. Particularly in reference to the previous example, loneliness as a type of aloneness is often identified with a sense of (self)exclusion. According to Julian Stern, loneliness expresses "the pain of being alone" and "the understanding is that you are rejected by others and believe that, in some sense, you deserve to be rejected and therefore reject yourself" (38). Hannah Arendt draws a line between the experience of loneliness and solitude, proposing that "[l]oneliness comes about when I am alone without being able to split up into the two-in-one, without being able to keep myself company," in contrast to solitude, which is "that human situation in which I keep myself company"(185). Solitude, as often observed in different shows of *Congregation*, is a form of aloneness that celebrates plurality by promoting engagement and attributing a creative, aesthetic and dialectical value to volitional withdrawal.

Over its touring years KMA's project has been exploring the tensions and exchange between "the individual and the collective, loneliness and togetherness" (*Congregation*, Brochure). At times the participants embody these tensions in very predicable ways, while at other times, their responses exceed the artists' expectations. The human-atom-like map projected on the ground with lines of light connects the participants to and separates them from the individual circular areas. Quite often participants break from their groups and pairs to playfully engage with their own game: either to occupy their digital imprint, observe the screen, or just be, stay still, lie or sit down. In doing so, they both establish and inhabit the performance space between a crowd and its singularities.

Reflecting on the instances when participants as singularities break from the collective, responding to the experience of *Congregation's* kinetic and interactive network, solitude appears as a choice, not as a punishment or rejection. The participants stand alone and draw their attention to themselves, to their co-players from a distance, and to their immediate performance and urban environment. And yet they are in-common. Indeed, these simultaneous moments of intersubjectivity define the audience's participatory activity.

Figure 9.6 Congregation, 2010, Tate Britain. Photo: Kit Monkman.

Hence, there is a need for participation to be kept in movement,[13] in circulation to avoid formulating an *operative* together or product of careful planning. In *Congregation*, passers-by move in and out of the performance space. They flexibly break from their temporary groups and pairs, or they choose to never join them and delineate their own individual space. According to Monkman,

> it is the intuitive network which adjusts to the participants' mobility. *Congregation's* invisible technology and public character liberates audience from a sense of "responsibility" that they have to stay until the end of the show to applaud the labour of the live performers.
> (Personal Interview)

The pressure and responsibility of meeting the conventions of spectatorship is partly lifted, as participants stage their in-common performance.

Solitude is a concept ignored in socially turned, community-orientated art and performance due to a cultural fascination with active collective participation, and the hypothesis that solitude—similar to loneliness (but crucially different)—appears as counter-cultural agent to sociability. Paul Tillich offers an explanation to the above phenomenon in relation to quotidian experiences:

> today, more intensely than in preceding periods, man is so lonely that he cannot bear solitude. And he tries desperately to become a part of

the crowd [...]. The same holds true of the forms of communal life, the school, college, office, and factory. An unceasing pressure attempts to destroy even our desire for solitude (8).

Yet, according to Sherry Turkle, solitude appears an imperative state that "refreshes and restores" (288). This type of aloneness is experienced fully as part of our networked life only when we are "able to summon" ourselves by ourselves:[14] "Otherwise, [we] will only know how to be lonely" (Turkle 288). The risk that contemporary (network) performance needs to take is to discover and devise new ways that allow audience members to enjoy their own company.

In *Congregation*, solitude appears as a "retreat" and "subtraction" of this pressure to destroy our right to be alone; which is to say that solitude is a retreat and subtraction of the exteriority of collective participation, when the latter becomes a *single thing*. Nancy writes that "retreat opens, and continues to keep open, this strange being-the-one-with-the-other, to which we are exposed" and "[c]ommunity is made of what retreats from it" (*The Inoperative Community* xxxix). That is, togetherness and participation could both become problematic "either as the product of the working community, or else the community itself as work" (*The Inoperative Community* xxxix). Retreat from "unicity" is necessary to prevent the diminution of the individual's contribution to the performance without interrupting the exposure and the opening to otherness.

Thomas Bernhard identifies a tension in the audience theater experience, according to which "[e]ach person wants to participate and at the same time to be left alone" (qtd. in Hoffman 11). While Bernhard underlines the impossibility of this tendency and the conflict that emerges from it, the in-common structure of *Congregation* seems to lie in the tension between aloneness and togetherness. Repeating Nancy's terminology, the audience's participation is also enabled from "what retreats from it." The participant's choice to act in solitude emerges from one's response to animate and inanimate stimuli, other participants, the environment, and the installation's interactive system.

KMA recognizes the participatory context of *Congregation* in "the physical and empathic connections that separate us, and conjoin us" (*Congregation*, Brochure). One of the incidents at the opening night of *Congregation* in Bournemouth shows aspects of the tension (rather than conflict that Bernhard describes above) between solitude and togetherness. In an utterly euphoric atmosphere the group made a heart shape with their bodies when a couple said that they had been married the previous week (KMA, "Blog").[15] The scene ended with a big round of applause. Reflecting on the specific incident of, no doubt, a well-intentioned gathering celebrating the collective, solitude (as withdrawal and disengagement from the euphoric group activity) was not absent. The giving of oneself during exposure to the other could reveal an ambivalent sense of aloneness between members of the audience, which is informed by constructive, uncertain, and even problematic communication. The heart-shaped arrangement of participants could be considered an amalgamation of all three. Certain participants joined the specific group, others remained observers to the participants' makings, and finally some were not interested and withdrew to look for different potential within the space.

Withdrawal and solitude in *Congregation* when one drops out of the performance or marks one's own separate space is very much interlinked with the participants' sense of belonging. So somebody may say, echoing the Derridean denunciation of community, "I am not part of this group. Don't count me in" (27), which also means that one wants to keep one's freedom and choose one's own way of engaging with an activity, group, and performance. Hence, the encounters between one and others are interrupted and often recuperated—strengthening the condition of in-common even through the choice of disengagement. We can decide to find solitude as a mode of participation that prevents audience members not only from losing themselves in the crowd but also from losing the *others* as well.[16] Solitude declares the participants' need for protection from what is expected that they offer back to the group, but also the need to engage with the performance alone or from a distance. For this reason, this type of withdrawal in *Congregation* does not take the form of loneliness—and I would identify loneliness with exclusion here. Rather, solitude defines a creative space that is part of the in-common of participants' openness and coexistence.

CONCLUSION

In *Congregation*, in-common is a topological encounter where a heterogeneous assemblage co-exists in "the noise"[17] of an initially nonshared space. Random pedestrians have, at first, no shared purpose. Yet their encounter is essential to the communication and making of an interactive participatory practice that attempts to test the grounds of social engagement within the public sphere, without forcing specific responsibilities, fees, or behavioral patterns on the audience. Of course, there are playful patterns, which audiences can choose to follow or not. Although KMA hardly ever mentions the concept of community to describe the company's interactive and participatory practice, their project "eagerly promotes inclusion and attempts to work creatively with exclusion" (*Congregation*, Brochure).

Philosophers and theorists often address with skepticism the good and benevolent intentions of community. In the face of historical and political distrust of the concept, as well as the commodification of artistic products, at a time when human singularities as part of the collective are reduced to numbers, there is a big question: why do we still care enough to talk about and theorize community, to devise work based on the challenging condition of community? Derrida offers a suggestion here when he argues that "[t]he desire to belong to any community whatsoever, the desire for belonging tout court, implies that one does not belong" (28).

As much we are convinced by the troubling context and exclusive character of community, there is a need to think of belonging or to "re-invent the stage" of participation, especially within a creative milieu. As Nancy would argue here, this is not about "innovation": we need to reinvent the staging of our co-appearance "each time, each time making our entrance anew" (*Being Singular Plural* 70–1). This is not to suggest that performance and art destabilize and challenge the pressures of cultural production by accommodating this *stage*. But I do find that *Congregation* amongst other public, social, and participatory artworks offers convincing and partial responses to these pressures. I willingly observe modes of solitude and social effective encounters within this interactive practice. If we can talk about a coincidental condition of in-common in *Congregation*, it is important to see community not simply as the product of the random participants' encounter; it is not just the sum of individuals having something in common. Rather, community in this interactive work is and could only be possible as a "désoeuvre," "inoperative" congregation of singularities.

The phenomenological discussion of the interactive public performance of *Congregation* reflects on the current infatuation with making *more* collaborative, *more* social, *more* inclusive performances. In response to economic, social, and cultural tensions, which in many ways are impossible to avoid, the intermissive structure of in-common offers a theoretical and material format that "reinvents the stage" of our human contact through displacement, solitude, and retreat. *Congregation* stages a place where participants are in-common, "only to discover that this 'in-common' cannot always be controlled by them and so eludes them" (Nancy and ten Kate 37). Nevertheless, this in-common condition, which sits in the bind between our connection to, and perception of, familiarity and difference, could still allow a sense of belonging to thrive, at least every now and then.

ACKNOWLEDGEMENTS

I am grateful to Kit Monkman (KMA) for his generosity and the provision of documented published and unpublished material for *Congregation*. I would like to thank my co-editors, Maaike and Jon, for their support, encouragement, and constructive feedback. Finally, I would like to thank Jenny Hall and the Yorkshire Innovation Fund, who enabled my discussions with KMA.

NOTES

1. Jen Harvie talks about "socially turned art and performance" in her *Fair Play: Art, Performance and Neoliberalism* reflecting on Claire Bishop's commentary on the "social turn" in contemporary art (see Chapter 1 in *Artificial Hells: Participatory Art and the Politics of Spectatorship*).
2. KMA. Website. 7 May 2014. <http://www.kma.co.uk>.
3. The description of the project is based on my own experience of different shows of *Congregation*, discussions with Kit Monkman and Tom Wexler of KMA, online reviews, KMA's website, documentation of different shows provided by

KMA, documented TV and radio interviews with the artists, discussion with members of the audience. Some of the on-line sources can be found here: *Market Square Public Art*. Web. 7 May 2014. <http://www.marketsquarepublicart.com/2014/>.
4. I am appropriating Bishop's latest book title called *Artificial Hells: Participatory Art and the Politics of Spectatorship*.
5. For some of the recent works that address "the hells and heavens" of participation, see Adam Alston, Claire Bishop, Laura Cull & Karoline Gritzner, Jen Harvie, Shannon Jackson, Susan Kattwinkel, Jo Machon, Nicholas Ridout, Nicola Shaughnessy, Gareth White.
6. Nancy borrowed this term (désoeuvré) from Maurice Blanchot to think community as a fragmented and interrupted entity.
7. For CBS Pittsburgh, Web. 7 May 2014. <http://pittsburgh.cbslocal.com/2014/02/21/unique-travelinglight-show-makes-pittsburgh-its-first-north-american-stop/>.
8. I refer here to Nancy's view that similar to community, being-in-common "cannot be presupposed. It is only exposed" (*The Inoperative Community* xxxix). Alan Read, discussing the political in theater, suggests that "[i]nverting the common velocity from individual to group, from self to collective, it is here the situation of 'being in common' that gives rise to the experience of being-self. It is only through such community that one is posed within an exterior, that one experiences an outside to one's self and you, in Nancy's provocative term, become exposed" (198). This negotiation between singularity and plurality as part of being-in-common in performance participation is discussed later in the chapter.
9. Jackson and Harvie expand on "social coordination" and "how art practices contribute to inter-dependent social imagining" (*Social Works* 14).
10. KMA. "Blog." Web. 7 May 2014. <http://www.kma.co.uk/blog/>.
11. Nancy talks about "clinamen […] an inclining from one toward the other, of one by the other, or from one to the other" (*The Inoperative Community* 3). Inclination enables the opening and exposure of one to another.
12. Drawing on Nancy's discussion of "co-appearance" it could be proposed that touching hands signifies the participants' "appearing to" themselves "and to one another, all at once" (*Being Singular Plural* 67).
13. By movement I mean here the *being-towards others* and the world.
14. Solitude signifies the value of spending time with yourself; being able to keep yourself company by choice. The analysis of this embodied *summoning of self by oneself* is beyond the remit of this chapter.
15. KMA. "Blog." Web. 7 May 2014. <http://www.kma.co.uk/blog/>.
16. Here I reflect on Derrida's sentiments against the "organic totality" imposed by the mechanisms of a community, family, a group etc. as described in his essay "I Have a Taste for the Secret" (27).
17. The "noise" of people who have nothing in common, according to Alphonso Lingis, in his book, *The Community of Those who Have Nothing in Common* (12,73,80,97,105). Lingis's view seems to echo Nancy's sentiment regarding limitation in communication, which obtains being-in-common in our everyday experience. Nancy argues: "I no longer hear in it what the other wants to say to me, but I hear that the other speaks and that there is an essential archi-articulation of voices which constitutes the being-in-common" (*The Inoperative Community* 76).

WORKS CITED

Alston, Adam. "Audience Participation and Neoliberal Value: Risk, Agency and Responsibility in Immersive Theatre." *On Value* Edition. *Performance Research* 18.2 (2013): 128–138.

Alston, Adam. "Damocles and the Plucked: Audience Participation and Risk in Half Cut." *Contemporary Theatre Review* 22.3 (2012): 344–354.

Arendt, Hannah. *The Life of Mind, Willing/Thinking.* San Diego: Harcourt, 1978.

Bishop, Claire. "Antagonism and Relational Aesthetics." *October 110*, Fall (2004), Ltd. and Massachusetts Institute of Technology, 51–79.

———, ed. *Participation.* London: Whitechapel Gallery, 2006.

———. *Artificial Hells: Participatory Art and the Politics of Spectatorship.* London, New York: Verso, 2012.

Bourriaud, Nicolas. *Relational Aesthetics.* 1998. Trans. Simon Pleasance and Fronza Woods with Mathieu Copelands. Dijon: Les presses du Réel, 2002.

Crawley, Dave. "Unique Traveling Light Show Makes Pittsburgh Its First North American Stop" Interview with KMA, CBS Pittsburgh, 21 Feb. 2014. Web. 7 May 2014. <http://pittsburgh.cbslocal.com/2014/02/21/unique-traveling-light-show-makes pittsburgh-its-first-north-american-stop/>.

Cull, Laura & Karoline Gritzner, eds. "On Philosophy & Participation." *Performance Research.* 16.4 (December 2011): Taylor & Francis.

Derrida, Jacques. "I Have a Taste for the Secret" *A Taste for the Secret.* Eds. Jacques Derrida and Maurizio Ferraris. Trans. Giacomo Donis. Cambridge: Polity P, 2001. 1–92.

Diprose, Rosalyn. "The Body Intermediating Community." *Intermedialities: Philosophy, Art, Politics.* Eds. Henk Oosterling and Ewa Plonowska Ziarek. Lanham MA: Lexington Books, Rowman & Littlefield, 2011. 119–126.

Harvie, Jen. *Fair Play: Art, Performance and Neoliberalism.* Basingstoke: Palgrave, 2013.

Heidegger, Martin. *Being and Time.* 1927. Trans. John Macquarrie and Edward Robinson. New York: Harper and Row, 1962.

Hoffman, Kurt. *Aus Gespauchen mit Thomas Bernhard.* Munchen: Deutsche Verlagsanstalt, 1991.

Ingram, David B. and John Protevi. "Political Philosophy." *Columbia Companion to Twentieth-Century Philosophies.* Ed. Constantin V. Boundas. New York: Columbia UP, 570–588.

Jackson, Shannon. *Social Works: Performing Art, Supporting Publics.* New York; London: Routledge, 2011.

James, Ian. *The Fragmentary Demand: An Introduction to the Philosophy of Jean-Luc Nancy.* Stanford, California: Stanford UP, 2006.

Kattwinkel, Susan, ed. *Audience Participation: Essays on Inclusion in Performance.* Westport, CT: Praeger Publishers, 2003.

Kit Monkman. Personal Interview. Feb. 2014.

Klanten, Robert, Sven Ehmann, and Verena Hanschke, eds. *A Touch of Code: Interactive Installations and Experiences.* Berlin: Gestalten, 2011.

KMA. "Blog." Web. 7 May 2014. <http://www.kma.co.uk/blog/>.

KMA. *Congregation. Brochure.* Pittsburgh. Jan. 2014.

KMA. Website. 7 May 2014. <http://www.kma.co.uk>.

Kwastek, Katja. *Aesthetics of Internaction in Digital Art*. Cambridge; MA: MIT P, 2013.
Lingis, Alphonso. *The Community of Those Who Have Nothing in Common*. Bloomington: Indiana UP, 1994.
Machon, Joshephine. *Immersive Theatres: Intimacy and Immediacy in Contemporary Performance*. Basingstoke: Palgrave, 2013.
Market Square Public Art, http://www.marketsquarepublicart.com/2014/ (last accessed May 2014).
Morin, Marie-Eve. *Jean-Luc Nancy*. Cambridge: Polity Press, 2012.
Nancy, Jean Luc. *The Birth to Presence*. Trans. Brian Holmes. Stanford, California: Stanford UP, 1993.
———. "Of Being-in-Common." *Community at Loose Ends*. Ed. Miami Theory Collective. Trans. James Creech. Oxford, Ohio: Minnesota UP, 1991. 1–12.
———. *Being Singular Plural*. Trans. Anne E. O'Byrne and Robert D. Richardson. Stanford, California: Stanford UP, 2000.
———. *The Inoperative Community*. Ed. Peter Connor. Trans. Peter Connor et al. Foreword by Christopher Fynsk. Minneapolis: U of Minnesota P, 1991.
———. *The Sense of the World*. Trans. Jeffrey S. Librett. Minneapolis: U of Minnesota P, 1997.
Nancy, Jean Luc, and Laurens ten Kate. "'Cum' … Revisited: Preliminaries to Thinking the Interval." *Intermedialities: Philosophy, Art, Politics*. Eds. Henk Oosterling and Ewa Plonowska Ziarek. Lanham MA: Lexington Books, Rowman & Littlefield, 2011. 37–44.
Read, Alan. *Theatre, Intimacy and Engagement: The Last Human Venue*. Basingstoke: Palgrave, 2009.
Ridout, Nicholas. *Passionate Amateurs: Theatre, Communism, and Love*. Ann Arbor: U of Michigan P, 2013.
Shaughnessy, Nicola. *Applying Performance: Live Art, Socially Engaged Theatre and Affective Practice*. Basingstoke: Palgrave, 2012.
Stern, Julian. *Loneliness and Solitude in Education: How to Value Individuality and Create an Enstatic School*. Oxford; New York: Peter Lang, 2014.
Tillich, Paul. *The Eternal Now*. London: SCM, 2002.
Turkle, Sherry. *Alone/Together: Why We Expect More from Technology and Less from Each Other*. New York: Basic Books, 2011.
White, Gareth. *Audience Participation in Theatre: Aesthetics of the Invitation*. Basingstoke: Palgrave, 2013.

10 Transracial Intimacy and "Race Performativity"

Recognition and Destabilizing the Nation's Racial Contract

Shirley Tate

INTRODUCTION

Starting from the love narrative of one Black British Caribbean man from the Windrush Generation and his White British wife featured in the documentary "Mixed Britannia 1940–1965" (BBC 2, 2011), this chapter focuses on the transformative potential and limits of transracial intimacy through looking at race performativity as a maker of bodies, psyches, and worlds. Thus, it orients us to how it is that transracial intimacy as an affective sensing of the other through gaze and touch can destabilize the Black/White binary because of its insistence on border crossings of the color line, bodies, and affect. This orientation focuses on the question of whether or not transracial intimacy may contribute to a transformation of how race is constructed by destabilizing the lived experience of the racial epidermal schema, which Frantz Fanon terms *l'expérience vécue noir*. Indeed, can desire for the raced other destabilize the Racial Contract (Mills)? Can transracial intimate recognition (Povinelli) and its destabilization of both the racial epidermal schema and the Racial Contract transform the national White social skin through race performativity? Can such a destabilization at the level of personal intimacy transform the construction of racial identifications in society at large?

If we see race performativity as *both* "the act by which a subject brings into being what she/he names [and] that reiterative power of discourse to produce the phenomena that it regulates and constrains" (Butler, *Bodies That Matter* 2; Tate, *Black Skins, Black Masks*), we already see these questions from a phenomenological perspective. This is so, as in thinking through "raced" inter-corporeality, heterosexual intimacy, and Blackness/Whiteness, phenomenology focuses on "the importance of lived experience, the intentionality of consciousness, the significance of nearness or what is ready-to-hand, and the role of repeated habitual actions in shaping bodies and worlds" (Ahmed, *Queer Phenomenology* 2). The phenomenological perspective being developed here through the lens of "race" performativity also bases its analysis on governmentality (Foucault, *The Birth of Biopolitics*), the biopolitics of "race" (Stoler, *Carnal Knowledge and Imperial Power*; Tate, *Black Beauty*), the operation of power/knowledge through "race" discourses (Foucault, *The Eye of Power*; Tate, *Black Skins, Black Masks*), and the place of affect in "raced" relationalities (Tate, *Supping It*). In moving closer to the other as we perform nearness across the color line, can we effect social change? The discussion of the couple featured in the documentary about the Windrush Generation exposes the tension between the destabilizing effects brought about by the transgressive character of their intimate relationship and what might be called the performative force of the Racial Contract. I will show that a phenomenology of the micro-practices of their daily life draws attention to how on the one hand their performance of quotidian personal intimacy transgresses the essentialist race binary by engaging in a relationship that was unthinkable and actively resisted in the colonial past, as well as in the continuation of this past in the ways in which racial politics are reiterated in postcolonial England. The chapter also elucidates how their transgressive intimacy meets with the performative force of the race binary, how from this perspective their intimate relationship is perceived as a threat and met with repression as well as silencing through exclusion from kinship. This transgression at an intimate and personal level and the responses of others suggest that rather than changing the Racial Contract, there is a reinforcement of its power. Can we perform daily life and personal intimacy across the color line to affect and change the racial norms we encounter? How can trans-racial intimacy change the performative force of the Racial Contract? First, let us move to the love narrative followed by an overview of the racialized post- war world of the Windrush Generation and its embedded understanding of the Black/White race binary. This helps us to see that the colonial past and 1940s present meant that resistance to Mary's and Jake's relationship was only to be expected as such resistance was always already part of the UK's social fabric.

RACE AND INTIMACY IN THE WINDRUSH GENERATION[1]

> Now in their mid-80s, Jake and Mary Jacobs have been together for 65 years. They met when Jake was playing his part in the war effort in the RAF and fell in love at first sight with Mary who was from Liverpool. For Mary it was exciting socializing with Black men because "we had never seen anyone like that before." For Jake the first time he saw her he thought, "jet black hair, tanned face, and beautiful eyes, what else more could you ask for?" After the war, Jake returned to Trinidad but kept writing love letters to Mary. On his return to England in search of work in 1948 he was sent to work in the Post Office in Birmingham. He experienced dirty jobs and the worse shifts but worked for 38 years. He confesses that he thought she was as beautiful as ever when he saw her again, even though Mary replies that she was never beautiful. For Jake being with Mary again was "like a new year for me, that's the only way I can put it. Like a new day in my life sort of thing. Something I had been looking for all of my life and I thought

I've clinched it." When asked by George Aligiah how he proposed to Mary, he said "my proposal [...] to be or not to be, will you marry me?" He quoted Shakespeare to woo her again, because Mary loved Shakespeare. However, Mary's relationship caused problems within her own family, as she says "my father wouldn't acknowledge it. He just didn't look at me, didn't say *anything* and I just didn't know what to do. Oh, I do remember him saying, whether it was at that point or earlier, I remember him saying now you've taken up with this young man from Trinidad, this *Black* man, you will never get a decent boyfriend, never. He said don't come back and I don't want to ever see you again. My mother and I were both crying and I came away thinking that was the end. I would never see my family again." Jake said that at their wedding in 1948 "no one was there, just friends, no family, and you look around and say to yourself is this what life is about?"

(Mixed Britannia, 2011)

As we see in the example, men in The Windrush Generation sailed from a colonial past into a colonial present in which the contribution of the Caribbean to Britain's economic development and the war effort were erased[2] and the national denial of transracial intimacy within the colonies and the metropole remained firm. This national denial extended from colonial anti-miscegenation regimes, which included laws, jurisprudence, and norms regulating the intimate sphere through constructing and manipulating race categories and boundaries (Thompson). These regimes had the Manichean task of removing Black pollution from Whiteness (Gordon, *Her Majesty's Other Children* 70). Thus, transracial intimacy was not solely about affect. It was about power, surveillance, securing racial dominance, disciplining bodies, and the management of life. Colonial intimacy regimes were, therefore, biopolitical (Foucault, "The Birth of Biopolitics"). In terms of heterosexual sex during slavery and colonialism, two discourses that kept White power in place were those of the intense desire of Black women for White men (Fanon) as well as the Black man as a potential rapist of White women and threat to the body politic. These discourses existed alongside the desire of White men for Black women's bodies and the policing, denial, and refusal of White women's desire for Black men (Francis). British colonial authorities ensured that Europeanness was class and "race" specific but also gender coded and bourgeois bodies defined their "healthy sexuality" in racial and gender terms (Stoler, *Carnal Knowledge and Imperial Power*).

Antigua was the only British colony in the Caribbean to legislate against miscegenation during the seventeenth and eighteenth centuries (Bush). These laws are historical evidence of the Empire's concern with regulating transracial marriages and the emergence of a mixed-race population with White fathers (Thompson) as is the "Johnny Newcome in Love in the West Indies" satire (JF). Earlier transracial intimacies that involved White women and Black men were erased from colonial memory (Francis). European women in the colonies were located in passionless domesticity, positioned as the desired object of colonized men, dissociated from the sexual desires of European men, and disallowed from being desiring subjects (Stoler). Thus, White desire for Black bodies was acceptable only as long as it was male and heterosexual, which aided Empire in constructing colonial citizens through the purity of White femininity and the heterosexual imperative. Indeed, in the nineteenth century in the UK the "most important miscegenated coupling" was Black women with White men (De Vere Brody 7). However, within this racialized intimate economy, European men and women were respectable if they steered their desires towards legitimate paternity, intensive maternal care, family, and conjugal love (Stoler, *Race and the Education of Desire*). Thus, anti-black racism was enshrined at the level of heterosexual intimacy, as "the inferior other becomes a fundamental project for the establishment of the superior self whose superiority is a function of what it *is*" (Gordon, *Her Majesty's Other Children* 70).

This was the existing racialized intimate economy into which the SS Empire Windrush sailed when it entered Tilbury Dock on June 22, 1948, with 492 Caribbean migrants on board. They came to help the mother country in post-war reconstruction from colonies that were themselves economically depressed after centuries of slavery, plantation agriculture, lack of investment in local infrastructure, repatriation of profits to the seat of Empire, and their contribution to the war effort. They came as citizens to a land that was as familiar to them as their own countries of birth. Yet these citizens were confronted by their absence because of the "binary world imposed upon [them] which functions as a constant source of evasion" (Gordon, *Her Majesty's Other Children* 72).

They did not cross territorial borders, but they encountered the continuing governance of the internal racial colony through extra-legal regimes based on reducing transracial heterosexual intimacy. For example, within Liverpool anti-black riots in June 1919 are blamed by Mark Christian (*The Fletcher Report*) on class, poverty, racism, and the White population's negativity about sexual relations between Black men and White women. The problem of "half caste" children in Liverpool took on greater significance after these riots and meant that the "mixed race" population was problematized. World War 2 prompted racialized responses by the British government to the presence of Black civilian and military personnel because of the interaction of mobilized White British women and mobilized men from the colonies and Black US GIs because of the problem of "half caste children"[3] (Winddance Twine, Carby). As early as 1942 the British Colonial Office worried about what the future population of Britain would look like in the face of the sexual invasion of Black soldiers (Carby). By 1947 "mixed race" orphans became "the lonely picaninny" (Carby, Winddance Twine). Thus, by the 1950s miscegenation "captured the descent of white womanhood and recast it as a signifier of the social problems associated with the black presence [and] emerged ahead of crime as a theme in the popular politics of immigration control" (Gilroy, *There Ain't No Black in the Union Jack* 79–80). This was illustrated in the summer 1958 "race" riots in Notting Hill and Nottingham, which were sparked by the threat of heterosexual transracial intimacy. Although anti-miscegenation laws were not enacted in the UK, like Canada, "an informal and extra-legal regime ensured that the social taboo of racial intermixing was kept to a minimum" (Thompson 354).[4] The extra-legal anti-miscegenation regime was continued in the mid-twentieth century color bar in public spaces that aimed to segregate White and Black populations and minimize the possibility of transracial intimacy[5].

This historical context both before and after the start of Jake and Mary's relationship meant that Black men were taboo for White women and such relationships would lead to women's subsequent loss of respectability and, indeed, their *un-whitening*. We can see this in Mary's father's insistence that no *decent man* [read White] would be interested in her now that she had been involved with a Black man and his need to shore up the respectability of the family by banishing her from it. The performance of Mary's father reiterates the "race" binary to keep the boundaries of the White social skin of the nation firm through keeping the family White as he marked her as abject. He also placed her as Black by association.

Taboos on transracial heterosexual sex were fundamental to state formation and to social stratification in the 1920s to 1950s (Winddance Twine). However, Mary's and Jake's behavior also demonstrates how individuals can transgress the norms imposed on them in choosing to go beyond the accepted norms of fundamental racial difference. Indeed, for Mica Nava women like Mary "played a central part in the social reconfigurations of the period" (94) through their attraction to otherness and

> Desire was, therefore, a part of these social reconfigurations as everything stems from the fact that in constituting itself as a whole the living subject rejects outside of itself the whole of which it is a part, it alienates itself from the world, which is why harmonious continuity becomes tension. However, it is from this tension that the relation is born, from this rejection that the phenomenal being of the world emerges.
> (Barbaras 120)

As we look at Barbaras's words, we see why it is that transracial intimacy has been and is still feared by Whiteness. It is through desire that Mary and Jake constituted themselves *as* a relationship rather than racial opposites.

Desire coupled with rejection of the always already known of "race" enables new racialized self/other relationalities and subjectivities to emerge and become the catalyst for change in intimate life. This change occurs because as desire is satisfied by its object, then it is reactivated rather than extinguished and increases one's commitment to the love object (Barbaras). White women's relationships with Black men declared an attraction to and desire for otherness, which created tension within the UK's biracialization.

In creating such destabilization of "race," the "race performativity" of transracial intimacy raises the question of if and how this destabilization at the level of personal life may also enable transformation at the level of society. Let us move to beginning to explicate this further by looking at transformations in the lived experience of the racial epidermal schema.

CAN TRANSRACIAL INTIMACY PRODUCE RACE DIFFERENTLY BY UNDERMINING THE LIVED EXPERIENCE OF THE RACIAL EPIDERMAL SCHEMA?

We live within repeated performances of Fanon's racial epidermal schema. In *Black Skin, White Masks* Fanon speaks about the historico-racial schema and the racial epidermal schema. In doing this he inserts both the coloniality of power and an analysis of racism, in terms of the colonial hold on the Black and White psyches, onto Maurice Merleau Ponty's deracinated reflections on corporeal schema. The historico-racial schema reveals how White colonial discourses on racial difference and their accompanying structuration of White racial dominance in societal structures and institutions, cultural consciousness, social practices, and knowledge production created "the Black man" as irredeemably other and "the White man" as inherently superior. The creation of this Black essential difference is the foundation for the racial epidermal schema, which ensures that the Black man is always already known, for example, as deviant, hypersexual, incapable of intellectual thought, and dangerous to White women's virtue. It is through the racial epidermal schema that Jake was read and understood as other, as stereotype rather than as an individual. Here we see the quotidian life of the colonial racial epidermal schema within the metropole as Mary's father's reaction to Jake enacts White superiority as it simultaneously denudes Jake's subjectivity, his complexity, and ensures that his Black body is denied personhood. Indeed, his reaction, his "white gaze renders the black body ontologically truncated, fixed like an essence" (Yancy, *Look, a White!* 152), acting as "a form of bodily fragmentation, 'visual mutilation,' and reduction" (153). It in effect splayed Jake out for enquiry as the always already known, irredeemable other. This White gaze, channelled through Mary's father, made the lived reality of anti-Black racism clear by placing Mary outside of the boundaries of Whiteness because of her transgression of anti-miscegenation norms and barring Jake's entry to a White family. Thus it is, that in transracial heterosexual intimacy love is not just about affect between an intimate pairing but a point at which the "race" binary is questioned.

This subverts the very basis of liberal society and mono-racial intimacy through acknowledging that

> the autological subject, the genealogical society, their modes of intimacy, and their material anchors emerged from European Empire as a mode and maneuver of domination and exploitation and continue to

operate as such [...] Thus the intimate couple is a key transfer point between, on the one hand, liberal imaginaries of contractual economics, politics and sociality and on the other liberal forms of power in the contemporary world [...] If the intimate couple is a key transfer point within liberalism, this couple is already conditioned by liberalism's emergence and dispersion in empire.

(Povinelli 16)

Liberalism is a carrier of anti-Black racism even as it makes us think that we are subjects free to make ourselves and delineates which forms of intimate attachment are linked to freedom or constraint. So, "love, intimacy, and sexuality are not about desire, pleasure, or sex per se, but about things like geography, history, culpability, and obligation; the extraction of wealth and the distribution of life and death; hope and despair; and the seemingly self-evident fact and value of freedom" (Povinelli 10). Mary and Jake's story demonstrates this point as it shows love is not just an interpersonal intimate event but it is also a deeply political one. Mary and Jake show us what happens when the "raced" expectations of heterosexual intimacy are not met.

Mary and Jake's intimacy, I argue, establishes a *"third space"* (Bhabha) or Edward Soja's *"critical thirding,"* which moves past binaries while being imbricated by them. This moving-past-but-imbrication dynamic is what instantiates the productive tension between Mary and Jake's performance of race and the normative performativity of the race binary. The empathetic identification of White women with Black men, and their construction of these racially othered men as desirable, momentarily destabilizes White superiority as new subjects emerge.

Mary's desire for Jake creates what Nava terms a "visceral cosmopolitanism" that is "in play in feelings of desire, sympathy, and hospitality towards cultural and racial others and the foreign" (63). Such desire for newly arrived Black men, however, subjected women like Mary to being seen as transgressive, to being "unwhitened" as a form of discipline (Nava, Winddance Twine). Such discipline was considered necessary because this transgressive desire, this unprecedented intimacy, poses a threat to the norm. Indeed, the intimate is a fleeting placeholder of an asubjective affectivity moving through ontologically variegated singularities; it is the figure that intuits and enacts the common, that which seethes beneath and is excessive of relations and communities founded on identitarian difference (Roach 15).

As the excess that seethes beneath identitarian difference transracial intimacy creates a space in-between and a zone of unbelonging that work to make the racial epidermal schema strange. Making the racial epidermal schema strange poses a challenge to the construction of the world by the Racial Contract that Charles Mills describes thus

> Both globally and within particular nations, then, white people, Europeans and their descendants, continue to benefit from the Racial

Contract, which creates a world in their cultural image, political states differentially favouring their interests, an economy structured around the racial exploitation of others, and a moral psychology (not just in whites but sometimes in nonwhites also) skewed consciously and unconsciously toward privileging them, taking the status quo of differential racial entitlement as normatively legitimate, and not to be investigated further (40).

The Racial Contract is biopolitical as it shapes bodies and worlds through repeated actions, discourses, governmentality, and distance/proximity. Indeed, Mills makes "race" and White supremacy central to nation-building (Holland). Further, race instantiates epistemologies of ignorance to which signatories of the Racial Contract must adhere (Yancy, *Black Bodies, White Gazes*; Mills), "producing the ironic outcome that whites will in general be unable to understand the world they themselves have made" (Mills 61, Sullivan and Tuana, Bailey). This is so because race is as constitutive of the Enlightenment and European colonialisms as it is of marking the White body as the somatic norm (Yancy, Mills, Holland). The Racial Contract extends to the intimate transracial couple. If White flesh as law and politics (corporeality) expects the materiality of White flesh (carnality), then transracial intimacy is already at odds with the norm. The Racial Contract also extends to affect as transracial intimacy makes visible the epistemology of ignorance focused on biracialization (Ifekwunigwe).

Epistemologies of ignorance are reminiscent of Merleau-Ponty's critique of empiricism. That is, that we have established an objective science of subjectivity because "we make perception out of things perceived. And since perceived things themselves are obviously accessible only through perception, we end by understanding neither" (50). Thus as (im)perceptible, racist action comes into the everyday as it "makes the system of racial differentiation work" (Holland 37). However, it does not work through ignorance but through an always present knowledge, though one which *denies knowing* White "race" power as differential entitlement (Tate, *Supping It*; Sullivan and Tuana). In other words, it operates through what Alison Bailey calls "strategic ignorance." Racism continues to make "race" matter (Holland) as much now as it did for the Windrush Generation men like Jake and the White women like Mary who became intimates.

What transracial intimacy illustrates is a refusal of the dictates of the Racial Contract's White corporeality and carnality, its social skin and epistemologies of ignorance through constituting other versions of what it is to be human. As we saw in the extract, Mary had to move away from the comfort of the familiar White social skin represented by her family to demonstrate her recognition of Jake's humanity by making her father's reaction *other*. To become familiar is to assert affective, physical, and material connections, a commonality denied by what Paul Gilroy (*After Empire*) terms "raciology." Transracial intimacy is about self-other relations that link individuals as much as it links families, communities, and nations. As we perform proximity across the color line, this very "moving" closer to the other as we envisage (Derrida, *The Politics of Friendship*) them as lover is productive of change. Such performance of proximity dismantles Whiteness as a master signifier. Dismantling is possible because performing proximity includes envisaging the beloved as human, equal, and thus brings new subjects into being. In this performance of proximity, the senses function as conduits of positive affects.

This thereby constructs

> a new subject out of the husk of the old and reset[s] the clock of the subject at zero. In your gaze, I become a new person, as do you in mine. This becoming anew is not by way of conversion, not by exposure to law or reason, not by persuasion or formal contract [...] Because the intimate event is hinged to nothing but itself merely by happening to us, by striking us, it happens. The truth of intimacy is that *we* know it happened to both of us, and the sign that it happened is that *we* have been transformed. It happening made us.
>
> (Povinelli 187)

Intimacy made us, and this making may destabilize and pose a threat to the world of the Racial Contract. We can locate this in the fear of Black touch during colonialism and slavery, for example, in the blood, on the skin, or in the politics of freedom. As such, touch encompasses both skin-to-skin contact and being emotionally touched (Derrida, *Le Toucher*). Both of these forms of touch encompass empathy, attachment, and the crossing of interpersonal racial boundaries that undermine the Racial Contract and question its prevailing epistemologies of ignorance as well as aesthetic norms. These all impact the phenomenal world.

CAN INTIMATE RECOGNITION TRANSFORM THE NATIONAL SOCIAL SKIN?

For Elizabeth Povinelli, without "the intimate couple, the national mass subject (We, the People), and its forms of critical reason and debate would not have been possible" (187). We have seen above that "We the people" is raced as White through the Enlightenment, slavery and colonialism as is the intimate couple as national subjects. This raises the question of whether or not the transgressive performance of the transracial couple also affects the givens of mono-racial love and intimacy at the macro-level of the national social skin. Can the intimate couple counter the *hegemonic representations* of love, intimacy, partnerships, and conjugal relationships characterized by the existence of an invisible color line?

We are in the grip of what Gilroy calls a "racial nomos—a legal, governmental, and spatial order" in which race is reified as embodiment, genetic inheritance, and an unseen force that determines one's current life chances and future prospects (*After Empire* 42). The Racial Contract continues to have affective and interpersonal impact extending to intimacy as it designates who is familiar, trusted, the same, and who is not. Transracial intimacy is imbricated with affect as much as it is with national governance. This latter generates its own discipline and recognizes the racialized other only through difference. The moment of transracial intimacy threatens such racialized recognition. The rejection and aggression experienced by Jake and Mary show how this in turn calls forth the demand for maintaining the White social skin. Their story shows how transracial intimacy does not automatically lead to redemptive national narratives or to post-race futures.

For Lewis R. Gordon the impossible relationalities of raced sociality are imbricated in the very category human. This is so as being human means going beyond the skin

> though not without one's outside. It is as Merleau-Ponty observed to have an 'other side' of one's body. Thus in typical human encounters, there is always a presumption of transphenomenal experience: There is always more to the human other than each of us can learn. With antiblack encounters, however, the mystery or riddle of blackness is a function of its supposed worthlessness.
> (Gordon, *Her Majesty's Other Children* 37)

The only body that is capable of asserting the presumption of *trans*phenomenal experience is the White, male, straight, middle-class, able-bodied one, as the racial epidermal schema and the Racial Contract denies the inside life of Black people and locates them as worthless (Gordon, *Her Majesty's Other Children*). They remain forever locked in infrahumanity and invisibility in the social world, a world that places itself outside of the boundaries of recognition within the relationality of the intimate couple, which is relegated to the private sphere. Here we come up against the limits of "race performativity" as a catalyst for the transformation of the national social skin.

CONCLUSION

A phenomenological perspective on transracial intimacy and the nation prompts us to consider the tensions between the normative performativity of discourses and practices of essential racial difference and the possibilities for transformation produced through performing race differently at a personal and intimate level. Thus, it makes us ponder how racialized distance/proximity and a "beyond" space can encourage us to think about the ways that moving through and across the body of the other reconstructs the nation through intimate recognition, even if only momentarily. The disorienting, re-racing movements and moments of this recognition instantiate a challenge to the hold of the Racial Contract and the racial epidermal schema over the micro-practices of everyday social life. This is because a choice is made that goes against the grain of biracialization. The challenge of transracial intimacy is that as *trans* it unfolds the nation of which it stands as the negation of the colonial racialized politics of intimacy, the ideal family/ citizen, and the nation as itself "racially" pure. The performance of transracial intimacy challenges the existing Racial Contract and racial epidermal schema through the intimate micro-practices of everyday life. As a result, the other becomes an uneasy part of the White nation, which as kin resists erasure while also continuing to be set apart.

NOTES

1. The arrival of the SS Empire Windrush at Tilbury Dock, Essex, England in June 1948 with 492 passengers on board from Jamaica, Trinidad, and Tobago and other Caribbean islands marked the beginning of post-war mass migration from the Caribbean. This has since been called the Windrush Generation.
2. Some contributions made by the Caribbean to the war effort were over 1 million troops, over £75,000 to the UK for general war purposes, an interest-free loan of £1,400,000, surgical supplies, food and clothing for British troops, investment in war bonds, £425,000 for the purchase of aircraft for the RAF, nearly £400,000 for war charities, and essential munitions and raw materials, such as oil and bauxite (Fryer).
3. In the first wave there were 125,000 volunteers, mostly Jamaican, who joined the RAF, worked in munitions factories and in forestry in Scotland. By 1942 there were 3 million American troops, 130,000 of whom were African American. The British government responded with measures to curb the flow of nonwhite soldiers. From these policies we can see the emergence of Britain as a modern racialized state (Carby).
4. The Indian Act in Canada was "designed to regulate interracial [Aboriginal and non-Aboriginal] marital relations and the categorization of mixed-race offspring." If women married non-Aboriginals, they and their children would be denied Indian status, whereas the opposite was the case for men who married non-Aboriginal women (Thompson 354).
5. The first full-length television documentary programme [on the BBC] to examine the problems faced by Black immigrants in Britain was *Special Enquiry: Has Britain a Colour Bar?* (31 January 1955). The programme implied that the primary reason for discrimination and a color bar was "cultural" difference rather than racism. Nevertheless, it provoked emotive responses from many White viewers who felt that it was a defence of Black people in its acknowledgement that racial discrimination existed in Britain. Many documentaries at this time such as *Black Marries White* (1964), *The Negro Next Door* (1965), and *People in Trouble: Mixed Marriages* (1958) focused on "racial problems" in British society from the (white) audience's point of view. Black people [...] were regularly located as the troubled subjects "stuck between two cultures" (Malik 360).

WORKS CITED

Ahmed, Sara. *Queer Phenomenology: Orientations, Objects, Others.* Durham: Duke UP, 2006.
Bailey, Alison. "Strategic ignorance." *Race and Epistemologies of Ignorance.* Eds. Shannon Sullivan and Nancy Tuana. Albany: State U of New York P, 2007. 77–94.
Barbaras, Renaud. *Desire and Distance: Introduction to a Phenomenology of Perception,* Trans. Paul B. Milan. Stanford, California: Stanford UP, 2006.
Bhabha, Homi. "The Third Space: Interview with Homi Bhabha." *Identity, Community, Culture, Difference.* Ed. Jonathan Rutherford. London: Lawrence and Wishart, 1990. 207–221.
Bush, Barbara. *Slave Women in Caribbean Society,1650–1838.* Indiana: Indiana UP, 1990.
Butler, Judith. *Bodies That Matter: On the Discursive Limits of Sex.* London: Routledge, 1993.
Carby, Hazel V. "Postcolonial Translations." *Ethnic and Racial Studies* 30.2 (Mar. 2007) 213–234.
Christian, Mark. "The Fletcher Report 1930: A Historical Case Study of Contested Black Mixed Heritage Britishness." *Journal of Historical Sociology* 21.2-3 (June/Sept. 2008): 213–241.
Derrida, Jacques. "Le Toucher/To Touch Him." *Paragraph* 16.2 (1993): 122–157.
———. *The Politics of Friendship.* London: Verso, 2005.
DeVere Brody, Jennifer. *Purities: Blackness, Femininity, and Victorian Culture.* Durham: Duke UP, 1998.
Fanon, Frantz. *Black Skin, White Masks.* London: Pluto Press, 1967.
Foucault, Michel. "The Eye of Power." *Power/Knowledge: Selected Interviews and Other Writings 1972–1977.* Ed. Colin Gordon. Brighton: The Harvester P, 1980. 146–165.
———. "The Birth of Biopolitics." *Ethics, Subjectivity and Truth: The Essential Works of Foucault 1954–1984, Vol 1.* Ed. Paul Rabinow. Trans. Robert Hurley et al. London: Penguin, 1994. 73–81.
Francis, Donna. *Fictions of Feminine Citizenship: Sexuality and the Nation in Contemporary Caribbean Literature.* New York: Palgrave Macmillan, 2010.
Fryer, Peter.*The Politics of Windrush.* Richmond, Surrey: Index Books, 1999.
Gilroy, Paul. *There Ain't No Black in the Union Jack: The Cultural Politics of Race and Nation.* London: Hutchinson, 1987.
———. *After Empire: Melancholia or Convivial Culture.* Abingdon: Routledge, 2004.
Gordon, Lewis Ricardo. "Existential Dynamics of Theorizing Black Invisibility." *Existence in Black: An Anthology of Black Existential Philosophy.* Ed. Lewis Ricardo Gordon. New York: Routledge, 1997: 69–79.
———. *Her Majesty's Other Children: Sketches of Racism from a Neocolonial Age.* Oxford: Rowman and Littlefield Publishers Inc., 1997.
Holland, SharonPatricia. *The Erotic Life of Racism.* Durham: Duke UP, 2012.
Ifekwunigwe, Jayne. *Scattered Belongings: Cultural Paradoxes of "Race," Nation and Gender,* London: Routledge, 1999.
JF. "Johnny Newcome in Love in the West Indies." London: William Holland, 1808.
Malik, Sarita. "Race and Ethnicity: The Construction of Black and Asian Ethnicities in British Film and Television."*The Media: An Introduction.* 2nd ed.

Eds. Adam Briggs and Paul Cobley. Harlow: Pearson Education Ltd, 2002. 357–368.

Merleau-Ponty, Maurice. *The Phenomenology of Perception*. London: Routledge, 2012.

Mills, Charles. *The Racial Contract*. Ithaca, NY: Cornell UP, 1997.

"Mixed Britannia." BBC 2. 2011. Television documentary.

Nava, Mica. *Visceral Cosmopolitanism: Gender, Culture and the Normalization of Difference*. Oxford: Berg, 2007.

Povinelli, Elizabeth A. *The Empire of Love: Toward a Theory of Intimacy, Genealogy, and Carnality*. Durham: Duke UP, 2006.

Roach, Tom. *Friendship as a Way of Life: Foucault, AIDS, and the Politics of Shared Estrangement*. Albany: State U of New York P, 2012.

Soja, Edward. *Third Space: Journeys to Los Angeles and Other Real-and-Imagined Places*. Oxford: Wiley, 1996.

Stoler, Ann Laura. *Carnal Knowledge and Imperial Power: Race and the Intimate in Colonial Rule* Berkley, CA: U of California P, 2002.

———. *Race and the Education of Desire: Foucault's History of Sexuality*. Durham: Duke UP, 1995.

Sullivan, Shannon and Tuana, Nancy. "Introduction." *Race and Epistemologies of Ignorance*. Eds. Shannon Sullivan and Nancy Tuana. Albany: State U of New York P, 2007. 1–10.

Tate, Shirley Anne. *Black Beauty: Aesthetics, Stylization, Politics*. Aldershot: Ashgate, 2009.

———. *Black Skins, Black Masks: Hybridity, Dialogism, Performativity*. Aldershot: Ashgate, 2005.

———. "Supping It: Racial Affective Economies and the Epistemology of Ignorance in UK Universities." *Integrated but Unequal: Black Faculty in Predominantly White Spaces*. Ed. Mark Christian. Trenton, NJ: African World P, 2012, 207–225.

Thompson, Debra. "Racial Ideas and Gendered Intimacies: The Regulation of Interracial Relationships in North America." *Social and Legal Studies* 18.3 (2009): 353–371.

Winddance Twine, France. *A White Side of Black Britain: Interracial Intimacy and Racial Literacy*. Durham: Duke UP, 2010.

Yancy, George. *Black Bodies, White Gazes: The Continuing Significance of Race*. Lanham: Rowman and Littlefield Publishers, Inc., 2008.

———. *Look, a White! Philosophical Essays on Whiteness*. Philadelphia: Temple UP, 2012.

11 Passing Period
Gender, Aggression, and the Phenomenology of Walking

Gayle Salamon

There is a story that came out around, I don't know, eight years ago. Of a young man who lived in Maine and he walked down the street of his small town where he had lived his entire life. And he walks with what we would call a swish, a kind of, his hips move back and forth in a feminine way. And as he grew older that swish, that walk, became more pronounced, and it was more dramatically feminine. He started to be harassed by the boys in the town, and soon two or three boys stopped his walk and they fought with him and they ended up throwing him over a bridge and they killed him. So then we have to ask: why would someone be killed for the way they walk? Why would that walk be so upsetting to those other boys that they would feel that they must negate this person, they must expunge the trace of this person. They must stop that walk no matter what. They must eradicate the possibility of that person ever walking again. It seems to me that we are talking about an extremely deep panic or fear or anxiety that pertains to gender norms [...] Someone says: you must comply with the norm of masculinity otherwise you will die. Or I kill you now because you do not comply.

(Judith Butler 2006)

I've always been obsessed with high heels but as a child I was not allowed to have them. Oftentimes I would sashay around on tip toes imagining that I had high heels on and I was constantly looking over my shoulders to make sure I didn't get caught or that I wasn't being judged. Let's face it, when you're a transchild you've got to watch your ass.

(Bond 2011)

THE BANAL ARTS: ERWIN STRAUS AND THE PHENOMENOLOGY OF WALKING

Erwin Straus is probably most frequently encountered today in Iris Marion Young's pathbreaking work of feminist phenomenology "Throwing Like a Girl," which gets its title, and fodder for its trenchant critique of phenomenology's treatment of women and the feminine, from Straus's 1952 piece "The Upright Posture." I'm not going to take up Young's critique here, not because I think it is not right or compelling; it is certainly both. What I would like to do instead is to read Straus's essay, "The Upright Posture," as offering an exemplary descriptive phenomenology, and one that is particularly useful for describing bodily movement in the performance of gender.

I would to like to consider phenomenology of this kind, which we might call following Edmund Husserl, a "descriptive and non idealizing discipline" (167), to ask how such a method might help us to apprehend bodies in times, places, and contexts other than Straus's own. That is to say, leaving aside the question of whether Straus's account is sexist—or even tabling the certainty that it is, to put it more strongly—I want to ask if it is possible to read past that gender bias to ask what tools such a phenomenological method might offer to all sorts of situations, even a situation in which gender is fundamentally at issue.

Straus is worth reconsidering because he gives us perhaps the most thorough phenomenological account we have of the act of walking. Here is how he describes it:

> Human bipedal gait has a rhythmical movement whereby, in a sequence of steps, the whole weight of the body rests for a short time on one leg only. The center of gravity has to be swung forward [...] human gait is, in fact, a continually arrested falling. Therefore an unforeseen obstacle or a little unevenness of the ground may precipitate a fall. Human gait is an expansive motion, performed in the expectation that the leg brought forward will ultimately find solid ground. It is motion on credit. Confidence and timidity, elation and depression, and stability and insecurity are all expressed in gait. Bipedal gait is, in fact, a balance alternating from one leg to the other, it permits variations in length, tempo, direction and accent (244).

The emphasis here is on that variation, the movement of walking, generated by the body creating an imbalance in itself that it then corrects over and over again. More crucially still, Straus is naming the wide range of mental and emotional states it can express.

But Straus does not begin the essay with walking, just as the human walker does not. "The Upright Posture" begins with a description of a body that is not even able to keep itself upright. "A breakdown of physical well being is alarming; it turns our attention to functions that, on good days, we take for granted. A healthy person does not ponder about breathing, seeing, walking. Infirmities of breath, sight or gait startle us" (Straus 232). He is not trying to describe illness here as much as he is endeavoring to show how illness can create a break in our seamless enmeshment with the world, and that this causes us to "ponder," in his words, what normally we simply, or not so simply, live. On a good day, neither our breath nor our sight nor our gait—and he deliberately lists them in that order—none of those things are present to us, we do not engage them through thinking and they are not features of our consciousness. That ordering of days in terms of the quality of their embodiment, some good and some bad, is his acknowledgement that infirmity, the breakdown of physical well-being, as he puts it, is a nearly universal experience. The "we" that he invokes take those functions for granted, but only on good days. What Straus opens with, however, is not a sense of continuity and community with similarly vulnerable bodily others, but rather of strangeness, of being startled, of feeling wary of and put off by that infirmity. Note the equivocation in the referent of that "us," which shifts suddenly. The "us" seemed to be continuous with the "we" who have bodies, but by the second sentence is designating a different group. "Among the patients consulting a psychiatrist, there are some who can no longer master the seemingly banal arts of standing and walking" (Straus 232).

The "us" who are startled are transported to a scene of patient and psychiatrist, and the assessment of the condition of that patient—they are not paralyzed—aligns the startled "us" with the observing psychiatrist. And it is that observational point of view that characterizes both the doctor and the philosopher in this moment, whose own bodies recede from view as they take up their function as those who attend to other bodies. He continues: "They are not paralyzed, but, under certain conditions, they cannot or feel as if they cannot keep themselves upright" (Straus 232). We see here Straus's interest in the *psychology* of the disorder. This is confirmed by a difference Straus asserts between not being able to keep oneself upright, and *feeling* that one cannot keep oneself upright. The distinction cannot be a phenomenological one. If I feel that I cannot keep myself upright, as opposed to merely fearing or anticipating that I cannot, then I cannot, in fact, keep myself upright. That distinction, the patient has the capacity to walk but feels he cannot, can only be made from an observational rather than an embodied point of view because the feeling of the body and its capacity converge in and as the body schema. He goes on to tell us that the significance of the upright posture is psychological and not merely physiological, and describes postural being as the site at which the relation between psychology and physiology can be clearly seen. "Obviously, upright posture is not confined to the technical problems of locomotion. It contains a psychological element. It is pregnant with meaning not exhausted by the physiological tasks of meeting the forces of gravity and maintaining equilibrium" (Straus 232). The upright posture is not just about the physical body, but about its interaction with that "psychological element" that renders the posture pregnant with meaning. It is a meaning not exhausted by the physiological tasks of action, and thus not coextensive with the physiology through which it is experienced.

But before the body has even arisen into uprightness, language has already taken up that meaning. "To be upright has two connotations. First to rise, to get up and to stand on one's own feet and second the moral implication, not to stoop to anything, to be honest and just, to be true to friends in danger. To stand by one's convictions and to act accordingly, even at the risk of one's life" (Straus 233). So for Straus the mapping of the meanings and, indeed the *moral valuations* that we attach to uprightness, spread into language. Straus seems to be insisting here on the psychological as a kind of interpenetration of the physiological and the meaningful. He insists that "the term 'upright' in its moral connotation is more than a mere allegory" (Straus 233), where that "more" is hard to figure unless we understand it to be referring also to something physical, something inescapably joined with the physicality on which the meaning is modeled. And, importantly, it is only once we get to language and have left the realm of strict physiology, or at least augmented it with language, that the stakes are heightened to the level of life itself.

There are, of course, some troubling moments in the description. When he writes "There is no doubt that the shape and function of the human body are determined in almost every detail by, and for, the upright posture" (Straus 233), it is hard to read his assertion of the seamlessness of the meshing of the form and function of the body, how little daylight there appears to be between "determined by" and "determined for" in that sentence, without hearing Iris Marion Young in our ears. But true to the task of descriptive phenomenology, he is interested less in asking *how did we get this way* and more in asking *what is this way that we are?* In keeping with what might be thought of as phenomenology's antigeneaological stance, he writes: "this writer's interest is in what man is and not in how he supposedly became what he is" (Straus 235).

Straus articulates what he calls a "biologically oriented psychology." That biologically oriented psychology, he clarifies, demonstrates that our experience of the world is necessarily tied to our physical orientation in that space and comportment as we move through it and we "must not forget that upright posture is an indispensible condition of man's self preservation. Upright we are, and we experience ourselves in this specific relation to the world. Men and mice do not have the same environment" (Straus 234). The stakes of uprightness are self preservation, are life itself, as he insists more than once. "Upright we are" posits uprightness as a fundamental to our human-ness. This suggestion that uprightness is not able to be dispensed with exists in rather remarkable tension with his clear articulation of standing, and walking, as achievements, even as biologically improbable ones, in the case of walking. Straus describes that tension this way: "Upright posture characterizes the human species. Nevertheless each individual has to struggle to make it truly his own" (236). If standing and walking are fundamental features of the human animal and also those banal arts that might be failed, then the stakes of this artistry, and the consequences for its failure, could not be any higher.

That specter of failure ensures that an individual's relation to uprightness is necessarily a struggle.

> Upright posture keeps us waiting [...] He has to learn it, to conquer it. The acquisition will pass through several phases, which although not completely separate, are sufficiently distinct. Progress is slow. It takes a number of years. This development will be followed here from the getting up, to standing, and finally to walking.
>
> (Straus 236)

The progress toward the upright posture is species-wide and it is teleological, inevitably aiming ever upward, at the same time that its species-specific characteristic is a certain amount of effort, of labor. So occupied is Straus with the inescapable significance of *work* in the banal arts of getting up, standing, walking that he muses that the significance of sex for the human species is the fact that it lets us stop resisting gravity and lay our bodies down: "sex remains a form of lying down" (239), he states categorically, comically.

All this, however, takes as its perspective the man who has gotten up, achieved upright posture and begun walking. The perspective of a child who has not yet quite done so is a different matter. Straus writes:

> In getting up, man gains his standing in the world. The parents are not the only ones who greet the child's progress with joy. The child enjoys no less the triumph of his achievements. The child certainly does not strive for security. Failure does not discourage him. He enjoys the freedom gained by the upright posture—the freedom to stand on his own feet and the freedom to walk upright. The upright posture, which we learn in and through falling, remains threatened by falls throughout our lives (238).

The child is untroubled by the prospect of falling. The exuberance of childhood that propels one toward walking, the drive to master it through repeated failures, means that the child must not be deterred by the fear of falling if he is ever to walk. Acquisition of the skill of walking is made possible only in the face of this falling that is not feared, even when it happens, and happens again. As he learns to walk, stumbles and falls, tries again, falls again, the child must comport himself with an unreasonable and unearned hopefulness about the success of his future efforts. He does so, at least in part, because walking brings the world to him, brings him things in the guise of things bringing themselves to him. He does not fear that his reach for mastery will exceed his grasp, even when he should. But the child does experience a fear of and fascination with the objects that walking brings into his path. The man who walks feels confronted by those objects by virtue of his placing himself before them, "he finds himself always 'confronted' with things," in Straus's words (240). The primary intentionality of our motor orientation toward the world means we can attribute a kind of agency, or a looking back, into the objects we survey.

In his delineation of childhood acquisition of motility, Straus articulates a teleology to an ever-straighter uprightness, but the goal is attained only if the walk is of a certain kind, has a certain character. A walk that is not sufficiently "dignified," to use one of his terms, or perhaps one that is not sufficiently upright, sufficiently straight, means that the body is not making good on the species progress toward ever-greater uprightness. The walk and the upright posture are expressive in many ways, and one of those ways,

Straus tells us, is sexual. The example that Straus gives about the sexual expressiveness of the body is worth close attention. He writes: "There is only one vertical but many deviations from it, each one carrying a specific, expressive meaning. The sailor pulls his cap askew, and his girl understands well the cocky expression and his 'leanings'" (Straus 241).

So we have a scene of sexual communication between a man and a woman, a sailor and a girl. Straus will insist that we do not ever have to be *instructed* in how to read such a situation, that "we have an intuitive sense of how to read what the body does in any given situation" (241). Straus offers the example to explain the eloquence of gesture, to show how meaning inheres in the sailor's gesture, that his meaning is instantly readable from his posture, that the girl understands both the "expression" of his cap askew, his gesture, and also his leanings. There is the interesting issue of bodily materiality and its insufficiency to transmit the meaning aimed at in this example. That is: this aspires to be an explanation of bodily posture, but the expressiveness of the body in this moment is achieved only through the bodily auxiliary of the cap. But perhaps the most startling thing about this particular example, as we read and understand it today, is that although the sailor's girl may be perfectly clear on the meaning of that cap pulled askew, we as readers may not be. I myself am not clear at all; to my eye that cocked hat is more likely to conjure Tom of Finland as it is to telegraph a heterosexual sailor with his girl or on the make, and the connotative dimension of that word "leanings" does nothing to lean my interpretation toward the latter image rather than the former. This may only demonstrate the danger of understanding the object to be already replete with its own meaning, and emphasizes the necessity of understanding that meaning as always relationally constructed.

If the tilt of the sailor's cap is a kind of persuasive discourse, then it will only succeed in persuading if the girl knows what it is suggesting. The tilt of the cap will not signify in the same way to every onlooker. Indeed, the girl may be perfectly clear on what the sailor means with the skew of that cap, and she may be perfectly wrong. We might imagine a scene in which the girl misrecognizes the tilt of the cap as her sailor soliciting her rather than, say, another male sailor, cap also askew, standing right behind her.

PASSING PERIOD

In 2008, Leticia King, a gender-transgressive 15 year old, was shot to death at E.O. Green Junior High School by her classmate Brandon McInerney. It was the first class of the day, Ms. Boldrin's English comp class. Leticia was seated at a computer, and Brandon was seated behind her. Twenty minutes into class, Brandon stood up, pulled a gun from the pocket of his sweatshirt and fired one bullet into Leticia's head. Leticia slumped down in her seat, bleeding profusely. Ms. Boldrin screamed: "What the fuck are you doing,

Brandon?!" Brandon stood up and fired a second shot into the back of Leticia's head.

Leticia King was more commonly known as Larry King, her given name, the one she answered to in school, in her family, and in the shelter where she was living at the time of her death. It was also the name used in the trial after the shooting that led to Leticia's death. The shooting took place after a long campaign of harassment targeting Larry's gender presentation and perceived sexual orientation, in which Larry's classmates bullied her for dressing, sounding, and walking "like a fag" and "like a girl." The defense in the subsequent murder trial attempted to rebut the accusations of bullying by suggesting that Larry was the perpetrator, rather than the victim, of bullying and harassment. Brandon McInerney and his lawyers claimed that Larry's dressing, sounding, and walking "like a girl" constituted harassment of those around him. Here we see one of the dangers of conflating gender identity and sexual identity; in this case, gender presentation becomes interpreted as a form of sexual behavior, and that "behavior" is marked and read as aggressive in order to legitimate the violence, violence with disciplinary and normativizing aims, visited upon the gender-transgressive person. The legal defense proceeded by way of reversal, a turning back against the trans child, the one who is murdered becomes the one who is judged and found guilty of aggression.

In the case that Judith Butler describes above, a young man in Maine is murdered for his queer walk, by boys who *"feel that they must negate this person, they must expunge the trace of this person. They must stop that walk no matter what"* (Judith Butler, 2006). His walk changes over time, its swish becomes more pronounced, more "dramatically feminine." The gender and sexual significations of his walk become more emphatic and distinct as he gets older, and it is this increase in his swish, and not simply the swish itself, that infuriates the other boys and drives them to murderous violence. So too with Larry King. His femininity made him stand out. In the seventh grade, when he still seemed to his classmates and teachers to be a boy, though perhaps a feminine one, few people could recall who he was. The increase in Larry's femininity was read and described, throughout the murder trial, as a "turning point" in his behavior.

We might pause to consider that turning. Gender here is understood as behavior, and as a volitional behavior, a matter of choosing, willing, deciding. Indeed Dr. Donald Hoagland, the defense psychologist, asserted that Larry's behavior, by which he meant Larry's femininity, was difficult for the other children to deal with and made them uncomfortable, particularly because at that point in adolescence students are coming to a sense of their own sexuality. The heteronormative scope of the developmental narrative invoked by is not understood to include Larry as well, but only to describe the presumptively heterosexual boys and girls he might have "confused" through his "behavior." One difficulty with the characterization of Larry's gender as a volitional act is its failure to recognize that Larry was coming into a surer and firmer sense of his gender as he approached adolescence, just as the rest of the boys were. Just as the rest of the girls were.

One of the primary ways that Larry's gender was read was through his way of walking. The walk and the gender are both real and both materially expressed, though neither can be reduced to the materiality that does the expressing. Gender and walk are situated between material body and immaterial inhabitation of the body. The walk resides in the hinge between the volitional (where my feet take me) and the nonvolitional (my walk as unintentionally disclosive of my gender or sexuality). The walk has a style that changes over time as it develops, even as its temporal dislocation points backwards as well, as an act I perform with the habit-body that I build up, over time, starting as a baby, with my first few toddling steps. This style that develops is unavoidably inflected with gendered meanings, meanings that strengthen and deepen and become more pronounced in adolescence, that develop like other characteristics of gender. That his walk was read as a manifestation of his gender, and as evidence of his improper inhabitation of gender, was recognized and demonstrated by Dawn Boldrin, the teacher in whose classroom the shooting occurred. When asked about Larry and what made him stand out from the other children, she suggested that it was something about gender, and articulated the ways in which the queerness of Larry's gender was easy to see but difficult to locate. She ended up locating gender in Larry's gestures. She was asked during the trial about the first time that she met him, the year before the shooting. "In terms of masculinity or femininity," asked prosecutor Maeve Fox, "where you would you put him on the scale?"

"He was obviously feminine" Boldrin responded.
"How so?" asked Fox.
"Um ..."[1] Boldrin paused.

During this time period Larry was in seventh grade, and Boldrin perceived him to be feminine. It is a femininity that was easy to see but difficult to locate. His femininity was discernible prior to the cross-gender accessorizing that would attract so much attention, and so much anger, in his eighth grade year. Prior to the makeup, earrings, and high heeled boots that he wore, sometimes singly and sometimes in combination, in the ten days prior to his death. She struggled to articulate this attribute of Larry's that was at once so discernible and so diffuse—so bodily and so not-quite-material. She offered: "I guess his size, his petiteness, by the way, his mannerisms, the way he carried himself, he had more of the qualities of a girl than a boy. Especially at that age, it's pretty distinct the boys vs the girls at that age." There was a distinct difference between the comportment of the boys and the comportment of the girls, said Boldrin, and Larry fell on the girls' side of that line. But the "versus" in that boys versus girls does more work than just indicate difference. Boys versus girls is a distinction that is oppositional and incompossible. Larry's girlishness was attributable to some things over which he had no control—"his size, his petiteness"—and other things that he was thought to be able to control, "his mannerisms, the way he carried himself." When asked if Larry's girlishness was apparent to everyone, Ms. Boldrin said that it was, to students and teachers alike. "Did that seem apparent to the other students?" Maeve Fox asked. Boldrin responded: "Oh yes. I don't think he was throwing it at people, but it was more his personality. You walk down the street and you see two men, I think you can distinguish which one is masculine and which one is feminine and that's just the way it is."

Gender here was figured as a potential projectile, something that Leticia could have been "throwing at people," but did not, at least not when she was in the seventh grade. Ms. Boldrin seemed to suggest that gender-as-thrown described gender as the province of the surface, of bodily appearance, of material aspects of the body that were more concrete than a walk or comportment. Those last are understood to be something more akin to "personality," to a way that one inhabits the body, an individuated style. Throwing it at people, she intimated, was what happened later, with the makeup, the earrings, and the boots. Boldrin here offered a reformulation of Sigmund Freud's assertion that the first thing you notice about someone walking down the street is whether s/he is a man or a woman. Freud conjures a solitary figure walking down the street, surrounded by people who singly and collectively form an audience for his or her gender expression, moving alone through this social setting in which gender is discerned and judged. In place of this solitary figure, Boldrin offered a pair, a couple, walking down the street, but rather than a heterosexual pairing of a man and a woman in which we would immediately know which was which, Boldrin substituted a feminine man for the woman. With that swap, the pairing of masculinity with femininity has been retained, as has the insistence that we all know difference. The insistence that we can all spot the girly boy, and immediately, and from twenty paces. We can tell that the girly boy does not quite pass for a boy, even in passing. Larry's gender was not only read off of his body, but also from what and how his body expressed itself, how he carried that body through the school. Boldrin described Larry's gender in eighth grade as "in full swing," a euphemism that seemed to refer to the femininity of the walk, that swing of the hip that constituted a swish, as much as anything else. And by a pair of boots, referred to invariably, and constantly, even obsessively, as "women's boots," with a "four-inch heel." When those boots were removed from the evidence bag and brought into the courtroom as evidence, this impressive heel height turned out to have been exaggerated through collective fantasy, as the heel on the boots was between one and two inches high.

On the morning of the shooting, Dawn Boldrin pulled Leticia aside at the beginning of class to talk with her about her academic progress. The class had a paper due that day, and Leticia had chosen protest songs of the 1960s as her topic, but the paper was not finished, perhaps not even started. Leticia, never a good student, was doing quite poorly this term, failing several classes, and was in danger of failing the eighth grade. "I told him," she said, "that eighth-grade graduation was coming up and if he wanted to walk, he would have to work on his academics." Boldrin's invocation of the walk here refers to a walk of a different sort, a metonymy for graduation, where the student's walk under a proscenium and across a stage signifies and performs the completion of his passage through some portion of his schooling, and his transition, in this case, to high school. The content of the conditional involved Larry's desire—"*if he wanted* to walk"—but its form intimated the likelihood of his failure. Boldrin suggested that the accomplishment of the walk was uncertain, and that his relation to the possibility of successfully walking was one of desire rather than probability. If he wanted to walk properly, if he wanted his walk to count as a walk at all, certain conditions would have to be met, certain conditions that Larry had failed in the past, certain conditions that, Boldrin was concerned, he would continue to fail, would keep failing. Because he kept failing, continued to fail, at his schoolwork, this other walk that signified in excess of itself, was weighted more than other walks, was also something that he would fail, another walk that he would not be able to accomplish.

The defense attorneys argued that Larry was harassing Brandon, and thus the shooting was a defensive rather than an aggressive act. This argument relied on the assumption that Larry's walk came to not only signify but actually to enact Larry's sexuality. That is, the case that the defense built rested on the assertion that Larry was harassing Brandon, and that Brandon killed him in an attempt to stop that harassment. The most surprising thing about the assertion of harassment is that the behavior characterized as harassment, in at least two instances, was in fact the walk itself. One incident they documented as an instance of Larry harassing Brandon was one in which Larry walked past a group of boys sitting on a bench. It sounds laughably innocuous thus described: how could simply walking past constitute harassment? As the defense attorneys and their expert psychologist took pains to show, it was the *way* Larry walked that was so provocative. Boys reported that they were uncomfortable around Larry, uncomfortable when he sat down at their lunch table, uncomfortable when he walked by. The defense explained that sexual harassment was behavior that made other people feel uncomfortable. Ergo: Larry was sexually harassing the boys in the school, because his sexual (read: gender) behavior made people uncomfortable. The conclusion was made possible through reading gender behavior as sexual behavior. When a queer style of walking becomes the target of aggression, that targeting legitimates itself by projecting aggression into the walk, and thus onto the person walking. The queer walk is treated as if it were aggression itself. One (uncorroborated) version of the story reported that Larry walked past the boys sitting on the bench, then paused to apply lip gloss. In that moment, behavior that is transgressing gender—that boy is putting on lip gloss!—is understood as harassment, as targeting the boys who are watching him. In the absence of any understanding that there could be such a thing as a boy who wears lip gloss, or, indeed, that Larry might be more of a girl than a boy, he was read as a boy who was choosing deliberate actions to make other boys uncomfortable. They called him faggot and ran away from him, or called him faggot and flattened themselves against their lockers to give him a ten-foot berth when he walked down the hallway, or called him faggot and left the lunch table when he sat down. The epithet is so commonplace that it did not register to the teachers as harassment. It was not unusual; it was every hour of every day that Larry was called a fag. Ken Corbett has noted that as an epithet, "Faggot operates as a projectile" (195) and one with projective force. It is a word that expresses the "general boyhood quest to be big and winning, not small and losing," (196) as Corbett makes clear. The word was directed at Larry with full awareness of its injurious capacity, at the same time as it was deployed with an almost casual contempt. It is not the word they, especially Brandon, were uncomfortable with; it was Larry. It was Leticia.

LOOKING AT "HOMOSEXUALITY IN AMERICA"

In this moment it is helpful to return to Straus and his contention that men and mice do not have the same environment because their postures are different. They do not inhabit space in the same way, and therefore they cannot inhabit the same space. I would like to extend this already extended metaphor, or perhaps more properly to contract it, to consider what happens when members of the same species have postural variations that make them take up space in a fundamentally different way. If a man and a mouse cannot be said to have the same environment, what about a man and a woman? That last was of course Iris Marion Young's challenge to Straus. My query here is similarly oriented but slightly askew: what about a man and a gay man? Or a boy and a not-quite-boy? Or a not-quite-man and a newly fledging transgirl? What happens when we consider the postulate of a different environment for the differently comported as it is conjugated through queer gender or transgender? Or to use Straus's own words, how might we think through the notion of "inclination, which just like leaning, means 'bending out' from the austere vertical. (from the Latin *clino*, to bend) (241), where inclination is read in its contemporary sense, of naming the direction or course of one's sexual desire? How, then, might we think of what use is made of the walk and the upright posture when examining the behaviors of those who might also bend in other ways? As we have seen, the walk is an elaborate and complex expression of embodied life, a rhythmic destabilization and reassertion of the vertical that propels us through the world, toward other people, or away from them. But embodied life also offers less elaborated deviations from the vertical, styles of bodily presentation that might function as a signal to others, that bring them into proximity or to keep them at a distance.

Let us reconsider Straus's sailor. Straus explains that the sailor's inclinations are communicated by his cap. His "leaning" does not inhere in the cap itself, but is communicated by how he wears it, the style of its wearing, the angle at which he sets it across his brow. This angle, the physical tilt that indicates an immaterial lean, is understood to be a sign of homosexuality, a code evincing a surprising cultural breadth and tenacity, Straus's unfamiliarity notwithstanding. The convention is apparently longstanding enough in American gay culture to have been referenced in the first mainstream magazine article to document "homosexual life" in 1964, and persistent enough that forty-five years later Larry's teachers could communicate their reading of his sexuality by describing his scarf as "jauntily tied," where once again the angle of the tie was more crucial in determining how the scarf and its wearing were read than any physical attribute of the scarf itself.

Two years before the publication of Straus's "The Upright Posture," *Life* magazine published that essay, "Homosexuality in America" (Welch). This piece, illustrated with photographs, documents the homosexual underground for the consumption of a heterosexual public assumed to be unaware of such a world. One of the venues described is a bar in the warehouse district of San Francisco in 1964. The patrons are leathermen, and the scene is described as conveying a certain amount of menace. One of the most noticeable things about the men described is the type of covers that they wear. Those caps are prominent in the images of the men in the bar, and also figure in magazine's descriptions of their masculinity. The leathermen in the unnamed bar are described this way: "The effort of these homosexuals to appear manly is obsessive—in the rakish angle of the caps, in the thumbs boldly hooked in belts" (Welch 70). As described, the accessorizing marks and enhances a certain kind of masculinity, but also detracts from it in implying that attention to dress and presentation necessarily slants that presentation toward the feminine. An overconcern with physical appearance, it is implied, queers even the most hyperbolically masculine gender, turns the unselfawareness that is the hallmark of masculinity into preening or dandyishness.

Each aspect of this dressing and accessorizing is freighted with meaning, in ways that are not always entirely apparent to a casual observer, even as it is implied that the language of gesture that governs the donning of those accessories is universal. An angle is always "rakish," or in Larry's case, "jaunty," rather than crooked, or sloppy. Thumbs are hooked in belts "boldly," thought it is unclear what exactly it is that is bold about the gesture.

These leathermen are portrayed as having an obsessive relation to their own manliness, but the article also introduces us to homosexuals who do not, who are described as "swishy" and "effeminate." These two groups of homosexuals are differentiated in terms of gender, the obsessively manly leathermen versus the effeminate softness of the boys in Chelsea and the Village, the opposed textures of California SM culture, leather, and

Chelsea boys, fluffy. If part of the pictorial describes the shadowy world of homosexuals that the world of heterosexuals could not possible fathom, another section describes homosexuals as they move through the straight world, and are encountered by heterosexuals. Indeed, the crux of the article is about those encounters between the heterosexual and homosexual worlds, where the index of the visibility of a homosexual world is a measure of its visibility to straights, and its increasing visibility is seen as fundamentally *about* heterosexuality, an aggressive movement out toward it.

The article offers two photographs depicting this other, more effeminate world of gays. The first shows the torso of mannequin displayed in a storefront window. He is dressed in a jacket and a long plaid scarf, one arm is crossed protectively over his midsection, and the other arm reaches up across the chest, one finger of the masculine resting on the collarbone in a delicately feminine pose. On his head is an outrageously oversized hat. The caption reads: "The window of this New York Greenwich village store which caters to homosexuals is filled with the colorful, offbeat attention-calling clothes that the 'gay' world likes" (Welch 68). The store window solicits our attention, and it does so, implies the analogy, in the same way that homosexuals solicit our attention, with color, outsized-ness, outrageousness. The agency is given to the clothing itself; it is the clothing itself that procures the attention that the homosexual is understood to crave.

This characterization of homosexuals as craving and demanding attention is another remarkably persistent stereotype. One of Leticia's teachers, Anne Sinclair, was giving testimony during the trial about the ways in which she understood Larry to be engaging in "negative attention seeking." She explained that this seeking of attention was something that could be felt the moment Larry entered a room. In her view, his entering a room was itself a demand for attention because of the way in which he entered it. And because the attention he received in school was almost invariably negative attention, Larry was necessarily demanding bad attention. That demand for attention was described as bodily but nonverbal. He "announces" through his manner of entering a room and his style of dress, both of which were described by the defense attorney Robyn Bramson as "flamboyant," a word Bramson offered to the teacher, who affirmed it in a string of assent. Flamboyant, here and elsewhere, functions as cipher for the word "homosexual," sometimes when the latter cannot be uttered.

BRAMSON: And you've described him as dramatic?
SINCLAIR: Yes.
BRAMSON: Coming into a room?
SINCLAIR: Yes.
BRAMSON: Announcing his presence?
SINCLAIR: Yes.

BRAMSON: And that he became a bit more flamboyant as well?
SINCLAIR: Yes.
BRAMSON: Would that be a good word?
SINCLAIR: Yes.
BRAMSON: In his style of dress?
SINCLAIR: Yes.

(Superior Court of the State of California 52–53)

Leticia, by all accounts, was a large presence. She knew how to enter a room. She liked to be noticed. She knew how to work it. If we read this form of embodiment movement as a demand, the question then becomes: what is this a demand for? And from whom is it being demanded? Sinclair understands it to be a demand that others give him negative attention; Larry was demanding an unhappy engagement with the other. In this view, if others then reacted to him with unhappiness, negativity, or aggression, they were only acceding to what he had demanded.

BRAMSON: Why you would say that he engaged in negative attention-seeking behavior?
SINCLAIR: Well, I was going to say I was always aware when he came into the classroom. I mean, it's not like—if I wasn't looking at the door, I mean, I would know that he had entered the room. I mean, some kids can quietly come into the room, and other kids kind of bring more attention to themselves when they come into the room.
BRAMSON: And you felt that Larry brought more attention to himself?
SINCLAIR: Right.

(Superior Court of the State of California 55)

What is occluded in this exchange between the defense attorney and the teacher is the teacher's own look, her own desire to look. We can read a hint of it in the ellipses that breaks off. "I mean, it's not like—" she stated, not finishing the sentence. What follows is her contention that she was not looking at the door when Larry came in. The words that are swallowed prior to that demurral cannot be read, as we are left with only the negative imprint of the thing about to be conjured ("it's not like"), followed by the impossibility of its formulation. It's not like she was looking at the door before he came in. *It's not like she wanted to look.* He made her do it.

With this we see some of the more pernicious consequences of understanding the performance of queer gender as a demand for attention, but also some of the dangers of reading the performance of gender as a demonstration of agency. If it was Leticia's own demand that drew Sinclair to look toward the door, a demand that provided cover for her own desire to look and to see, then she was not responsible for acknowledging or attending to her own desire. The attribution of "negative attention seeking" to Larry meant that the scene of her turning to look was a story of Larry's agency, rather than a story of her own desire to look, which was both satisfied and occluded by her turn toward Larry.

The *Life* magazine piece, too, tells a story, or several, about the complex circuits of desire and disgust, recognition and retraction, that are at play when straight people look at queer people. One of the photographs shows two couples passing each other as they walk through what looks to be Washington Square Park. The first couple appears to be two young men, and the camera captures them from the back in the left of the frame as they walk away from us. Walking toward them and toward the viewer is a second couple, a middle-aged woman and a balding man. The first couple is looking straight ahead. The second couple is looking at the first, the man with a hard, sizing-up stare, and the woman with a not-quite-legible gaze. There is a shadow between her brows, and a hint of flare and raise in her nostrils. Her look may be unkind; it may be curious. It may be compassionate, it may be fearful. The most readable aspect of her embodiment is not her face but her hands. One white-gloved hand clutches her pocketbook and the other clutches her husband, curling around his elbow. His hands are unreadable, pushed into the pockets of his pants, but his face is anything but inscrutable. His brow is furrowed, his eyes are narrowed, his stare is hard, and his tongue is pushed into his lower lip. It is a look of judgment, of disapproval, of contempt.

The photograph's caption reads: "Two fluffy-sweatered young men stroll in New York City, ignoring the stare of a 'straight' couple. Flagrant homosexuals are unabashed by reactions of shock, perplexity, disgust" (Welch 68). The photograph's caption understands the image to capture homosexuals' desire and their flagrancy, even as the only physical evidence of desire captured by the photograph is the desire of the straight couple to look at the gay one. The young men are looking ahead, not returning the openly hostile stare that is directed at them. They walk through the park, side by side but not touching. Their sweaters are soft, as are the stances; the young man closest to the center of the frame slightly contrapposto, caught mid-stride in the play of balance that is human bipedal gait. Each has his arms closed protectively around his own torso, contained, containing. They are not soliciting attention in their comportment, their bodies evidencing rather the opposite, a kind of proprioceptive retraction. Nor their gazes: straight ahead, slightly down, non-challenging. Yet it is the homosexual couple who is characterized as seeking attention, soliciting stares, flagrantly and brazenly courting the attention of the straight couple, a characterization that would free the slack-jawed onlookers from having to face their own desire to look. With the insistence that homosexuals are "unabashed" by the "shock, perplexity, disgust" of the onlooker, the chief complaint against these homosexuals is advanced: not that they are violating norms of gender or sexual behavior, but that they are doing so without a sufficient sense of shame, a charge whose workings in this case I have explored elsewhere.[2]

THE TURN

The period of time after class allotted to the students to walk from one classroom to another is called the passing period. The day before the shooting there was an incident between Brandon and Larry during the passing period. "The passing period," said Dr. Hoagland, the defense psychologist, "was the trigger incident" in the case. Brandon recounted that he was walking along the hallway with his friend Keith L. Brandon saw Larry approaching, walking down the hallway. Brandon bent the arc of his path wide, veering away from Larry. In Brandon's telling, he was trying to steer clear of Larry. Dr. Hoagland says: "He was not wanting any trouble. He tried to avoid him. They passed each other and then the defendant turned around and looked at him and the victim said something." The victim said something but no one is certain what it was. Brandon did not hear all the words. His friend Keith did not hear the words. Brandon heard only the word at the end: "baby." After the shooting, he said that Larry might have said: "What's up, baby?" Or that he might have said: "What's wrong, baby?" Brandon was not sure. He could not remember exactly what was said. This incident was, according to the defense, the defining moment in the case. Larry called Brandon "baby," and Brandon reported that this was disgusting, the worst thing anyone had ever said to him. "I have never been disrespected like that," Brandon said.

Dr. Hoagland was asked why such a seemingly innocuous comment would be reacted to in such a violent manner: "Was it the comment, what was it about this incident that upset Brandon?" Dr. Hoagland responded:

> There are multiple things. One was that this boy who was dressing as a woman and secondarily who was gay that was coming up and saying this kind of provocative things to him in front of many other people. I think Brandon said that was the straw that popped the balloon.

Which was indeed how Brandon described his feelings after the incident, "the final straw that popped the balloon," mixing the metaphor in order that he not be the camel with a broken back, but rather the balloon popping, a noise that several of the children thought they heard that morning in the classroom, and only realized, once they smelled gunpowder and saw Brandon standing over Larry's body aiming to fire a second shot into his head, that it was not a balloon at all.

Brandon agreed with Dr. Hoagland's assessment that it was Larry's gender transgression, rather than his sexual orientation, that provoked him toward violence. That gender transgression was primary, and Larry's sexual orientation was only "secondary." "I knew he was gay," Brandon said of Larry. "But he took it to a whole other level. What the hell, high heels and makeup and hairdo? It was surprising and disgusting." Brandon, in fact, did a quite precise job of articulating the fact that his hatred of Larry stemmed from the fact that Larry was violating gender roles. Prosecutor Fox asked: "Did you talk to him about why he found it so disgusting?" Hoagland responded: "Yes. He said that it was such a disruption of what was expected from a male that simply seeing that was upsetting and disturbing."

The events of the "trigger incident," however, deserve a second look. Brandon and Leticia passed each other in the hall, apparently without incident. No words were exchanged, nothing was reported. After they passed one another, Brandon reported that he turned to look. *Brandon turned to look.* He did not say why. We do not know what motivated that look. It was not words between them. It was not physical contact. It was not, so far as anyone can tell, anything that Leticia did. For some reason after they had passed one another, Brandon turned around to look, and what he reported in that moment was that Leticia was looking at him. Leticia's look was one that Brandon would not have perceived had he not turned around and looked himself, so it was his own act of turning and looking that occasioned Leticia's look, and that offered him as receptive to her look. The "triggering incident" began with some desire of Brandon's, a desire that oriented his body back and behind, turned himself toward Leticia. He was hailed in the moment after he had turned to look, with an unheard utterance and the word "baby." If we are to understand the disgust, the revulsion, the blinding rage that Brandon reported feeling at this moment, must we not understand the disgust to be formed not just around the half-heard utterance, but also Brandon's own turn, his own solicitation of that utterance with his body and his look?

During the murder trial, the court was half-full of people: the lawyers, the jury, the gallery, the accused: all eyes to the judge. The entrance was in the back of the courtroom. Every time someone opened that door to enter the courtroom, the hinge on the double door squeaked. When court was in session and that door opened, and a bailiff or a witness or a family member entered the courtroom, Brandon turned around in his chair. Every time. He swiveled his head around with his face to the gallery to see who had entered, then quickly turned back around to face front. It was as if the sound and the feeling of someone coming in and standing behind him was unbearable. That feeling of being the object of someone's gaze, a someone that he could not see, shifted him and turned him around in his chair. When he turned around, he rearranged his body with the turn, insuring that he was not in the same position relative to whoever was entering the room that Leticia was when Brandon shot her: seated, blind from behind, his back and the back of his head offering themselves as one target.

NOTES

1. I attended the Brandon McInerney trial in the summer of 2011; all quotations of testimony are from my personal notes unless otherwise specified.
2. See Salamon, "Humiliation and Transgender Regulation."

WORKS CITED

Corbett, Ken. *Boyhoods: Rethinking Masculinities.* New Haven: Yale UP, 2009.
Husserl, Edmund. *Ideas Pertaining to a Pure Phenomenology and to a Phenomenological Philosophy.* Trans. F. Kersten. Dordrecht: Kluwer Academic Publishers, 1998.
Judith Butler: Philosophical Encounters of the Third Kind. Dir. Paule Zadjermann. Arte, 2006. Film.
Salamon, Gayle. "Humiliation and Transgender Regulation: Reply to Ken Corbett." *Psychoanalytic Dialogues,* 19.4 (2009): 376–384.
Smith, Robert. "Justin Vivian Bond: Childhood, Revisited." Interview with Justin Vivian Bond. *Lambda Literary.* 12 Sept. 2011. Web. 18 Oct. 2011 at http://www.lambdaliterary.org/features/09/12/justin-vivian-bond-childhoodrevisited/
Straus, Erwin. "The Upright Posture." *Phenomenology and Existentialism.* Eds. Richard Zaner and Don Ihde. New York: Capricorn Books, 1973.
Superior Court of the State of California for the County of Ventura. *People of the State of California vs. Brandon David McInerney,* Case No. 2008005782, Reporter's Partial Transcript of Proceedings, Testimony of Anne Sinclair, 29 July 2011.
Welch, Paul. "Homosexuality in America." *Life* 26 June 1964: 66–74, 76–80.
Young, Iris Marion. *Throwing Like a Girl and Other Essays.* Bloomington, Indiana UP, 1990.

12 Doing Phenomenology

The Empathetic Implications of Crew's Head-Swap Technology in 'W' (Double U)

Sigrid Merx

"Did you ever wonder what it would be like to look out from another persons' head?" This is how CREW, a Belgium techno-theatre company, introduces *'W' (Double U)* on their website (CREW). In this performance the question at hand is not addressed reflexively or thematically; instead CREW sets out to find an answer by having its audience "do" what the question suggests: to virtually look through someone else's eyes. *'W' (Double U)*, first presented in 2008, is an immersive performance experiment for two participants in different geographical locations, based on what CREW calls their "head-swap" technology. With the use of their self-developed omnidirectional video system, the vision of both participants is swapped, allowing them not only to perceive the world from each other's point of view, but to actually move in each other's field of vision. Both equipped with a pair of video goggles that fully covers their sight and a live recording camera on top, the participants are confronted with live footage filmed from the first-person perspective of the other participant that is fed onto the video display inside their goggles (Figure 13.1). A head-tracking sensor allows for the images to adapt to the movements of the participants, creating for the participants an experience of actually moving around in the filmed environment. This sensation of being "inside" or "there" is further enhanced by the fact that the video goggles are constructed in such a way that any other visual trigger besides the video images is blocked. The goggles fully cover the sight of the participants, and the size of the video display reaches to the same parameters as the angle of their visual field. As a result the images on display appear unframed to the participants, creating an illusion that one is not looking at projected images but actually is present in that world. Depending on each other's instructions, they physically try to find their way in each other's field of vision. The "head-swap" is yet another step in CREW's investigation of immersive technologies and the effects they can produce.

Returning to CREW's question, I must admit I have wondered what it would be like to look at the world from someone else's perspective, as I have wished from time to time that people could see the world from my point of view. "Try to see things from my perspective" is a phrase most of us undoubtedly use when we want to convince others of our ideas or beliefs,

Figure 12.1 Participant in *'W' (Double U)* equipped with technology. © Santi Fort, 2009.

or to have them understand us better or empathize with us a bit more. The expression "to look at things from my perspective" can be considered a metaphor that tells us something about how our culture links seeing and understanding, and at the same time implies that for a "true" understanding we need to adopt another perspective, in this case "my" perspective. What is presupposed in this metaphor, I would like to suggest, is a particular form of *empathy*, the human capacity to engage intersubjectively with others, to understand others, to be able to relate to their feelings and experiences.

According to philosopher Matthew Ratcliffe, we can roughly distinguish between two different theoretical strands with regard to empathy within the context of phenomenology. Some stress that empathy foremost is an intentional *perceptual ability*, an attitude towards others that enables people to perceive human behavior as an expression of (part of) someone's mental states (Stein 14–23; Zahavi 37). We perceive experiences of others as being "theirs" and therefore the other as "that-which-is-not-I." Others argue that empathy is rather a form of simulation that entails the ability to project ourselves in the situation of others (Goldman 17; Stueber 4). Through an *act of imagination*, we attribute our own experience to the other "as-if-it-was-Me." Understood as simulation, empathy points to the possibility of accessing experiences of others from a first-person perspective, that is, our own perspective (Ratcliffe 3). When we understand empathy as a particular perceptual ability, a third-person position is implied. We can only relate to the experiences of others from the outside.

However, whether we understand "looking at things from someone else's perspective" as a form of simulation or as a type of perception, from the point of view of embodiment it does not stop being a metaphor. Clearly we are not actually physically able to adopt someone else's perspective as an embodied position from which we can see. Nor is the field of vision that is produced by such a perspective an actual space in which we can move around. No matter how well-developed our empathic capacities, physically speaking we are bound to our own embodied perspective, the point of view it implies and the spaces it opens up for us. In this respect we are unable to experience from a second-person perspective, from a "you-that-is-I." This is where we meet the limits of our perception. It is precisely at these limits that CREW's work, more particular 'W' *(Double U)*, can be located.

In this chapter I want to investigate what CREW's "head-swap" could mean within a phenomenological context, more particular from the perspective of empathy. We can start answering this question from two sides, depending on if we approach the head-swap first of all as a technological tool or as a phenomenon that can be experienced by the participant. Either we start with the technology used to switch perspectives or we choose to begin with the participant's behavior or attitude in relation to seeing the world from someone else's perspective. Obviously technology and experience are closely related and any analysis of 'W' *(Double U)* needs to take both into account. However, I hope to demonstrate that these two different starting points allow for two slightly different readings of what it might mean to look at the world from someone else's perspective.

Analyzing the performance from a technological point of view, it becomes clear the technology produces a *simulation of someone else's perspective* that in the end interestingly enough creates a new bodily *experience of one's own presence*. From the point of view of the actual behavior and attitude of the participant, however, a different understanding of the work comes to light. It can be argued that being confronted with *a perspective that is not yours* it is not so much one's own presence that is emphasized, but our co-presence with others. These two different readings relate to the two different possible understandings of empathy as discussed before.

Approaching the performance and the experiences it produces from a technological point of view, matters of subjectivity become prominent. This line of reasoning can be found in CREW's own reflections on their work, as represented in various articles from theatre scholars Vanhoutte and Wynants, who are affiliated with CREW and write from an inside perspective.[1] What is emphasized in their reflections is the relationship between the technology and individual experiences of presence. However, if we analyze the performance from the participant's point of view, what is emphasized is the intersubjectivity of the experience of the head-swap. I believe these social implications of the head-swap technology in 'W' *(Double U)* have not been addressed enough and could be stressed more.

Both readings raise questions about what is at stake when we look at the world from someone else's perspective. What does empathy imply in terms of how we find ourselves present in the world? What is empathy all about ultimately? Is it about me, you, us, or all of that at the same time? As I suggested at the beginning of this chapter, the performance does not touch upon these questions thematically or reflexively; instead the performance invites its participants to experience the possible answers. As such 'W' *(Double U)* can be understood as a specific form of phenomenological research, or as Don Ihde would put it, a case of "*doing phenomenology.*"

DOING PHENOMENOLOGY

'W' *(Double U)* is presented as a performative experiment. Not only this performance, but CREW's work in general, seems to be the artistic embodiment of the answer to a question philosopher Don Ihde puts forward in *Experimental Phenomenology*: "what if a phenomenological inventor began to explore deliberate variations, playfully engaging each to see what resulted?" (167). As the title of his book indicates, Ihde calls for an experimental phenomenology, arguing that phenomenology is above all "an investigative science, an essential component of which is experiment" (4). Experimental phenomenology, according to Ihde, is a way of "doing phenomenology." Most of his work explores how to do phenomenology as praxis and stresses that doing phenomenology is vital to understand phenomenology. Learning phenomenology is to learn by doing, by example, and by experience. Experimental phenomenology, Ihde suggests, engages in "experience-experiments" (5). Phenomenology is put forward here as a means of practical investigation, the actual practice of a phenomenological analysis.

> A phenomenological analysis (or description, as it is technically called) is more than mere analysis. It is a probing for what is genuinely discoverable and potentially there, but not often seen. Phenomenology is the door to the possible, a possible that can be experienced and verified through the procedures that are, in fact, the stuff of experimental phenomenology.
>
> (Ihde, *Experimental Phenomenology* 13)

Phenomenology as research praxis is a manifestation of what Ihde has coined "post-phenomenology." Whereas classical phenomenology is dominated by descriptive (transcendental phenomenology) and interpretative (hermeneutical phenomenology) methodologies, the post-phenomenological approach is utterly pragmatic. Instead of or next to describing or interpreting human experience, presence, perception, and meaning making, post-phenomenology suggests that the most pertinent vocabulary to speak about these things is the vocabulary of practice and action (117).

It is important to note that Ihde locates post-phenomenology and the phenomena and experiences it should study firmly within the context of contemporary techno-culture. Ihde stresses that human bodies today are always bodies in relation to technology. According to Ihde, the classical understanding of interrelational ontology as the ontological relationship between the human experiencer and his life-world, as theorized both in pragmatic philosophy and phenomenology, needs to be expanded to include technology because technologies profoundly change this relationship in how they mediate our consciousness of our environment. Building further on his idea of an interrelational ontology of human-technology relations, as developed in *Technics and Praxis* back in 1979 and further unpacked in *Postphenomenology and Technoscience* in 2009, Ihde claims that technology "transforms and translates our embodiment into our reach through instruments [...] thus into what we can experience and know of the world" (142).

Ihde's interest in technologies and instruments is closely related to his assumption that technologies can help us discover and experience the limits of our perception. "How do I discover my 'limits'?" Ihde asks in "Stretching the In-Between: Embodiment and Beyond." "My answer is *by means of technological, instrumental mediation*" (110). In this context Ihde is particularly interested in immersive imaging technologies, for example video games, point of view in cinema and virtual reality. CREW's omnidirectional video system can be considered as such an immersive imaging technology. The potential of these technologies, Ihde stresses, resides in how they can simulate or present phenomena that lie beyond the perceptual capacities of human bodies and that would not be available to our perception if it were not for the technological mediation (*Experimental Phenomenology* 140–1).

Precisely because of the influence of technology on human experience, Ihde suggests that investigating technology-human relationships can help us to develop a better understanding of phenomenological issues. In his account of experimental phenomenology, Ihde emphasizes its playfulness, a constant testing and exploring of new phenomenological variations. This playfulness, according to Ihde, is particularly enabled by technology. This is very much the case in the work of CREW where different variations of new immersive technologies are tested within the context of a live performance to playfully discover the limits of our perception and explore new possibilities of experience, in 'W' *(Double U)* for example, the experience of looking at the world from someone else's perspective. In many respects we can consider CREW the "phenomenological inventor" Ihde is calling for, and their performative experiments, a specific case of doing phenomenology (167).

And if we follow Ihde, who claims that postphenomenology "finds a way to probe and analyze the role of technologies in social, personal and cultural life that it undertakes by concrete —empirical—studies of technologies in the plural," we could even argue that CREW's work is not only a case of doing phenomenology, but also of postphenomenology (*Postphenomenology* 23).

Let's have a closer look at how CREW uses immersive technologies to create new experiences for their participants and make an attempt to characterize these experiences.

THEATRE AS TECHNO-LAB: VARIATIONS AND PROCEDURES

Although structurally subsidised as a performance company, CREW is not a theatre company in the traditional sense of the word. It intends to operate on the border between art and science, between performance art and new technology. CREW might be better described as a multidisciplinary team of artists, researchers, and technicians using live performance and installations as medium to test, play with, and reflect on the aesthetic possibilities and implications of innovative immersive technologies. More specifically CREW's artistic research focuses on aspects of presence, spectatorship, interactive narration in virtual environments, and their relations.

Creation and research go hand in hand at CREW as becomes manifest in CREW_lab. As a research component of CREW, the lab is where both technological and academic research into immersive technology is undertaken, in close collaboration with partners such as academic research institutes, manufacturers of digital technologies, and media companies. This ongoing research feeds directly into the creative work and vice versa. Not only CREW_lab, but also CREW performances themselves can be understood as experimental settings. "Theatre as a laboratory" is how Vanhoutte and Wynants characterize the work of CREW in their article "Performing Phenomenology" (277). CREW's focus on questions of presence, embodiment, and perception is thoroughly phenomenological in its orientation turning CREW's work into a phenomenological laboratory.

Since 2004, starting with the performance *CRASH*, CREW has developed and improved one technological system in particular that lies at the heart of their dramaturgy: omni-directional video.

> Omni-directional video allows the spectator a surround video display. Equipped with an orientation tracker this HMD [head mounted display, SM] shows a sub-image of the panoramic video that corresponds with the spectator's view direction and desired field of view. ODV thus places the viewer physically in a video-captured surrounding imagery, generating a very lively environment. Consequently, the filmed image becomes a space in which the viewer can dwell (277–78).

In most CREW performances individual participants are equipped with this ODV system and experience another world (see Figure 13.1). The participant is unable to look beyond the frame of the video display and cannot escape the images presented within this frame, as these are fully occupying his field of vision. As such the participant, or, as CREW calls her *immersant*, is truly encapsulated by technology, as the helmet and the goggles are literally surrounding her head. Visually speaking, the immersant cannot experience an "outside" of the images; the images become her 3D environment in which she is immersed. Technology takes over her sight.

Most of CREW's performances can be considered a series of test versions of this particular technology. Through the years the system has radically improved, particularly in terms of its responsiveness. Whereas in the first immersive experiments, the participant needed to be in a fixed position because the system was not able to adapt to changing positions, over time the immersant became much freer to physically move around in the virtual environment. The head-swap technology in *'W' (Double U)* was yet another step in expanding the technological possibilities. However, what is tested and experimented with in these versions is not only what the technology itself can do and how it can perform better, but also what kind of meaningful experiences that technology can help to produce for the immersant that is hooked up to that technology. For this purpose, and this is where CREW's research also becomes artistic research, the use of technology, and therefore also the immersant equipped with that technology, is framed within a specific narrative and theme.

Reflecting on CREW's different projects for example in *CRASH* (2004), the immersant hears a story on her headphones gradually suggesting that she might have crashed, now waking up and not knowing where she is. In *EUX* (2009) there is a suggestion that one suffers from agnosia, a loss of ability to recognize objects, persons, shapes, and smells. *LINE-UP* (2010) invites the immersant to believe that the world around her is the product of her own imagination. Using themes such as memory loss, dementia, schizophrenia, and dreams, these stories, together with the technology, cater to unstable experiences of presence, identity, and reality. The immersant wonders who she is, where she is, and if what she sees and feels is real or not.

Whereas immersion, especially in the context of virtual reality, often is connected to out-of-body experiences that entail a transition from a physical reality to "somewhere else," in the live performances of CREW physical space and virtual space coincide. Consequently, the physical presence of the participant in virtual space is never denied. Partly this feeling of presence is triggered by the kind of images CREW feeds to the immersant. This footage, both live and pre-recorded, is shot mostly on location and therefore is familiar and recognizable. Even more important is that these images, thanks to the orientation tracker, respond and adapt to the movements of the head and the body of the participant, strengthening the experience of being surrounded by an environment in which one can move, instead of just looking at two-dimensional imagery from a fixed position. Moving through virtual space, the physical presence of the immersant and his experience of an actual here and now are continuously emphasized, even intensified further by the use of omni-directional audio feedback and tactile sensations corresponding with the imagery:

> By mixing real and virtual experiences in novel ways, this technology offers the possibility to extend the traditional categories of experience: the virtual space coincides with the embodied own space, integrating thus the story world into the physically perceived world of the spectator, installing a new intimacy and a high degree of presence.
> (Vanhoutte and Wynants, "Performing Phenomenology" 278)

Although the virtual space and the physical space do coincide, CREW is careful not to let them fully collapse into each other. Full immersion is not what CREW is after (279). Instead they look for ways to problematize and disturb the embodied presence of the immersant. Vanhoutte and Wynants speak in this respect of an "ontological ambivalence" (279).

CREW has developed different ways to unsettle the immersant and the way she finds herself in the world. One of their strategies is to trigger the participant in believing that pre-recorded images are live. Using both live and pre-recorded footage from the actual location of the performance allows CREW to subtly mix these without the immersant knowing it. For example *EUX* (2008) provides the immersant with a truly uncanny experience when one is moving around in a virtual environment and all of the sudden unexpectedly encounters one self. The immersant is confronted with an image of herself looking around and walking towards and by her, footage that has been recorded at an earlier stage before the start of the performance, and is now fed into the video goggles as if live. Seeing an "I" that is "not-my-body," but neither just a reflection, is a confusing, alienating, and indeed ontologically ambivalent experience in which one's physical presence is not denied but doubled in a virtual counterpart that has a presence of her own.

Another strategy of disturbance is the so-called "rubber hand illusion" based on a well-known scientific experiment that has demonstrated that seeing how a rubber hand is being stroked, while one's own invisible hand is stroked simultaneously, triggers a feeling of ownership of the rubber hand. The "rubber hand illusion" is an example of how conflicting sensorial input stimulates a person to bring these conflicting senses together in a meaningful experience (Vanhoutte, Wynants, and Bekaerts 161; Vanhoutte and Wynants, "Performing Phenomenology" 282). In their performances CREW deliberately creates similar moments of sensorial friction between what the immersant sees and what she feels.

For example in *CRASH* (2004), loosely based on Ballard's novel with the same title, the immersant lies on a table while on her display she sees how another body on a table surrounded by doctor-like figures, undergoes a weird kind of surgery, where materials hard to identify are taken out of what seems to be a (her) belly. Simultaneously one of CREW's members, whose presence the immersant is not aware of, shines an infrared light on her abdomen. The sense of warmth triggers the immersant to connect the image of the surgery "out there" with her own body "right here," negotiating between what she sees and what she feels.

Vanhoutte and Wynants argue that in mixing embodied and disembodied perspectives CREW creates "a transitional space: an environment in-between embodied and perceived reality" (281). Similar to the rubber-hand experiment in which it becomes clear how vision is dominant over other sense systems, in CREW's performative experiments the immersant is triggered to match these tactile sensations with what he sees. A similar perceptual confusion can be found in 'W' *(Double U)* in the sense that something that is physically speaking "not-I" is experienced as something that somehow can be embodied, in this case someone else's field of vision.

'W' *(DOUBLE U)*

As described in the introduction in 'W' *(Double U)* two participants in different locations—in some tests in different parts of the same building, in others in different cities, even countries—are equipped with the omni-directional video system as described before. In this particular case the technology is used to swap the participants' field of vision, enabling them to perceive the world through another person's point of view and to actually move in each other's vision. Unlike other performances 'W' *(Double U)* lacks a fictional narrative frame. As a result the focus is much more on the technology of the head-swap itself. In this respect 'W' *(Double U)* is more experiment than performance, indeed a performative experiment.

The performance starts with a variation on the rubber-hand illusion. Through their headphones the participants receive an instruction to stretch out their hands, which are captured live by the camera on their head and fed into the display. Consequently both participants see their own hands. The muscular sensation of stretching the hands and the visual stimulus are perfectly in tune. At that moment the personal view of both participants is switched off, resulting in, as Vanhoutte and Wynants describe, "a temporary state of sensory deprivation" (281). When the video is switched on again, the head-swap has been executed and now, with their hands still stretched out, the participants see an image of hands that are not theirs. But to whom do these perceived hands belong? Now the participants feel how their own hands are being touched (by a CREW member) while they simultaneously see how the visually represented hands are being touched (Figure 13.2). Both are triggered to create an embodied understanding of their new reality and their presence in that reality. This understanding however remains unstable throughout the performance because even the simplest instructions over the headphone to look around or to take a few steps, seem almost impossible to execute. The environment as perceived by the participant through her video goggles is

Figure 12.2 Hands of participant in 'W' *(Double U)* touched by CREW member. © Eric Joris, 2009.

filmed by the camera on top of the other participant, and therefore consistent with the position, movement, and point of view of that other participant, but not necessarily in sync with her own movements and embodied presence.

Looking or moving around in a virtual environment that you experience from a point of view that is noticeably not "yours" is an unsettling experience. If the space you are moving in is not responding to or corresponding with your movements but with someone else's movements, you are finding yourself in a world that does not belong to you and that you seem unable to truly occupy. Instead this world seems to belong to someone else, the "other" who is not there physically, but whose presence is implied in the space you perceive, a being-there that you can sense spatially. In order to be able to perform in this alien world, the participants need to sustain and guide each other verbally via microphone and headset, trying to synchronize their positions, movements, and directions of looking.

Slowly the immersants adapt from the perspective of a "body-out-there" to a "here-body"(Vanhoutte and Wynants, "Performing Phenomenology" 281). Very different from other CREW performances, however, the reconciliation of conflicting perceptions is only achieved in a collaborative effort:

> Participants seem to seek for a consistent experience in synchronizing and tune their movements to each other, in order to almost

> "hypercorrect" or counterbalance the incongruence of the digital dance.
>
> (Vanhoutte and Wynants, "Performing Phenomenology" 282)

It is only in moving *together* that one gradually appropriates the required visual domain and can finally shift from a disembodied to an embodied perspective towards the virtual space. However, most of the performance is played out precisely at this shift. The immersants have to operate together in an unstable in-between. As a consequence they are constantly confronted with the otherness of their current perspective and as a result simultaneously with themselves and the other. Obviously looking from someone else's perspective implicates both the one who is looking and the one whose perspective is involved. But how exactly do these two relate?

In the beginning of this chapter I argued that "to look at the world from someone else's perspective" can be understood as a particular form of empathy because it entails an engagement with experiences of others. Drawing on Ratcliffe, I distinguished between two different understandings of empathy within the context of phenomenology: on the one hand empathy as simulation, an act of imagination in which we project our own experiences on others, and on the other hand empathy as perceptual ability, an openness to the experiences of others. I connected empathy as simulation with a first-person perspective, relating to the other as-if-it-was-Me, whereas empathy as a perceptual ability was related more closely to a third-person perspective, engaging with the other as a that-which-is-not-I. However, I also stressed that the particular experience of looking at the world from someone else's perspective, whether understood as simulation or as type of perception, is limited from the point of view of embodiment because we are not able to physically adopt someone else's perspective as an embodied position from which we can see. This is where we run into the limits of our perception. I suggested that if we were able to actually embody such a position, this would imply a very particular second-person perspective: a you-that-is-I.

The question is: has '*W*' *(Double U)* been able to somehow lift these limits and create such a perspective? In the next paragraph I will explore these questions in more detail from the perspective of empathy. What could it mean to look at the world from someone else's perspective? I will approach this question from two different directions: on the one hand from Ihde's technological point of view, on the other hand from Ratcliffe's socio-psychological point of view.

SIMULATING PERSPECTIVE

For Ihde, the potential of immersive technologies, such as CREW's omnidirectional video system, resides in how they can simulate or present phenomena that lie beyond the perceptual capacities of human bodies and bring them within our perceptual reach through technological mediation. Ihde's thoughts about technology and embodiment start from the assumption that instruments are able to extend the bodily and perceptual capacities of human bodies and can help us to experience beyond the limits of our experiential horizons ("Stretching the In-Between" 110).

In 'W' *(Double U)* embodying someone else's perspective is perceptually brought into reach through the use of omni-directional video technology. The cameras, filming live from the top of the heads of both participants, capture the environment from their respective positions in space and feed these images into their head-mounted video displays. The technology *simulates* the participants' perspectives and then swaps these simulations, offering them first-person point of view shots similar to what a viewer or gamer might encounter in a film or videogame. However, the combination of video technology with orientation trackers allows for an experience that moves beyond such still limited point-of-view experiences where the viewer or player physically speaking is not only in a fixed position, but also always remains outside the screen. In 'W' *(Double U)*, because the visuals are omni-directional and fully occupy the participant's field of vision, appearing unframed and unmediated, the participant is not looking at the projected world, but is virtually surrounded by that world. Moreover, she is able to physically move around in that virtual world, creating a particular presence. It is interesting to see how this technologically advanced simulation relates to empathy as simulation.

According to Ratcliffe empathy as simulation is an act of imagination in which we project our own experiences on someone else, creating a first-person access to the other's experiences. From a "me" we try to relate to a "you," by imagining that this you is *as* me. In 'W' *(Double U)* this process seems to be radically reversed. The reversal can be located on the level of who is imagining what. The participant does not have to imagine what the other participant as a "you" and her experiences are like, or as in this particular case what her perspective is like. Instead it is the technology that offers the participant a simulation of that perspective. It is from this simulated perspective the participant needs to consciously negotiate her own presence in a transitional and unstable space and to somehow ground herself.

In 'W' *(Double U)* because of the technologically induced swap of vision we could argue a *second-person access* becomes available to one's *own* experiences: a "you" from which one can experience oneself. This perspective is not so much the product of an act of imagination on the part of the participant, but on the part of technology. The technology being used simulates someone else's first-person perspective and projects it "on" the visual field of the participant. The result is a perceptual clash. As I have described before, the inherent "otherness" of this perspective, and the participant's conscious perception of this otherness, triggers a process of perceptual negotiation in the participant who needs to bring her own embodied perspective in congruence with the projected, simulated perspective.

From the perspective of its technology, 'W' *(Double U)* reveals that a swap of vision in the end can result in a renewed and intensified corporal awareness of one's own presence in the world. It also suggests that, dramaturgically speaking, the swap of vision is not steering towards an empathetic understanding of the other as a subject, but rather towards a corporal understanding of the otherness of the world one finds oneself in and needs to cope with. This line of reasoning allows for framing the performance within the cultural context of our mediatized society. We could argue that the experiment demonstrates how innovative immersive technologies both help to create new (virtual) realities that we can live in, and function as particular interfaces that mediate our access to those realities, allowing (or forcing) us to find ourselves in the world in new ways. What 'W' *(Double U)* through the strategy of the head-swap helps to make tangible on an experiential level for its participants is how both our reality, and our presence in it, are no fixed givens, but unstable perceptions that need to be actively negotiated in order to make sense.

Discussed from this point of view, it seems that having participants look at the world from someone else's perspective CREW is using this "other" perspective merely as a tool to create and provide access to that world. However, the act of relating to the "otherness" of this perspective is not addressed as a theme or experience that in itself is worth engaging with. Still we could argue that the performance produces a particular kind of empathy, if we approach empathy as a form of simulation. Interestingly enough, despite the obvious differences between the technological simulation of a particular point of view, as we can find in 'W' *(Double U)*, and human simulation as an act of imagining what another subject might experience, as discussed by Ratcliffe, the effect empathically speaking appears to be the same: the engagement with someone else's perspective implies primarily an engagement with our own perspective and our own experiences and as such in the end seems to be a truly first-person affair.

But does 'W' *(Double U)* also allow for a kind of engagement that is not directed toward a more intense and conscious understanding of our own presence, but to a better understanding of the other? In the next paragraph, drawing on Ratcliff's ideas about "radical empathy," I will introduce an alternative reading of empathy in 'W' *(Double U)*, foregrounding its intersubjective dimensions.

RADICAL EMPATHY

Like Ihde, Ratcliffe is particularly interested in the supposed limits of our perception. However, whereas Ihde emphasizes the role technology plays in locating and maybe even surpassing these limits, Ratcliffe focuses on a particular attitude from which to experience what might seem to be out of our perceptual reach. Ratcliffe argues that some forms of experience remain unintelligible for others, unless we adopt what he calls "a phenomenological stance" (473). Instead of accepting that some forms of experience are out of bounds to phenomenology, Ratcliffe suggests that these need to be approached as a "phenomenological challenge." Ratcliffe calls for a kind of engagement that moves away from empathy as a first-person act of imagination: "[p]henomenological enquiry needs not be an exclusively first-person affair; it can incorporate a distinctive kind of engagement with the experiences of others" (474).

Adopting a phenomenological stance according to Ratcliffe can amount to a way of "doing phenomenology" that enables "radical empathy," a distinctive kind of empathy that requires letting go of our habitual understanding of the world around us, and "allows us to contemplate the possibility of structurally different ways of 'finding oneself in the world'" (474). Although Ratcliffe focuses mainly on forms of experience that occur in psychiatric illness and points to the therapeutic significance of empathic understanding, his ideas are interesting with respect to the work of CREW, especially when we consider that CREW claims on its website that 'W' *(Double U)* creates a "*schizophrenic* relationship with your immersive counterpart" (CREW, Performances & Installations).

If we analyze 'W' *(Double U)* from the perspective of radical empathy, we can see how the performance entails a phenomenological challenge, confronting its participants with an alienating experience—perceiving the world from a perspective that does not align with their own embodied position—that can only become intelligible if they are willing to adopt a phenomenological stance and to let go of their habitual understanding of the world. The performance invites its participants to experience, to contemplate and to actively deal with what it means to look from someone else's perspective, a radical other way of finding yourself in the world. As such the performance stretches the boundaries of phenomenological enquiry as an exclusively first-person affair.

The participants depend on each other for their sight. They have to collaborate in order to create a stable vision for both of them. Not only, as Vanhoutte and Wynants stress, do they tend to unify the divergent ontologies of the real and the virtual to a meaningful experience in a process of synaesthetic negotiation, more importantly they come to an unified understanding of the actual situation *with each other*. Looking through each other's eyes simultaneously implies moving along with one another, tuning in to each other movements, striving for a shared understanding of the situation, and opening oneself up to the other, sharing experiences. 'W' *(Double U)* therefore is as much about negotiating co-presence as it is about negotiating presence.

The performance reminds us that we cannot think about subjectivity, without taking into account intersubjectivity. I agree with philosopher Christopher Seel, who suggests that it is only within the context of a presupposed communality in the life experiences of others that we can experience and reflect upon our own subjectivity (Kattenbelt 31). Ratcliffe argues that in phenomenology, this communality is often taken for granted or even denied:

Our phenomenology incorporates much that is not specific to interpreter or interpreted, much that is not experienced as 'mine' in contrast to 'yours' or vice versa but taken for granted as shared. Important aspects of our experience are therefore eclipsed by an exclusive focus upon what a person attributes to herself as opposed to others. Radical empathy, in contrast, involves suspending the world that heterophenomenology[2] and other approaches take for granted as a backdrop to interpretation. In the process the sense of belonging to a shared world comes to light as a phenomenological achievement, one that is prone to considerable variation in structure. It thus reveals a realm of interpersonal difference that otherwise eludes us (490–91).

'W' *(Double U)* is an experiment that brings its participants in a situation in which their sense of belonging to a world is disturbed on the level of embodiment. In order to regain that sense of belonging, they have to act together. I would like to suggest that 'W' *(Double U)* as an experimental case of "doing empathy" in a radical practical way raises an embodied awareness in its participants of how their world is first of all a shared lifeworld. Moreover, it allows them to experience how their sense of belonging to the world is neither a given nor a fixed state of being, but something that indeed needs to be achieved in actual relation to and in collaboration with others—others with whom we share the world but from whom we differ radically nonetheless.

From the perspective of the actual behavior of the participants looking at the world from someone else's perspective implies a thorough commitment with and involvement in the world we live in with others. As such this performance creates a phenomenological stance from which a radical empathy with others, other perspectives, and other experiences becomes possible.

MOVING BEYOND THE METAPHOR?

'W' *(Double U)* starts out from the phenomenological question what happens if two people switch their field of vision. On their website CREW wondered what it would be *like* to look out at the world from someone else's head. Using the world "like" already indicates that CREW was well aware of not being actually able to have people look out from someone else's eyes.

However CREW's experiment is an attempt to *simulate* this experience, using innovative technology to move beyond the limits of human perception. How do you simulate an experience that lies beyond our perceptual reach? Necessarily such simulation is grounded in certain assumptions about what this particular experience *might* entail. Some insight in the assumptions CREW has been working on might be gained from asking what the technology is actually simulating in this performance.

In discussing the head-swap technology in their article about *'W' (Double U)*, Vanhoutte and Wynants speak both of "fields of vision" and "perspective," terms that I have used interchangeably. However, although clearly related, there are some differences between both terms that are worth accounting for. I follow Maaike Bleeker here who suggests that it is "important to distinguish between three different subjects involved in the event of visuality" (Bleeker 10). Bleeker speaks of "the subject seen" (that what is there to be seen), "the subject seeing," and lastly the "subject of vision" that mediates between the two as a position from which to see (10). The concept of perspective therefore not only entails what is there to be seen from a particular position, but also the subject position. Obviously the actual subject seeing, her subjectivity, is influencing what is there to be seen. Precisely this subjectivity of the one who is seeing, I would argue, is remarkably absent in *'W' (Double U)*.

As I mentioned before in *'W' (Double U)*, the environment is filmed from the top of the head of each participant. The images that are the result of this live recording are all shot from this radical first-person perspective and function as a simulation of the field of vision of the participant. Technically we can say the field of vision of the camera is roughly similar to that of the participant because what is there to be seen is the same for both the camera and the participant. In this respect *'W' (Double U)* indeed entails the switch of fields of vision between two participants, although strictly speaking it is the simulations of these fields of vision that are swapped. And it is precisely for this reason that we cannot speak of an actual switch of perspective because perspective is not only about what is there to be seen for a subject from a certain position, but also implies the subject seeing.

In *'W' (Double U)* perspective is limited to a (simulated) spatial position from which to see and experience. However, how we see and what we see from a particular perspective clearly is not only a matter of position, but also of whom we are as biological, cultured, gendered, and historical beings. What the performance technologically is unable to simulate is the subjectivity of the participant to whom the perspective belongs. The participant is not looking from someone else's perspective but from someone else's simulated position. Obviously, not only human perception has its limits, so has technology. *'W' (Double U)* might allow its participants to embody a position that originally is not their own, and that is made available through technology. In that respect the performance does offer them a new perspective. But the participants cannot embody the subjectivity of that position, nor can they escape from bringing their own subjectivity into their experience.

So we might conclude that the subjectivity of others by definition cannot be experienced from an inside, even not from a simulated inside, perspective. Indeed, the metaphor "to look at the world from someone else's perspective" necessarily remains a metaphor. Nonetheless even then the experiment does shed light on what is at stake when people are forced to look at the world from a position that is not theirs. As we have seen, the experiment opens up to two different kind of experiences that are inextricably bound to each other: on the one hand an intensified awareness of one's own presence, on the other hand an intensified awareness of one's co-presence. In both cases this heightened awareness is the result of being positioned in an unstable reality, a world to which we do not seem to belong and that needs to be actively negotiated both by ourselves and in relation to others. Whereas it could be argued that CREW "does" the head-swap, switching the fields of vision for the participants, the participants are in the end "performing" it, actively and physically acting out a new reality. Looking, as the swap of vision demonstrates, is revealed as a never "just looking," but also always embodied *act* through which we not only make ourselves present in a world but also present to others.

If we cannot relate to the subjectivity of others, to their particular understanding and experiencing of the world from the inside, we'd better approach it from the outside using our empathetic capacities. This implies that on the one hand we need to present ourselves and our experiences to others, whereas on the other we need to be open to their experiences. And if radical differences between people's perception cause trouble in understanding and relating to the other and her world, we need to be willing to let the other guide us in her world, so that we can find out about other ways of being in the world. This is what 'W' *(Double U)* as a particular experimental case of both doing and performing phenomenology can remind us of.

NOTES

1. An interesting but concise overview and analysis of CREW's work by Vanhoutte and Wynants can be found in their "Instances: The Work of CREW with Eric Joris".
2. Heterophenomenology, a term introduced by Dennett in *Consciousness Explained* (1991), refers to a phenomenological approach where "first-person descriptions are treated as fictional narratives that are ultimately accounted for in non-phenomenological, third-person terms" (Ratcliffe 490).

WORKS CITED

Bleeker, Maaike. *Visuality in the Theatre. The Locus of Looking*. Houndsmill: Palgrave MacMillan, 2008.
CREW. "Performances & Installations." Web. June 2014. <http://www.crewonline.org/art/projects>.
Dennett, Daniel C. *Consciousness Explained*. London: Penguin, 1991.
Goldman, Alvin. *Simulating Minds: The Philosophy, Psychology, and Neuroscience of Mindreading*. Oxford: Oxford UP, 2006.
Ihde, Don. *Postphenomenology and Technoscience*. New York: SUNY P, 2009.
———. "Stretching the in-between: Embodiment and Beyond." *Foundations of Science* 16.2 (2011):109–118.

———. *Experimental Phenomenology. Multistabilities*. 2nd edition New York: SUNY P, 2012.
Kattenbelt, Chiel. "Intermediality in Performance and as a Mode of Performativity." *Mapping Intermediality in Performance*. Eds. Sarah Bay-Cheng, Chiel Kattenbelt, Andy Lavender and Robin Nelson Amsterdam: Amsterdam UP, 2010. 29–37.
Ratcliffe, Matthew. "Phenomenology as a Form of Empathy." *Inquiry* 55.5 (2012): 473–495.
Seel, Martin. *Die Kunst der Entzweiung: Zum Begriff der ästhetischen Rationalität*. Frankfurt am Main: Suhrkamp, 1985.
Stein, Edith. *On the Problem of Empathy*. Trans. W.Stein. Washington: ICS Publications, 1989.
Stueber, Karsten. *Rediscovering Empathy: Agency, Folk and the Human Sciences*. Cambridge MA: MIT P, 2006.
Vanhoutte, Kurt, Nele Wynants, and Bekaert, Philippe. "Being Inside the Image: Heightening the Sense of Presence in a Video Captured Environment through Artistic Means: The Case of CREW." *Presence 2008*. Eds. A. Spagnolli and L. Gamberini. Padova: CLEUP, 2008. 157–162.
Vanhoutte, Kurt and Nele Wynants "Instances: The Work of CREW with Eric Joris." *Mapping Intermediality in Performance*. Eds. Sarah Bay-Cheng, Chiel Kattenbelt, Andy Lavender and Robin Nelson Amsterdam: Amsterdam UP, 2010. 69–74
———. "Performing Phenomenology: Negotiating Presence in Intermedial Theatre." *Foundations of Science* 16.2 (2011): 275–284.
Zahavi, Dan. "Expression and Empathy." *Folk Psychology Re-assessed*. Eds. D.D.Hutto and M.Ratcliffe. Dordrecht: Springer, 2007. 25–40.
———. "Empathy, Embodiment and Interpersonal Understanding: From Lipps to Schutz." *Inquiry* 53 (2010): 285–306.

13 Performance as Media Affect
The Phenomenology of Human Implication in Jordan Crandall's *Gatherings*

Mark B. N. Hansen

In his 2011 prize-winning, critical-creative performance piece, *Gatherings*, media artist Jordan Crandall addresses a crucial challenge posed to performance studies by the development of what I have elsewhere called "twenty-first-century media" (Hansen, *Feed-Forward: On the Future of 21st Century Media*). As a form of media that operates predominately beneath or beyond the registers of human sense experience and for purposes other than storing such experience, twenty-first-century media would seem to fall outside the "scope of capture" of the performing body as it has been articulated by performance theorists over the last several decades. The question I want to pursue here is whether this situation—the disjunction between media's operationality and the scope of human phenomenology—marks the end of the line for performance studies' extraordinarily fruitful investment in the body as a nexus for capturing the richness and variety of the sensory world; or if, by contrast, it constitutes a productive challenge that calls on us to rethink, and to radicalize, some of our assumptions concerning the functioning of the phenomenal body and its correlation with the environment/world.

To explore this question, and the imperative it would seem to institute for a "shift" in the phenomenological experience of the performing body that would somehow broadly parallel the shift to twenty-first-century media, I propose to track the shifting vicissitudes of Crandall's performance as he submits his own performing body to forces of a media environment that operate predominately outside his attentional registers and modes of conscious control. More precisely, I want to track the development of Crandall's performance as the activity of his performing body becomes *implicated within* broad, though specifically technical, environmental confounds—"diffuse, 'animated' surrounds" that offer "cognitive and ontological supplements to human agency" (Crandall, "Performance Interface for *Gatherings/Gatherings* Player")[1].

"Implication" introduces a counter-concept to phenomenological intentionality. Like the latter, implication designates a relation between an experiential event and an objectivity informing that event, but it differs fundamentally from intentionality on the question concerning the status of that objectivity. Eschewing any phenomenological reduction designed to transpose worldliness into a content of consciousness, implication involves the causal impact of worldly materiality on an experiential unity that cannot be reduced to the pure status of consciousness. More simply stated, implication marks an infiltration of agency that is the precise opposite of the phenomenological *epoché*: in implication, worldly materiality operates on and through an agent (or unity of experience) in ways that evade capture, mastery, or direct presentification by or to that agent.

Gatherings is a one-person critical performance piece in which the protagonist, Crandall himself, performs a theoretical text in conjunction with a shifting background of media feeds detailing various appearances or presentifications of technically gathered data. The piece stages an encounter of the gradually evolving, internally generated yet outwardly expressed content of Crandall's lived experience with an externalized, omnipresent technical system of surveillance and computational analytics that continuously feeds multiple flows of information into the present situation across diverse scales and domains. The interest of the work, and hence its role as exemplar for phenomenology's shifting status in contemporary performance, concerns how the influx of technically gathered environmental information transforms the qualitative flux of intimate lived experience.

I experienced Crandall's performance, in a version entitled *Gatherings 1: Event, Agency, and Program*, at the *Transmediale* festival in Berlin on February 3, 2011. The performance took place in a large auditorium, with a sparsely equipped stage featuring the artist sitting at a desk, rigged-up with a microphone, and surrounded by a set of screens of different sizes and dimensions. As the performance proceeded, and in seeming mimetic correlation with the increasing frenzy of the media flows surrounding him, the artist abandoned his sitting position and came to pace, sometimes in slow wide movements, sometimes in more frenetic, close-range motions, all around the stage area. Through this kinetic assimilation of bodily movement to the rhythm of the informational flows, as well as through the ideational flux of Crandall's theoretical incantations, the performer's bodily integrity and separation from the environment of media flows gradually gave way to an interpenetration of his perspective and footing with the technical viewpoints of the data fed into the performance space in the form of images on screens and auditory information. The result of this process of boundary dissolution is the shift from an intentional distance on environmental information to a mode of implication where the performer's body-mind itself arises within *and* from out of the data flows surrounding it and where it can be thought of as a composition with and of such flows. It is the process of this transformation from intentionality to implication that I am seeking to theorize here.

Supplementing this experiential account of the performance with the artist's own descriptions as well as his extremely prescient reflections on the situation of contemporary media,[2] we can understand Crandall's performance as an opportunity for experimenting with media as the vehicle for a certain reduction (*epoché*) of what we might well call "the bodily attitude." What is at stake in it, as I have already noted, is the possibility to *reverse* the phenomenological method: to move from intentionality to implication, understood as a fundamental *non-differentiation* of body and world that necessarily underlies any intentional distance.

This approach to *Gatherings* finds corroboration in Crandall's description of the performance's aim: to induce compositions that exceed the bounds of the intentional correlation. *Gatherings*, Crandall notes, is designed as:

> [a] performative study of the nature of the event and the new forms of awareness, cognition, and material agency that are emerging in data-intensive environments. It is about how things come together *as matters worthy of attention*: how actors assemble, relate, and affiliate in entities and phenomenal occurrences that are more than the sum of their parts.
> (Crandall, "Summary of *Gatherings*," emphasis added)

The question of "how things come together as matters worthy of attention" is the key here, and, though it remains implicit in this passage, it is precisely *the status of attention* that comes into question in Crandall's performance. Not only, that is, does the gradual implication of Crandall's performing body within broader techno-environmental networks displace consciousness from its position as the experiential frame of reference, but—more radically still—his implication puts into question the assumption that attention comprises the achievement of a single, unified or coordinated, higher-order system. In the place of such a view, implication introduces a model of attention as a confluence of operations occurring at various levels, timeframes, and with reference to a number of distinct systems, which only come into one during the movement of performance itself.

In my study of twenty-first-century media, I have referred to this situation as "operational overlap," where consciousness operates in overlap with the (from its perspective) "more primitive" processes comprising its components (*Feed-Forward*). On this account, and in direct contrast with the paradigm of emergence that has cascaded outward from the sciences of complexity into the social sciences and humanities, the "total situation" of consciousness comprises the modes of attention distinctive of consciousness *plus those modes particular to the more primitive forms of bodily contact with the environment* that occur simultaneously with, and in quasi-autonomy from, consciousness proper.

By thematizing the transformation of Crandall's own modes of awareness, *Gatherings* provides an example that can help us to reconceptualize human attention beyond its historic limits. *Gatherings* submits the body-mind of its protagonist to a process of enworlding—implication into environmental media fluxes—that opens up modes of contact between body and environment that can no longer be captured by the perceptual and intentional circuits central to phenomenological modes of theorizing. The reconceptualization of attention at issue in *Gatherings* thus centers on the complexification of consciousness itself: supplemented by "data of sensibility" that lie outside its scope of capture—data that place the bodymind in "direct," non-perceptually mediated contact with what I have elsewhere called "worldly sensibility"[3]—consciousness comes to enjoy a split vocation. While it continues to exercise its traditional function as sense perceiver, consciousness also increasingly comes to operate in a supervisory role with regard to the embodied and environmental impact of another domain—worldly sensibility—that is beyond its direct grasp.

Another, and perhaps more fundamental, element of such a reconceptualization of attention involves the relationship between embodied performance and the expanded scope of sensibility that is made available—and manipulable or "programmable"—by and through twenty-first-century media. Crandall's performance foregrounds the body's continuous contact with the sensible environment—its non-perceptually accessible, direct sensory proximity to the world—and, via the recursive circuits enacted by his performing bodymind with the informational flows surrounding him, mobilizes this contact as the basis for a new mode of "being-in-the-world." Put more simply, *Gatherings* not only foregrounds technical accessibililty to non-phenomenal elements of experience, but it also, and most crucially, folds the data thus gathered back into embodied performance, where it appears not as contents of consciousness but as data concerning feelings and affects generated by the body's environmental dissolution.

In this sense, we can say that *Gatherings* treats the performing body as the locus for an expanded operation of attention, one that is both perceptual (as it has always been) and in the sense we have just begun to specify. With respect to the phenomenology of performance, it is this second, bodily sensible dimension of attention that deserves attention: Crandall's performative self-implication into media circuits of sensibility exposes a bodily sensible form of attention that has been largely unavailable prior to the advent of twenty-first-century media. By gathering data concerning the body's ongoing engagement with worldly sensibility and by allowing such data of sensibility to contribute *directly* to the ongoing process of the performance, Crandall's deployment of twenty-first-century media transforms the body's contact with sensibility into a form of attention in its own right.

A NEW PHENOMENOLOGY FOR PERFORMANCE?

It is with respect to this bodily dimension of attention that, I suggest, we can begin to take stock of *Gathering*'s contribution to extant work at the nexus of performance and phenomenology. Let us consider the fundamental claim that opens Sally Banes's and André Lepecki's introduction to their 2007 anthology, *The Senses in Performance*:

> Performance practices [are] privileged means to investigate processes where history and body create unsuspected sensorial-perceptual realms, alternative modes for life to be lived. To carry out the task of analyzing "the senses in performance" is also to carry out bio-political investigations of the many critical thresholds where the corporeal meets the social, the somatic meets the historical, the cultural meets the biological, and imagination meets the flesh (1).

From my perspective, the crucial insight of this passage is that performance—or more precisely, the encounter of body and environment—produces possibilities for knowing, experiencing, and living *that are only accessible sensorily*, that can only take place in the medium of sensibility.

Yet, almost as soon as they have made the important gesture to open sensibility as a new frontier of experience, Banes and Lepecki undercut its radicality by linking sensibility to appearance:

> But what still needs to be articulated more clearly if we want to build a theory of the performance of the senses is that any such performance generates and reveals subjacent economies and politics of appearing. Indeed, whether this appearing, this stepping of the sensed object or subject into the fore of perception, happens visually, or happens rather as an olfactory, or tactile, or proprioceptive, or gustatory, or aural experience (or as a combination of, or synesthesia between, different sensory organs), the imbrication of sensory perception with language and memory makes the senses a matter of urgency for understanding the conditions under which the body interfaces with and assigns privileges to certain modes of the perceptible while condemning other modes to the shadows of the imperceptible and the valueless (2).

The focus on how sensory perception is "imbricated" with language and memory makes clear how much Banes's and Lepecki's phenomenological investment in the sensory is, as it were, always already compromised. For, so long as the role of the sensory is limited to how it affects the line dividing the perceptible from the imperceptible, and so long as the sensory is reduced to the operations of already extant sense organs operating in the service of producing sense perception, the promising conjunction of performing body with worldly sensibility remains—and cannot but remain—effectively untapped.[4]

This double reduction becomes a problem when the performing body is called upon to materialize elements of worldly sensibility that do not and cannot manifest directly to perception—that do not and cannot take the form of perceptual or phenomenological *appearances*. Such is the situation of our contemporary mediasphere.

Here we confront a definite limit to Jacques Rancière's post-Foucauldian theorization of a "distribution of the sensible," which would seem to be motivating Banes and Lepecki's development of a performance theory of the senses, and which arguably forms the basis for most contemporary conjunctions of phenomenology and performance.[5] Taken as the basis for an aesthetic program, the political agenda of Rancière's project—to confront reigning distributions of the sensible—can have no goal other than that of a phenomenological expansion, a widening of the scope of the perceptible. Yet this goal is precisely what becomes problematic in a world where the sensible itself has become operative—and has become fully manipulable—*without any need to cross over into the domain of perception*. From the standpoint of twenty-first-century media, and of the opening up of non-perceptible elements of sensibility it affords, the crucial question appears to be less that of how the sensible is distributed, than of how it is materialized in bodily performances and experiences *without ever entering directly into the domain of appearance at all*.

In light of this situation, let me propose a different conjunction of performance and phenomenology, one that eschews the Foucauldian-Rancièrean theme of sensory distribution in favor of a direct linkage between performance and sensibility. Following such a conjunction, the performing body shifts its role: no longer an object relative to a larger sensory distribution, the body instead becomes an element among others within a larger matrix of sensibility. Alongside this shift in the role of the body, we must revise our understanding of performance: no longer a capacity *of* the body, performance now designates an environmental event that involves but is not exclusively channeled through the body—an event that *implicates* the human through its robustly embodied contact with worldly sensibility. With performance theorist Sha Xin Wei, we must follow the turn to the body in phenomenology all the way down, or perhaps better, all the way out; we must, that is, embrace the "deeper turn to action, and to performance," and must follow this turn beyond the human, to a "less anthropological" understanding of performance "as the primordial flow of matter holding in suspension the problematic distinction between living and the inert" ("From Technologies of Representation to Technologies of Performance").

What does it mean to theorize performance as the production of an event that implicates the body without making it the center or agent of sensory processing? This is precisely the question Crandall poses in regard to his own "sense of control" over his own bodily "situation" in a recent essay simply entitled, "Something Is Happening." Crandall writes:

> The situation involves not only how I see, but how I am seen. It involves not only an image of control but a sense of it [...] The situation is the apprehended totality of the happening-event—the assembling-event as sensed and known. It includes not only my subjective position, but my own sense of self-in-movement; not only my objective position, but my

moving self as sensed by others. It includes not only my position but my sensory-corporeal movement as sensed from within and without: my passage.

("Something Is Happening")

Crandall's *Gatherings* stages an experiment with bodily implication in the situation in just this sense, by allowing his own bodily contribution to the situation to coalesce with its happening, and thereby to embrace the imperceptible fluxes of sensibility materialized by the technical elements of the situation and to let his own embodied experience be carried along by it.

That is why Crandall's *Gatherings* exemplifies the promise of performance in a world newly activated by technologies of sensibility, following the account of artist and media critic Chris Salter. According to Salter, twenty-first-century performance breaks with the machine paradigm in a decisive manner—by eschewing the body as the site of a technical infiltration in favor of a dispersion of body into larger, technically mediated or information environments:

> As photography and motion pictures in the fading moments of the nineteenth century appeared, suddenly revealing the microfluctuations of human movement, the raw body soon became the perfect machine embodiment of the new industrial age of socialism. With the reigning machine paradigm for the technologized body forming the start of the twentieth century, the prostheticized, computationally augmented or *data-formed* body frames the twenty-first. No longer conceived as a machine in the traditional sense of an organized heterogeneous assembly of parts, performance theorists and practitioners now see the contemporary body as something incorporated into larger than human systems—as something to be transcended through implants, prosthetics, sensors, actuators, and even genetic invasion.
>
> (*Entangled* 221)

Though I would stop short of characterizing the contemporary provocation of the body in performance as "transcendence" (hence my introduction of the concept of "implication"), Salter's account perfectly grasps how contemporary performance theorists and practitioners approach and deploy the body less as the site for the materialization of a linguistic or performative artifact than as an open-ended surface of contact with an environmental domain of sensibility that operates largely outside the restricted traditional channels of sense perception and conscious attention.

For art historian Amelia Jones, it is the world-disclosing power of the body that makes Merleau-Ponty such a resonant source for body artists in the 1960s and 1970s:

> The performative self, whose meaning and significance is not inherent or transcendent but derives "from the whole scene of his action,"

dramatically overturns the Cartesian self [...] The lived body, Merleau-Ponty observed in his [...] *Phenomenology of Perception*, is not discrete from the mind as vessel but is, in fact, the "expressive space" by which we experience the world (39).

Jones's concept of "expressive space" perfectly captures the way the body serves as host for multi-valenced, recursive flows of information subtending any and all subjective experience of the world. Body art, concludes Jones, "does not *illustrate* Merleau-Pontian conceptions of the embodiment of the subject and theories of the decentered self that we are now familiar with from poststructuralist theory; rather, it *enacts* or *performs* or *instantiates* the embodiment and intertwining of self and other" (38).

With this gesture toward Merleau-Ponty's late work, Jones points us to where performance theory should have gone all along in its effort to integrate the insights of phenomenology: the intertwining of flesh and world that is Merleau-Ponty's own answer to the impasses of his early conception of bodily intentionality. With his conceptualization of the intertwining or "chiasm," Merleau-Ponty gestures towards a non-intentional conception of co-implication of body and world that would overcome the impasse of his earlier method: "The problems posed in *Ph.P.* are insoluble," he writes in an important *Working Note* from 1959:

> because I start there from the "consciousness" — "object" distinction— —Starting from this distinction one will never understand that a given fact of the "objective" order (a given cerebral lesion) could entail a given disturbance of the relation with the world—a massive disturbance, which seems to prove that the whole "consciousness" is a function of the objective body— —It is these very problems that must be disqualified by asking: *what* is the alleged *objective* conditioning? Answer: it is a way of expressing and noting an event of the order of brute or wild being which, ontologically, is primary.
> (*The Visible and the Invisible* 200)

Rather than investing the body as the site for an activity that intends the world (the payoff of the notion of bodily intentionality as "I can," a notion Merleau-Ponty borrows from Husserl), co-implication centers around the body's implication within the flesh of the world. The body is itself flesh and is part of the flesh of the world.

The ensuing methodological shift from a phenomenology of bodily constitution to a bodily phenomenology of worldliness has been excavated by contemporary French phenomenologist Renaud Barbaras in a series of recent studies.[6] Barbaras's work has, in turn, served a primary role in my own effort (*Bodies in Code*) to theorize an account of technics in the late Merleau-Ponty that would update and move beyond the prosthetic approach of the *Phenomenology of Perception*. If we bring this shift to bear on the question of performance, what we encounter is an imperative to problematize the link between body and presentation or appearance—the very link that has been the most obsessive focus of recent efforts to conjoin performance with phenomenology. Whether in the form of Elin Diamond's or Bert States's respective accounts of how the bodily performance gives body to the theater,[7] or of Stanton Garner's provocative analyses of how Beckett's late plays challenge the limits of such embodiment,[8] or even of Jones's expositions of body art as an engagement with the flesh of the world, the attention of performance critics has remained firmly focused on the body as a site of production and constitution, and on the *presencing* of bodies in space as the *origin* of the phenomenon that is performance.

It is precisely this coupling of body activity and presence that *Gatherings* puts into question. The project seeks to invest the body as a *participant* in a larger operation of environmental eventuality, and not as the *agent* of the presencing of this event. *Gatherings* does not *channel* the environmental event *through* the body, but rather *inserts the body's experience into or within the larger operation of the environmental event*. In this respect, *Gatherings* takes up the trajectory opened by recent critics like Giannachi and Benford and Bay-Cheng et al., who foreground the continuum linking bodies to ecologies as an expanded terrain for the genesis of performance. For example, when Steve Benford and Gariella Giannachi theorize "hybrid time" and "temporal trajectories," their effort serves to correlate, in a robustly "open" manner, the construction of temporal experience with an "ecology of interfaces" that freely mix "different activities" and "flexible temporal structures" in order to "engage and disengage" participant experience "according to the circumstances of their everyday lives" (93).[9] Similarly, by shifting focus to the perception of observers, Robin Nelson expands the terrain for the genesis of performance in another, complementary direction: specifically, Nelson demonstrates how the interactions between perceiving bodies and media ecologies "challenge established modalities of experience" by, for example, demanding "modulations of the entire human sensorium" (16–17).[10]

Like these theoretical accounts, Crandall's performance foregrounds the fundamental transformation in the correlations linking the body to the environment. Thus it is no longer the time of the body that *constitutes or hosts* the presencing of the event. Rather, the environmental event operates a plurality of presencings that only partially overlap with the body's lived presence. Nevertheless, they operate as "causally efficacious" (Whitehead 168ff) elements informing this presence, as it were, from underneath.[11] To put this another, perhaps more direct, way, *Gatherings* engages and supplements the body in a *resolutely non-prosthetic* manner. Rather than expanding the body's capacity to take in and process the environment, *Gatherings* stages an encounter between body and environment in which the body is "exfoliated" precisely in order to become implicated in a process far vaster than itself.[12]

Gatherings thus forges a new link between phenomenology and performance, one focused not on how the body materializes—makes present—a script or idea, but on how the body itself operates within and as part of a larger environmental event. *Gatherings* makes central the way in which the body, in the very process of its implication into a larger environmental process, nonetheless furnishes a specific, highly partial, vantage point on that event. Rather than providing a sense of presentification (to employ Alfred North Whitehead's term for the self-referential immediacy of sense perception) of his own experience as it is occurring, Crandall's bodily experience functions more like an expression of the new situation in which he finds himself. What *Gatherings* explores is precisely whether and in what ways we can still think of this now extremely partial vantage point as a privileged one.

By performatively enacting the human bodymind's implication into mediated circuits of sensibility, Crandall's work discovers—indeed, *inaugurates*—new modes of "acting," in which the *propensity* of the situation as a whole holds sway over any delimited agency that may operate, already fully constituted, within it, including the agency of a human subject understood as a minimally transcendent or otherwise separable constituting force. Put more directly: as the performance proceeds, the agency driving Crandall's performing body gradually exteriorizes itself from his bodymind into the environment itself in which this latter is implicated and from which it is composed. Crandall's performing body thereby becomes the *expression* of a larger circuit of forces.

By correlating the process of implication with a new, technically mediated form of appearance, Crandall's *Gatherings* contextualizes the bodily phenomenology of worldliness against the backdrop of twenty-first-century media. When today's microcomputational sensors and predictive analytic systems feed data of sensibility forward into futural consciousness, they introduce technical mediation into the very heart of phenomenal appearance, and in so doing, call into question the autonomy of the transcendental subject of orthodox phenomenology. By technically contaminating the operation of appearance, a bodily phenomenology of worldliness contrasts explicitly with the phenomenology of constitution still central to much contemporary work in phenomenology: where the latter looks to consciousness to *constitute* phenomena, the former looks instead to the world—to the constant "depresencing"[13] of the world—as the source for the total situation within which appearances arise and can be made manifest to consciousness.

On this understanding, any appearance of worldly sensibility as a content of consciousness—as an element *constituted by* the activity of a separated and self-contained consciousness—is, at best, a derivative phenomenon, and one that has become increasingly superfluous in the environments of twenty-first-century media. Or, to put it more starkly, we could say that the inaugural dream of phenomenology—of consciousness coinciding with itself at the very moment of its constitution—has run its course: confronted with the networks of twenty-first-century media, consciousness has been forced to relinquish any operational role it may have in *creating* sensible presencing. In the worst case scenario, consciousness relinquishes this role to the marketing campaigns of contemporary data and cultural industries that do everything they can to bypass the domain of consciousness.[14] And in the best case scenario, one that is central to my argument in *Feed-Forward*, consciousness relinquishes its hopes to constitute the present and accepts a new, supervisory role over the complex process through which worldly sensibility presences. In this scenario, consciousness opens itself to the presentification of data of sensibility that it cannot experience directly, perceptually, and phenomenologically. Such data of sensibility is, as I have put it, fed-forward—from the moment of its sensible happening—into consciousness and, as such, comprises an expanded picture of the sensible field that is at issue in any attentional delimitation. *Feed-Forward* thus explains the mechanism whereby consciousness is permeated by the environmental outside: presentified to consciousness in the form of data from outside consciousness, data of sensibility can thus be said to "contaminate" the "intimacy" of consciousness with artifactually produced "contents" that are resolutely *not* "contents of consciousness" —that not only haven't been lived by consciousness, but that *cannot take a form that could ever be lived by consciousness* (Hansen, "Technics Beyond Technical Object").[15]

GATHERING AS IMPLICATION

Crandall's performance begins with the artist adopting the persona of a familiar figure, a man sitting at a café watching people pass by. Reminiscent of that icon of modernity, Poe's "man of the crowd," this figure is almost immediately displaced as the artist quickly swaps it out for that of an "observational expert sitting at the interfaces of an intelligence agency, interpreting movements on images, maps, and screens" (Crandall, "Summary"). No more than a third of the way into the performance, this figure is displaced in turn, as the specialized eye of the observational expert finds its agency surpassed by "the vast reservoirs of datasets" that yield their "patterns" only to a "calculative seeing" (Crandall, "Summary").

Enacting these discrete stages in the displacement of human seeing by machine vision, the performance features Crandall narrating the transformations of human agency and subjectivity—of his own agency and subjectivity—as various screen-based images and videos as well as environmental sounds materialize the agency of the environment and bring it to bear on his experience. The three main sections of the performance describe three stages in the advent of a hybrid agency composed of human elements implicated within larger technical circuits. As we witness the assimilation of the artist's subjective point-of-view into a broader environmental perspective, we participate in the gradual displacement of "the centrality of the human agent in the process of tracking" (Crandall, "Summary"): Within the broader environmental picture materialized by technical tracking, human agency enjoys no *de jure* privilege and can lay claim to no transcendence or mastery.

Gatherings pays careful attention to the ways in which the technification of the urban environment has modified the modes in which humans act, perceive, and sense. More specifically, and most crucially, it directly engages the operation of sensibility at the level of the total environment. With his self-implication into media fluxes beyond his perceptual grasp, Crandall accepts, indeed welcomes, the transformation wrought by twenty-first-century media, and he takes as the very basis for his practice some of the concrete ways in which today's microsensors and data-mining capabilities catalyze a wholesale revolution in the economy between narrowly subjective sensation and worldly sensibility.

In *Gatherings*, Crandall approaches this general transformative potential of twenty-first-century media through the specific lens of tracking technologies that tap into movement at a level common to all phenomena and operative *beneath* perception proper. Crandall's performance explores how the "algorithmic procedures" and "automated systems" of contemporary tracking systems operate within complex "distributed network environments" that vastly expand its scope. Augmented by microsensors and location-aware technologies that are typically embedded into mobile devices, automobiles, buildings, and urban spaces, contemporary tracking systems induce fundamental modifications not simply in how humans experience lived environments, but also, crucially, in how environments *themselves* directly contribute to the genesis of "environmental events." "Environments," Crandall explains, "become able *to directly sense* phenomena and respond to what they apprehend, in ways that complicate distinctions between body and space, as well as between human, artifact, and computer" ("Summary").

Consider how Crandall's piece eschews any simple thematization in order to implicate the agency of the human subject within the technological shift it chronicles. In contrast to theoretical writing, his own not excepted,[16] Crandall's performance is able to *express* the impact of this shift literally— *as* the progressive modification undergone by the artist (and, by extension, the spectator) across the duration of the performance. *Gatherings* advances a subtle, indeed subterranean, argument that the impact of the interoperationality of twenty-first-century media *can be accessed only via a logic of expression*, a logic that directly implicates embodied and enworlded modes of experience independently of their upward (and necessarily selectional or reductive) sedimentation into discursive conceptualization. Put another way, *Gatherings* engages the continuum between body and ecology first and foremost through and by means of the bodymind's transformation as it becomes implicated within its broader environmental logic.

To understand why, we need only consider Crandall's rejection of the media theoretical figure of the interface in favor of implication. As he sees it, the figure of the interface only serves to reinforce longstanding philosophical divides—between subject and object, human and world—that themselves stand in the way of a fuller theorization of what is at stake in twenty-first-century media. That is why *Gatherings* approaches the new sensing capacities of the technologized environment not "in terms of formed and distinct objects or subjects" but "in terms of their complexes of practices," which, moreover, it understands "as involving affective transmission and absorption"—elements that break down the separation between human and world—far more than "reflective distance" (Crandall, "Summary").

Displacing the "interface," which can only impose distance, Crandall installs what he calls the "program." More than simply algorithmic, the program is "a guiding principle of structural inclination" that is equally technical, social, and practical. Every program, claims Crandall, "is sensitive to the patterns, rhythms, and affects of its surrounding environment—speeds, material constitutions, and regulations; flows for pedestrians, vehicles, information, utilities, and goods." In this sense, every program operates as "a mechanism of awareness, as vast as the streets themselves, whose flickering presence it both gathers, reflects, and incorporates" (Crandall, "Performance Interface" Section 1.5). The program thus furnishes an alternative principle of organization—of *gathering*—that differs fundamentally from the figure of the subject: rather than synthesizing the environmental outside into a subjective construction, the program *implicates* subjectivization into the broader ecology of process.

In one description of how implication occurs, Crandall draws attention to the way the interoperationality of today's media environments compel human agents to attune their activity to the "inclinations" of larger compositions:

> In order to endure, I must continually "update," extend, maintain and be maintained in continuing moves. I must affiliate, cultivate my modulation in gatherings that can carry me forth. As I do so, I must negotiate adherence to the demands for movement and attendance that these affiliations seek. I must push forth and be pulled forth through gatherings and adjust myself to the prevailing terms of their movement-constitution, their structural inclination
> ("Performance Interface" Section 1.8).

Taken in its full radicality, Crandall's notion of attunement would require him to put the "I" in parentheses or under suspension, since it, the "I," emerges precisely and always transitorily from out of the process of gathering. In this it makes common cause with the conceptualization of affective attunement proposed by developmental psychoanalyst Daniel Stern: for Crandall no less than for Stern, what is at issue is precisely a process of attuning—a *gathering*—that occurs prior to and beneath the level of any self-referential, substantial subject or "I."

Like the experience of subjectivity as understood by Whitehead, the "I" of Crandall's performance is itself a composition, a *gathering*, of a host of agencies that act on one another and thereby generate intensity. Operating in the mode of "superjective potentiality,"[17] these agencies are in excess over their own proper subjective power. Actors, Crandall tells us at the end of Section 1

> solicit one another, act upon one another, recruit one another, harness and channel one another's transmissions. They are agency of one another. Concentrated and networked. Analytical and active. Objective and immersive. They band and disband, accumulate and release. They extend and consolidate. They attune [...] to the sensory, rhythmic and atmospheric exchanges that compose them.
> ("Performance Interface" Section 1)

With his claim that gatherings are *"agency of one another,"* Crandall taps directly into the power of the Whiteheadian superject: by hosting or staging superjectal relations, gatherings facilitate the interoperability—the inter-agency—of the world's worlding.

APPEARANCE AS TECHNICALLY ACCESSED SENSIBILITY, OR THE WORLD IS SELF-SENSING

With its conjunction of implication and potentiality, Crandall's performance helps specify how the transformation of human subjectivity explored here—its becoming-implicated within the propensity of a total, "originally environmental" situation—finds its source in the potentiality generated by twenty-first-century media's direct modulation of sensibility. To the extent that potentiality comprises the mode in which the settled world—worldly sensibility—expresses its power to create future worlds, the conjunction of implication with potentiality calls for a conception of subjectivity as *the power of superjectal potentiality*. Put very schematically, superjectal potentiality designates the power that accrues to process not because of any internal, subjective organization and processing, but because of its operation as direct expression of heteroaffective environmental forces. Superjectal potentiality thus constitutes nothing less than the power of the environment acting on and through delimited elements of its becoming, which is to say, in the mode of implication. It is precisely this dimension of superjective power that the bodymind deploys—or better, that is deployed *as bodymind*—when the latter is implicated by, though, and into the environment.

What remains to be explored is how this liberation of the propensity of the total, "originarily environmental" situation yields a notion of subjective implication that breaks with the orthodox phenomenological commitment to subjective transcendence. To this end, I shall consider a challenge recently advanced by Barbaras against Merleau-Ponty's final ontology, and that would by extension apply to any post-phenomenological ontology whose aim is to dissolve subject-object dualism and extend subjectivity beyond higher-order phenomenological beings.

The crux of this challenge concerns what Barbaras takes to be the failure of Merleau-Ponty's "monism of the flesh" to overcome the dualist impasse of *The Phenomenology of Perception*. For Barbaras, the flesh of the body and the flesh of the world cannot interpenetrate because the world cannot sense itself, the world is not itself sensible ("Les Trois Sense de la Chair" 23).[18] Because of this failure, Barbaras tells us that the body and the subject can never coincide. They designate what he considers to be distinct, and to some extent, non-correlated operations: on one side, the immanent, ontic body senses itself; on the other, the transcendental, ontological subject receives the appearance of the world. To Barbaras's mind, accordingly, the final result of Merleau-Ponty's ontologization of phenomenology can only be an "inconsistent concept:" a "doubling" of the flesh into two fleshes—flesh of the world and sensing flesh—that simply cannot be brought together.

Confronting Merleau-Ponty with Whitehead allows us to question precisely what remains unquestionable for Barbaras: the purported impossibility for the world to sense itself. What Whitehead brings to the table is an account of superjective subjectivity—and thus a source of sensing prior to any self-other split—that does not have to be possessed by a subject separate from or transcendent to the world. Subjectivity, for Whitehead, is generated from out of the world's worlding or depresencing, from the intensities produced by its vibratory tensions. On this score, Whitehead helps to reveal the radicality of Merleau-Ponty's final ontology, and in particular, to see precisely how it overcomes the subject-object split that attaches to any commitment to transcendence. Indeed, by excavating how worldly sensibility continuously gives rise to novelty, and thereby to its own renewal, Whitehead's account of process lends a concreteness to Merleau-Ponty's notion of the *écart* and to the "dehiscence" between sensing and sensed that it informs.

In their own account of Whitehead's proximity to Merleau-Ponty, philosophers William Hamrick and Jan Van der Veken focus on how Merleau-Ponty's final ontology of the flesh centers around a fundamental displacement of synthesis in favor of metamorphosis. The fruit of Merleau-Ponty's effort to dispense definitively with Edmund Husserl's concept of constituting consciousness, this displacement is intended to yield "a contact with being across its modulations or its reliefs," a contact that *would not be mediated* by any subjective *synthesis* (in Hamrick and Van der Veken, *Nature and Logos* 189). In the place of synthesis, what is needed is a subjectivity without a transcendental subject—a radically democratic, if still differentiated, distribution of subjectivity to all elements of worldly sensibility.

Conceptualized in relation to Whitehead's larger account of process, where both concrescences and superjects wield subjective power (Hamrick and Van der Veken 89), Merleau-Ponty's account of the *écart* and reversibility between sensing and the sensible helps to flesh out what is involved

Performance as Media Affect 237

in a conception of subjectivity without subject: specifically, it accords subjectivity, in other words, the power of sensing, to every entity in the world. Merleau-Ponty's reversibility thereby liberates superjectal subjectivity and installs it as the source of power of worldly sensibility. On his account, not only would every actual occasion become "on the basis of its sensibility to its past actual world that it incorporates within it," (89) as Hamrick and Van der Veken point out, but it would become because of the power of the sensibility *of all past actualities now operating as superjects*. Following such a reading, the power of superjectal subjectivity becomes autonomous from and broader than its operation within subject-centered concrescences: this power designates nothing less than the capacity for the world to sense itself, to be a primordial sensibility from which all else springs.

In preserving the distance between sensing and sensed without relying on intentionality to do so, Merleau-Ponty's conception of the *écart* in turn sheds light on the "oneness" of Whitehead's account of concrescence and of the superject: in both cases, it is precisely the structure of oscillation or reversibility that accounts for the force of sensibility. Understood in this way, reversibility helps to elucidate an important Working Note in which Merleau-Ponty specifies that the flesh of the world "is not self-sensing *like my flesh*" (*The Visible and the Invisible*, in Barbaras 26). Far from marking an either-or relation (being self-sensing or not), as Barbaras maintains it does (26), this specification might better be read as an opening onto a continuum of differentiation, a plethora of modes of self-sensing, only one of which is that of the human body ("my flesh"). By saying that the flesh of the world is not self-sensing *like my flesh*, Merleau-Ponty does not mean that the world is not self-sensing, but rather that the flesh of the world *is* self-sensing *in a different way than my flesh*, or more precisely, that it is self-sensing *in a host of ways all of which differ from that of my flesh*. We can thus conclude, with Hamrick and Van der Veken, that the world is not univocally or indifferently self-sensing, but also, *contra* Barbaras—and this is the fundamental point—that the world *is* self-sensing:

> [...] there are various degrees and modalities of reversibility depending on the degree of sentience possible. A 'univocal sense of flesh' would mean one kind of flesh with many modalities. [...] with regard to Merleau-Ponty's monism some entities, such as the pen, are clearly not sentient in the ways that we are. Others—such as the experiences of higher life forms—are very like our fleshly reversibilities. And there is a vast array of lower life forms with various degrees of sentience and, therefore, reversibilities (189).

As the fundamental operation of temporalization, sensible reversibility informs every actuality in the universe, from the most miniscule speck of dust to the greatest achievements of collective consciousness. At every level and scale of being, this reversibility yields a subjectivity *without* any subject, a superjectal subjectivity *prior to* and *necessary for* the emergence of any higher-order subject, including the transcendental subject of orthodox phenomenology.

CONCLUSION: A BODILY PHENOMENOLOGY OF IMPLICATION

As a specification of superjectal subjectivity, reversibility opens onto a sensibility produced by the causal efficacy of the world itself in all its variety. That is why reversibility makes up the general texture of worldly sensibility. Reversibility characterizes the human relation with the flesh of the world *in the same way* as it does any other relation. All sensible events, including human and human-implicating events, are concrete productions of worldly temporalization, of sensibility's self-proliferation.

The convergence of Whitehead's superjective subjectivity with worldly sensibility allows us to treat sensations as elements of the world, even when they are experienced (or "lived") by perceiving consciousnesses. Following this convergence, subjectivity can be accorded to *any entity that is capable of reversibility*—to any entity that is produced from other-sensibility and that generates further worldly sensibility on the basis of its own operation.

This transformation—of other sensibility into worldly sensibility—furnishes a recipe for conceptualizing how the proliferation of "objective" sensation accompanying the advent of mobile media and ubiquitous computing is able to generate an intensification of our properly *human* sensibility *that is at the same time* an expansion of the domain of *worldly* sensibility from which it arises. With the unprecedented capacities of our digital devices and sensors to gather information about behavior and about the environment, we literally acquire new "organs" for excavating extraperceptual dimensions of experience—our own as well as that of other entities.

By experimenting with the potential for the sensibility of twenty-first-century media networks to catalyze new forms of human experience, Crandall's *Gatherings* foregrounds the *exteriority* and *technicity* of these new organs in relation to the human body. Displacing his own agency as the privileged channel for media to enter experience, Crandall implicates his sensibility within the circuits and flows created by the ubiquitous media surrounding him precisely in order to open new possibilities for experience. Specifically, his self-implication allows this media environment to express its potentiality directly, as primary elements in the very gatherings in which Crandall himself is implicated and, importantly, to which he can bear (partially though illuminating) witness.

With this clarification, we arrive at a solution to—or rather a dissolution of—the problem posed by Barbaras. Far from requiring a subject that transcends the appearing of the world and that would have the duty of giving subjectivity to it, Crandall's bearing-witness entails nothing more than a "going-along-with" the gathering of potentialities. The subjective perspective his witnessing introduces is simply one perspective among others, and, as such, it remains partial and immanent to the gathering within which it emerges. If this perspective enjoys a privilege, it is one that differs in kind from the privilege Barbaras claims for the transcendent subject of phenomenological manifestation: for whereas the latter privilege sets the subject off from the world that manifests itself through it, the provisional privilege claimed by Crandall's performance positions the subject—or rather the coalescence of subjectivity that occurs around every human-implicating event of gathering—as fully immanent to the world and as directly responsive to the total situation of a concrete gathering.

Far from being a mere accident of its particular configuration, the partiality of the witnessing at issue in Crandall's piece is an endemic aspect of the experience of any gathering whatsoever. And what his performance underscores so effectively—here in marked contrast to most contemporary theorizations of computational networks and sensor technologies—is how the specifically *human* experience of gatherings remains central. By repositioning the human witness as a phenomenon that is partial and expressive in relation to the larger environmental event to which it responds and within which it arises, Crandall's performance manages to capture *both* the particular marginalization of the human subject that occurs as human bodyminds are implicated within twenty-first-century media networks *and* the continued, if repositioned, centrality of human witnessing that alone can make this implication, and the greater expansion of environmental agency it betokens, both apparent to and meaningful for *human experience*.

As a model for a new performative relation with the environmental outside, as well as a new conceptualization of the relation between performance and phenomenology, Crandall's *Gatherings* enacts the movement from treating media as a source for a human-centered mode of performance to an engagement with media as environmental in a radical, and as we put it above, non-anthropological sense. Media operate on and within the environment before they impact our narrow subjective acts, and they impact these acts not simply by providing them a "content" but by placing our bodyminds into a robust contact with worldly sensibility. We might thus want to speak in terms of a process of "reembodiment" and view such a process as the result of non-anthropocentric performance within highly mediated environments. For what happens across the duration of Crandall's performance—again as exemplar for experience in general—is a gradual disembodying of experience understood as a channeling of sensory fluxes through the filter of the body and a processual re-embodying of experience in the myriad fluid vectors that comprise the environment's performativity and that encompass the subjectivities informing bodymind phenomenality. The body thus undergoes a fundamental transformation, an emptying out of its synthetic constructions of environmental flux in favor of a thorough becoming-environmental: the body thus becomes a conjunction without synthesis of all of the ecological elements informing the situation in which it is implicated.

It is precisely through this dis- and re-embodying of experience that Crandall's *Gatherings* brings the fruits of a radicalized bodily phenomenology of worldly sensibility to bear on twenty-first-century media environments. His performance performs the shift from a phenomenology of performance that invests in the body as the site of presencing to a more complex model that views the body as a hinge linking environmental performativity (non–perceptually-accessible domains of sensibility) to bodily performance. The fundamental contribution of *Gatherings* cannot be dissociated from the impact it has on us *as media affect*: by way of its introjection of media into the very process of attention, *Gatherings* implicates us, its viewer-participants, into a larger, technically dispersed environmental performance. In this way, Crandall's *Gatherings* urges us to take seriously the significance of the post-anthropological mediation of worldly sensibility for thinking—and for *living*—our own self-reference. The hope his work inspires is the possibility for performance to engage phenomenology in a nonanthropocentric mode that brings the resources of phenomenology to bear not on some reduced subjective space but on the entirety of the mediated environment informing all experience. To follow this hope to its fruition, we must find ways to make its lesson bear on our own sense of self. Following our re-embedding within the multiscalar complexity of an always flowing, massively technified world, together with the re-embodying of our consciousness as superjectal subjectivity, we come to enjoy an expanded sensory contact with worldly sensibility that allows us, occasionally and always partially, to experience from the standpoint of environmental performativity, or more precisely, from the standpoint of our implication within such performativity.

NOTES

1. *Gatherings* was awarded the 2011 Vilém Flusser Theory Award for outstanding theory- and research-based digital arts practice, by the Transmediale Festival in collaboration with the Vilém Flusser Archive at the University of the Arts, Berlin.
2. See, for example, his article, "The Geospatialization of Calculative Operations," which engages many of the concepts deployed in *Gatherings*.
3. In *Feed-Forward*.
4. This same reduction can be found in contemporary phenomenology. For Don Ihde, for example, sensibility is always already subsumed into perceptual histories that correlate it with larger human and cultural configurations: "The histories of perception teach us that every version of microperception is already situated within and never separate from the human and already cultural macroperception which contains it" (Ihde 42). This point, of course, goes back to Heidegger's arguments concerning the "context of involvements" that surround sensations in any existential situation. On this point, see my essay, "The Primacy of Sensation."
5. See, for example, their historical account of the correlation of the senses and appearance: "In other words: as the senses shift in relation to social and cultural changes, what they also change are the political conditions of possibility for

entities, substances, bodies, and elements to come into a being-apparent" (Banes and Lepecki 2–3).
6. See, in particular, Barbaras, *Desire and Distance*, especially Chapters 2, 3, and 4; *Vie et intentionalité*, Chapter 1.
7. Diamond, "The Violence of the 'We;' States, *Great Reckonings in Little Rooms* 35.
8. Garner, *Bodied Spaces* 28.
9. I thank Eirini Nedelkopoulou for drawing my attention to this work.
10. I thank Eirini Nedelkopoulou for drawing my attention to this work.
11. The term "causally efficacious" refers to Whitehead's concept of "causal efficacy," which he introduces as an expansion of the domain of perception beyond sense perception.
12. On the concept of "exfoliation," see Gil, *Metamorphoses of the Body*.
13. Husserl's final assistant, Eugen Fink, coins the term "depresencing" [*Entgegenwärtigung*] to name the primordial operation by which the world continuously passes out of the present, out of its own self-prescencing. "Depresencing" features prominently in my "Ubiquitous Sensation."
14. I analyze the process of bypassing consciousness in *Feed-Forward*, Chapter 3.
15. The feed-forward structure of consciousness radicalizes Bernard Stiegler's understanding of tertiary retention as technical memories that are not lived by consciousness. What is, in Stiegler, a limitation due to consciousness's finitude—the fact that it can only live a small amount of content—becomes here a limitation of capacity: human consciousness can *never* live the contents or data of sensibility because these latter occur at levels of experience to which consciousness has no direct access. See Stiegler, *Technics and Time*, vol. 3. For an extended development of this criticism of Stiegler, see my essay, "Technics Beyond the Technical Object."
16. Crandall is, in his own right, an extremely acute critic of contemporary visual and sensory media. I discuss his theoretical work at length in *Feed-Forward*, Chapter 3.
17. Whitehead distinguishes two aspects of subjectivity—the subject and the superject—while insisting that they are both always involved in any subjective activity. The "subject" designates the process of subjectivity that is involved in "concrescence," Whitehead's term for the genesis of new actual entities (actual entities are the units of reality that are the topic of Whitehead's speculative account of how the universe must be in order for experience to be what it is). The "superject," by contrast, is a name for the subjective power that attaches to actual entities once their narrowly subjective genesis is complete, and they become elements of the settled world. Superjects are elements of the experiential world that have the potential to be revivified in new concrescences and in the experiential entities Whitehead calls "societies."
18. "It makes no sense to say that the world senses itself, is present to itself as is my flesh" (Barbaras, "Les Trois Sense de la Chair" 23).

WORKS CITED

Banes, Sally and André Lepecki. "Introduction: The Performance of the Senses," in *The Senses in Performance*, Eds. Sally Banes and André Lepecki. New York: Routledge, 2007.

Barbaras, Renaud. *Desire and Distance: Introduction to a Phenomenology of Perception*. Trans. P. Milan. Stanford: Stanford UP, 2006.

———. "Les Trois Sense de la Chair: Sur une Impasse de l'ontologie de Merleau-Ponty," *Chiasmi International* 10 (2008): 19–32.

———. *Vie et intentionalité: Recherches phénoménologiques*. Paris: Vrin, 2003.

Benford, Steve and Gabriella Gannachi. *Performing Mixed Reality*. Cambridge: MIT P, 2011.

Bay-Cheng, Sarah, Chiel Kattenbelt, Andy Lavender and Robin Nelson, eds. *Mapping Intermediality in Performance*. Amsterdam: Amsterdam UP, 2010.

Crandall, Jordan. "The Geospatialization of Calculative Operations." *Theory, Culture & Society* 27.6 (2011): 68–90.

———. "Performance Interface for *Gatherings/ Gatherings* Player." Web. July 2014. <http://jordancrandall.com/main/+GATHERINGS/index.html>.

———. "Something Is Happening." *Code Drift: Essays in Critical Digital Studies*, *C-theory*. 21 Apr. 2010. Web. July 2014. <www.ctheory.net/articles.aspx?id=637>.

———. "Summary of *Gatherings*." Web. July 2014. <http://jordancrandall.com/main/+GATHERINGS/index.html>.

Diamond, Elin. "The Violence of the 'We': Politicizing Identification." *Critical Theory and Performance*. Eds. Janelle G. Reinelt and Joseph R. Roach. Ann Arbor: U of Michigan P, 1992.

Garner, Jr., Stanton B. *Bodied Spaces: Phenomenology and Performance in Contemporary Drama*. Ithaca: Cornell UP, 1994.

Hamrick, William and Jan van der Veken. *Nature and Logos: A Whiteheadian Key to Merleau-Ponty's Fundamental Thought*. Albany, NY: SUNY P, 2011.

Hansen, Mark B. N. *Bodies in Code: Interfaces with New Media*. New York: Routledge, 2006.

———. *Feed-Forward: On the Future of 21st Century Media*. Chicago: U of Chicago P, 2014.

———. "The Primacy of Sensation." *Theory Aside*, Eds. Stout, Daniel and Jason Potts. Durham: Duke UP, 2014.

———. "Technics Beyond the Technical Object." *New Formations* 77 (2012): 44–62.

———. "Ubiquitous Sensation: Towards an Atmospheric, Impersonal and Microtemporal Media." *Throughout: Art and Culture Emerging With Ubiquitous Computing*. Ed. Ulrik Ekman. Cambridge: MIT P, 2012.

Ihde, Don. *Technology and the Lifeworld: From Garden to Earth*. Bloomington: Indiana UP, 1990.

Jones, Amelia. *Body Art: Performing the Subject*. Minneapolis: U of Minnesota P, 1998: 39.

Merleau-Ponty, Maurice. *The Visible and the Invisible*. Ed. Claude Lefort. Trans. Alphonso Lingis. Evanston: Northwestern UP, 1968.

Nelson, Robin. "Prospective Mapping" in *Mapping Intermediality in Performance*, eds. Sarah Bay-Cheng, Chiel Kattenbelt, Andy Lavender, and Robin Nelson. Amsterdam: Amsterdam University P, 2010.

Salter, Christopher. *Entangled: Technology and the Transformation of Performance*. Cambridge: MIT, P, 2010.

Sha, Xin Wei. "From Technologies of Representation to Technologies of Performance." *Critical Digital* 2. Harvard Design School. Apr. 2009. Web. June 2014. <http://topologicalmedialab.net/xinwei/papers/papers.htm>.

States, Bert O. *Great Reckonings in Little Rooms: On the Phenomenology of Theater*. Berkeley: U of California P, 1985.

Stern, Daniel. *The Interpersonal World of the Infant*. New York: Basic Books, 2000.
Stiegler, Bernard. *Technics and Time* vol. 3: *Cinematic Time and the Question of Malaise*, Trans. S. Barker. Stanford: Stanford UP, 2010.
Whitehead, Alfred North. *Process and Reality: An Essay on Cosmology*. New York: The Free Press, 1978.

List of Contributors

Maaike Bleeker is a professor of theatre studies and the head of the School of Media and Culture Studies at Utrecht University, The Netherlands. She graduated in art history, theater studies and philosophy at the University of Amsterdam and obtained her Ph.D. from the Amsterdam School for Cultural Analysis (ASCA). She is also active as dramaturge in theater and dance. She is the author of *Visuality in the Theatre* (Palgrave, 2008). She has published extensively in international journals and edited volumes and several books, including *Anatomy Live: Performance and the Operating Theatre* (AUP, 2008). Bleeker is the president of Performance Studies international (PSi, psi-web.org) and was the organizer of the 2011 world conference of Performance Studies international, titled "Camillo 2.0: Technology, Memory, Experience." www.theatrestudies.nl

Pannill Camp is an assistant professor of performing arts at Washington University in St. Louis, USA. His research interests are performance theory, theater architecture, and the historiography of modern western theater. His book *The First Frame: Theatre Space in Enlightenment France* (Cambridge University Press, 2014) examines the use of optical geometry in the theater architecture reform movement that unfolded in the second half of the eighteenth century in France, and argues that theater spectatorship during this period both helped articulate and was informed by empirical natural philosophy's encounter with the natural world. His dissertation won the Joukowski Family Foundation's Award for Outstanding Dissertation in the Humanities at Brown University in 2009, and his articles have appeared in *Theatre Journal*, the *Journal for Eighteenth-Century Studies*, the *Journal of Dramatic Theory and Criticism*, and in *Anatomy Live: Performance and the Operating Theatre* (Amsterdam University Press, 2008).

Jon Foley Sherman, Ph.D., is an independent scholar and an award-winning actor and deviser. His book, A Strange Proximity: Stage Presence, Failure, and the Ethics of Attention, is forthcoming from Routledge in 2015. Jon's articles and reviews appear in Performance Research, New Theatre Quarterly, Theatre Topics, Theatre Journal, and TDR, and he is has contributed a chapter to the forthcoming Routledge Companion to Jacques Lecoq. Jon has performed and directed in Europe and the United States, most recently debuting This Is Not For You at Fringe Arts in Philadelphia. You can find more on Jon at jon foley sherman.com.

Mark Hansen is a professor in the program in literature, the program in media arts and sciences, and the Department of Art, Art History and Visual Studies at Duke University, USA. His research, writing, and teaching focus on the role played by technology in human agency, environmental process, and social life. In work that ranges across a host of disciplines, including literary studies, film and media, philosophy (particularly phenomenology), science studies, and cognitive neuroscience, Hansen has explored the meaning of the relentless technological exteriorization that characterizes the human as a form of life. Hansen is the author of *Bodies in Code: Interfaces with New Media*, *New Philosophy for New Media*, and *Embodying Technesis: Technology Beyond Writing*. His book, *Feed-Forward: On the Future of Twenty-First-Century Media*, forthcoming from University of Chicago Press, explores the role of computational processes in today's media and their diffuse, nonperceptual impact on human experience.

Susan Kozel is a professor at the School of Arts and Culture at Malmö University, Sweden. She works at the convergence between philosophy, dance, and digital technologies. She has an active artistic practice and has published widely. Solely authored books include *Closer: Performance, Technologies, Phenomenology* (MIT P, 2007) and *Mobile Choreographies: Affect and Encryption in Urban Spaces* (in process). She is project leader of the Swedish Research Council's funded research project *Living Archives* and is on the advisory board of the Swedish School for Artistic Research.

Sigrid Merx is an assistant professor of theatre studies at the Department of Media and Culture Studies, Utrecht University, The Netherlands. In June 2009 she completed her Ph.D. thesis on video and the (re)presentation of time in theater. Her current research focuses on performative interventions in public space. Sigrid was convener of the IFTR working group Intermediality in Theatre and Performance from 2010–2013 and board member of PSi (Performance Studies international) from 2011–2014. She is currently one of the artistic directors of Platform-Scenography.

Joslin McKinney is an associate professor in scenography at the University of Leeds, UK. Joslin has a first class degree in theater design and ten years of professional experience as a set and costume designer. In 2008 she was awarded a Ph.D. for her practice-led study into the communication of scenography. She is lead author of the *Cambridge Introduction to Scenography* (Cambridge University Press, 2009), and she has published articles and chapters on the spectacle of scenography and the body of the spectator, empathy, and exchange in scenography and scenographic research methods. Joslin was co-director of the Performance Studies international (PSi) conference in Leeds, UK, 2012 and a member of the PSi board from 2011–2013. She is currently working on a book for the Palgrave Readings in Theatre Practice series entitled *Construction*, a critical investigation of the history and concepts of structures, objects, and materials in theater and performance practice.

Eirini Nedelkopoulou is a lecturer in theater at York St John University, UK. Her research interests are interactive art, digital media performance, and audience participation. She is co-editor of the special issue "Hybridities: The Intersections between Performance, Science and the Digital" (*International Journal of Performance Arts & Digital Media*, Taylor & Francis, Sept. 2014). For the last three years Nedelkopoulou has been co-convenor of the Performance and New Technologies Working Group for TaPRA (The Theatre and Performance of Research Association).

Philipa Rothfield is an honorary senior lecturer in philosophy at La Trobe University, Melbourne, Australia. She writes on philosophy of the body largely in relation to dance. She has looked at the work of Merleau-Ponty, Nietszche, Klossowski, and Deleuze, to see what each of these philosophers can bring to dance and also to see what dance brings to philosophy. Alongside these commitments, she has engaged in an ongoing but intermittent performance project with Russell Dumas (director Dance Exchange, Australia). She is a member of Footfall Ensemble (director Alice Cummins). She also reviews dance for RealTime, Australia and *Momm Magazine*, Korea. She is head of the editorial board for Dancehouse Diary and is the Dancehouse creative advisor. She is currently writing a monograph on philosophy and dance.

Gayle Salamon is an associate professor at Princeton University, USA. Salamon specializes in phenomenology, gender and queer theory, critical theory, and visual culture. She is the author of *Assuming a Body: Transgender and Rhetorics of Materiality* (Columbia University Press, 2010) on embodiment and transgender subjectivity. Recent articles include "Transfeminism and the Future of Women's Studies" in *Women's Studies on the Edge*, (Joan Scott, ed., Duke University Press, 2008) and "Justification and Queer Method, or: Leaving Philosophy" in *Hypatia: A Journal of Feminist Philosophy*, Vol 24 No. 1, winter 2009. She is currently at work on "Chronic Pain and the Language of the Self," a manuscript exploring narrations of bodily pain in contemporary memoir.

Peta Tait is a professor of theater and drama at La Trobe University, Australia. She is an academic scholar and playwright with a background in theater, dramatic literature, performance theory, and creative arts practice. She researches in the interdisciplinary humanities fields of emotions, body theory, and gender identity. She is the author of (among others) *Circus Bodies: Cultural Identity in Aerial Performance* (London Routledge, 2005) and *Performing Emotions: Gender, Bodies, Spaces, in Chek-*

hov's *Drama and Stanislavski's Theatre* (Aldershot Ashgate, 2002), and the editor of (among others) *Body Show/s: Australian Viewings of Live Performances* (Amsterdam: Rodopi, 2000). She was a member of the executive board of Performance Studies international from 2005–2009, and her visiting professorships include NYU Performance Studies in 2000 and the University of Helsinki in 2010.

Shirley Anne Tate is an associate professor in race and culture and director of the Centre for Ethnicity and Racism Studies in the School of Sociology and Social Policy at the University of Leeds, UK. She is also visiting professor in the Institute for Reconciliation and Social Justice at the University of the Free State in South Africa. Tate is the author of *Black Skins, Black Masks: Hybridity, Dialogism, Performativity* (2005) and *Black Beauty: Aesthetics, Stylization, Politics* (2009). She is particularly interested in exploring the intersections of "raced" and gendered bodies, "race" performativity, critical "mixed race," and Caribbean decolonial theory within the Black Atlantic diasporic context.

Phillip Zarrilli is emeritus professor of performance practice at Exeter University, UK; artistic director of The Llanarth Group; and research fellow at the Freie Universitat, Berlin. In 2015 he will direct Ota Shogo's *The Water Station* in Norway. In 2014 he directed Kaite O'Reilly's *The 9 Fridas* (Taipei Arts Festival). He is completing a new book, *(Toward) A Phenomenology of Acting*.

Index

Abstraction 9, 35–38, 44–48, 50, 148; Lived abstraction 9, 36, 45–46, 50
Actor 9–11, 21, 26, 31–32, 51, 75–94, 95n11, 123–124, 142–148, 235
Actor Training 10–11, 80, 83; Psychophysical 10, 75–76, 80, 83–84, 86, 88–89, 92, 95n10; *See also* Alexander Technique
Affect 3, 10, 14, 54, 56, 62–63, 68, 69–70, 72n4, 73n10, 173–174, 175, 178, 180–182, 222, 234, 240; Affective 56, 63–4, 68–70, 71, 173, 180, 182, 234, 235 (heteroaffective); Affectivity 179
Affordance 45, 51n8
Agency 11–12, 68, 70, 97, 99, 100, 102–103, 106, 108n2, 121–122, 125–128, 134–136, 190, 198–199, 222, 223–224, 231–233, 235, 238–239; Objects 9–12, 20, 22–28, 30–33, 33n1, 33n4, 39, 41–42, 64, 69, 82, 94n4, 115–116, 121–122, 124–128, 130, 133–134, 136, 190
Ahmed, Sara 7, 173; Queer Phenomenology 173
Alexander Technique 11, 97–102, 105–107, 108n7, 109n12; Inhibition 95n8, 99–101, 102, 105–106, 108n11; Contraction 99–100; Directions 99–101, 102, 106; Role of teacher in 100; "Means whereby" 100, 101, 102
Alexander, F. Matthias 97, 99–101
Ambiguity 1, 112, 142
Animals 11, 111–119; Dead 11–12, 111–115, 117–119; Skin of 114, 116–118; Entrails of 112–113; Rights of 113; In art 112–113; Taxidermy 114–115
Apprehension 23, 25, 27–29, 32, 123

Appearances (phenomenological) 21, 23, 26, 29–31, 226, 231
Arendt, Hannah 165
Attention 3, 5–10, 13, 15, 40–41, 63, 69, 70, 72n3, 76–78, 80–89, 91–93, 94n6, 116, 126, 130, 133, 136, 144, 146, 191, 193, 197–200, 224–225, 228, 230, 240
Austin, J.L. 31

Barad, Karen 6
Barbaras, Renaud 10, 177, 229, 235–239, 241n6, 241n18
Behavior 5–7, 14, 26, 33, 118, 177, 192, 195, 199, 205–6, 218, 238; Normative 7, 200
Bennett, Jane 121–122, 126–128, 135, 137
Bergson, Henri 37, 43–44, 47–48
Berthoz, Alain 47, 51n10
Bishop, Claire 13, 157, 159, 160, 170n5
Body 3–8, 11–2, 15, 21, 32, 37–39, 44–49, 51n7, 63–64, 68–70, 75 (brain-body), 81, 85, 89, 93, 94n4, 97–107, 108n2, 109n12, 109n20, 111–112, 114–119, 121, 126, 136, 140, 143–145, 148, 158, 161–163, 178, 180, 182, 187–191, 193–194, 201–202, 210–213, 222, 224–231, 233, 236–240, 241n12; Phenomenal 15, 79, 222; Body-mind 79, 81, 86, 97, 108n2, 114, 223–225, 231, 233, 235, 239
Boldrin, Dawn 191, 193–195
Bourriaud, Nicolas 16n2, 50n4, 157; Relational aesthetics 13, 16n2, 50n4, 157, 159–160
Bracketing 2, 9, 20, 33, 42, 56
Brannigan, Erin 36–37
Burrows, Jonathan 49
Butler, Judith 6, 173, 186, 192

Chiasm 121, 229
Choreography 9–10, 36, 44, 45, 46–50, 59–61, 72n6; Choreographer 35, 44, 57, 59, 62, 64, 72n6, 97, 109n12; Choreographic 9, 37, 39, 46–50, 93, 109n12
Cognitive science 10, 75, 78–80, 94n1, 94n5; Cognition 1, 3, 79, 224; Extended cognition 3; *See also* Mirror neurons
Community 5, 7, 13, 152, 157–169, 170n6, 170n8, 170n16, 170n17; Inoperative (community) 158–160, 162, 167, 170n8, 170n11, 170n17; Exclusion 163–164, 168; Inclusion 163–164, 168
Consciousness 2, 4, 6, 9–12, 20–23, 41–42, 75–79, 81–83, 87–89, 92–93, 95n8, 103, 104, 109n20, 135, 173, 178, 187, 208, 223–225, 229, 231–232, 236–237, 240, 241n14, 241n15; Aesthetic consciousness 29; Common consciousness 32; Embodied consciousness 76; Image-consciousness 21–33, 33n3; Being-in-the-world 2, 158, 225; Stage consciousness 21–22, 26–31; Perceptual consciousness 6, 14, 22–23; Pure consciousness 20
Crandall, Jordan 222–224, 227–228, 232–235, 238–240, 241n16; *Gatherings* 14–15, 222–225, 228, 230–231, 233–235, 238–240, 240n1, 240n2
CREW 14, 204–220
Cunningham, Merce 39

Dance 1, 35–50, 55–56, 58–59, 62, 72n2, 93, 95n11, 105, 107, 108n6; Dancer 39–40, 49–50, 57–59, 62, 67, 72, 97–98
Davis, Tracy 20, 51n6
Deleuze, Gilles 37–38, 43–44, 50n2, 97–98, 103–106, 108n3, 109n15, 109n17, 109n18, 109n19, 109n20; Deleuzian 11, 106; movement-image 37, 43–44, 47; time-image 37
Depresencing 231, 236, 241n13
Derrida, Jacques 2, 72n3, 168, 170n16, 181; Community 168, 170n16; Phenomenological reduction 2, 6, 9, 20, 29–32, 42, 222
Desire 108n11, 143–144, 173, 175–177, 179, 195–196, 199–200, 202, 241n6

Diprose, Rosalyn 7, 163, 165
Drama 21, 26, 124; Dramatic representation 36; Dramatic theatre 9; Drama theory 21, 24, 26
Drawing 57, 61–63, 65–68

Écart 236–237
Embodiment 3–4, 6–7, 13, 15, 38, 42, 44, 76–77, 87, 98, 144, 146, 148, 181, 187, 199–200, 206, 207, 208–209, 214–215, 218, 228–230, 239 (reembodiment)
Emotion 69, 129
Empathy 14, 181, 205–207, 214–218
Epidermal schema 173, 178–179, 182, 183
Epistemology 180
Epoché 2–3, 8, 20, 22, 29, 223–224; *See also* bracketing
Ethnographic 64, 67
Expectation 22–24
Experience 1–12, 14–16, 20, 23, 25–28, 30, 35, 36, 38, 41–43, 47, 50n2, 51n7, 54–55, 60–68, 72n4, 75, 76, 79–83, 87–88, 94n3, 94n4, 121–122, 125–126, 129, 132, 134, 137n3, 152, 156–157, 159, 161–162, 165, 170n8, 170n17, 173, 178, 182, 204–218, 222–234, 237–240, 241n15, 241n17; Experience (*the verb, not the phenomenon*) 56–58, 60, 64, 67–69, 145, 148, 149; Out-of-body-experience 210
Expression 14, 62, 69, 107, 130, 136, 191, 194, 196, 231, 233; Clothing 198

Fanon, Frantz 173, 175, 178
Féral, Josette 20–21, 30, 51n6
Fischer-Lichte, Erika 4, 36, 122
Foster, Susan 46–47
Forsythe, William 48–50
Franko, Mark 2
Freud, Sigmund 194
Fried, Michael 41–42

Garner, Stanton 4, 123, 230, 241n8
Gaze 20, 21, 72n7, 84–85, 88, 92–93, 118, 173, 178, 181, 200, 202
Gender 1, 7, 13–14, 142, 175, 186–187, 191–197, 199, 200–202; Effeminacy 197–198
Gibson, James J. 45, 51n8
Goebbels, Heiner 122, 124–126, 132

Goffman, Erving 5, 6
Graham, Dan 48, 157
Graham, Martha 39
Grosz, Elizabeth 7, 108n4, 128

Habit 7, 10–11, 15, 57, 69, 97–103, 106, 107, 108n6, 109n16, 115, 193
Hansen, Mark 3, 14–15, 45–46, 51n9, 222–242; *Bodies in Code* 229
Harvie, Jen 157, 159, 169n1, 170n5, 170n9
Heidegger, Martin 2–3, 11, 20, 57, 158, 240n4; *Being and Time* 158; Being-in-the-world 2, 158, 225; Mitdasein/Mitsein 158; Ready-to-hand 2, 173; Revealing 2–3; Technology 2–3
Heywood, Niki 111, 116–118, 119n5
Husserl, Edmund 2, 6–9, 20–33, 56–57, 141, 187, 229, 236, 241n13; *Époche* 223–224; Physical Image 23, 25, 28; Image consciousness 21–33; Image object 23–28; *See also* bracketing

Ihde, Don 3, 14, 207–208, 214–216, 240n4; *See also* Post-phenomenology
Imagination 10–11, 15, 22, 55, 69, 71, 76, 82, 83, 85–87, 92–93, 125, 205, 210, 214–215, 217, 226
Immersion 29, 63, 76, 88, 101, 210–211; Immersive Performance 204
Implication(s) 14–15, 206, 209, 222–225, 228–229, 231, 233–235, 238–240; Being implicated 9, 41–42, 45–46
Improvisation 49, 56, 67; Improvisational 67 (exercises)
Ingold, Tim 12, 80–81, 121–123, 125–128, 130, 132, 134, 136–137
Intentionality 7, 15, 43, 79, 87–88, 101–102, 105–106, 173, 190, 222–224, 229, 237
Interactive Performance 13, 142, 156–160, 163, 165, 167–169
Intercorporeality 128
Intersubjectivity 8, 165, 206, 217
Intimacy 13, 163, 173–183, 211, 232; Interracial 183n4; Transracial 173, 175–183
Intuition 25, 27–28, 30

Jackson, Shannon 7, 170n5, 170n9; Synchrony 7
James, William 78

Kantor, Tadeusz 122, 124, 125–126, 137n2
ten Kate, Laurens 13, 158, 164, 169
Kattenbelt, Chiel 4, 35, 217
Keersmaker, Anne Teresa de 49
Kinetic 37, 153, 155, 165, 223
King, Larry/Leticia, 191–192
Kirby, Michael 26
KMA 13, 172–190
Kozel, Susan 4, 10, 54–73, 129
Krauss, Rosalind 9, 41–42, 46, 51n5,

Lambert-Beatty, Carry 9, 36, 38–40, 42–43, 47–48
Leder, Drew 15
Lehmann, Hans-Thies 36, 124–125
Lilja, Efva 54, 61–65
Liveness 55, 111, 116–117
Loneliness 13, 164–168

Martin, John 47
Manning, Erin 50n2, 55, 72n2
Massumi, Brian 9, 36, 50n2, 73n10
Materiality 4–5, 12, 115, 121, 127, 134, 136–137, 180, 191, 193, 223; Assemblage 12, 135, 137, 152, 158, 168; Aristotle 122; Hyle 122; Materializing/e 70, 226–228, 231–233; Materials 12, 22–23, 121–137; *See also* Bennett; Ingold
McInerney, Brandon 191–192, 202n1
McKenzie, Jon 5
Meaning 3–4, 6, 8, 10, 21, 41, 64, 70, 78, 123, 124, 126, 130, 135, 141, 147–149, 150n3, 188–189, 191, 197, 207, 228
Media 3, 5, 9, 15, 35–38, 43–46, 48, 222–225, 227–228, 230–231, 233–235, 238–240, 241n16; Media culture 9, 35–36, 43–46; Cinema 36–38, 43–45
Medium 21, 25, 29, 32, 209, 226
Memory 15, 22–24, 31, 33n3, 56–57, 63, 71, 112, 124, 137n2, 142, 175 (colonial), 210, 226
Merleau-Ponty, Maurice 1, 3, 10–12, 20, 57, 79, 81–82, 89, 98, 101, 103, 109 n13, 115–118, 121–123, 125, 128, 132, 135–137, 140–142, 145, 182, 228–229, 236–237; Chiasm 121, 229; Consciousness 12, 81, 135, 229, 236; Embodiment 20, 98, 229; Flesh, the 116, 121, 128, 136, 180, 226, 229–230, 236–238,

241n18; Lived body 11, 98–99, 101, 103, 115, 229; Motor Intentionality 101–102, 105–106, 229 (bodily intentionality); Perception 80–83, 97, 115–117, 121, 123, 132, 134–136, 180; *Phenomenology of Perception* 1, 80–82, 101, 115, 116, 123, 135, 140, 229–230, 236; Subjectivity 78, 98, 101–2, 180; Time 140–142, 145–149; *The Visible and the Invisible* 3, 11, 69, 89, 121, 128, 132, 136, 229, 237

Minimalism: Minimalist 40–42, 48–49; See also Morris, Robert; Graham, Dan

Mirror neurons 47

Morris, Robert 40, 48

Movement 3, 5, 7, 9–12, 14, 26, 35–51, 56, 80–81, 89, 95n9, 97–107, 123, 126, 130, 166, 170n13, 187, 198, 199, 213, 223–234, 227–228, 232–233, 239; As Harassment 192, 195; Gender and 176–182; Inhibition 95n8, 99–102, 105–106, 108 n11; Motor intentionality 101–102, 105, 106, 229; Movement as object of perception 35–50; Non-doing 97, 99–102, 105; Qualitative dynamics of movement 10, 42, 46; Sensorimotor schemata 37; Style 193, 194–196; Voluntary 83; Walking 13–14, 186–190, 192–195, 200–201; *See also* Affective dimensions of movement

Muybridge, Eadweard 43–44, 48

Nakedness 143–144

Nancy, Jean-Luc 13, 55 (philosophical anaesthesia), 56, 64, 70, 71, 72n3, 158–164, 167, 169, 170n6, 170n11, 170n17; Being-in-common 13, 152, 158–160, 164, 170n8, 170n17; *Being Singular Plural* 158, 161–162, 164, 169, 170n12; Co-appearing (compearance) 161, 163; Désœuvrement (inoperativeness) 159, 160; *The Inoperative Community* 158–160, 162, 167, 170n8, 170n11, 170n17; *Listening* 72n3; Retreat 167, 169; Subtraction 167

Natural attitude 6, 9, 29–31, 42, 44, 46

Neo-Futurists 12, 140–149; Chicago 12, 142–144; New York 12, 142–143, 146, 149

Nietzsche, Friedrich 97, 98, 102–107, 108n2, 108n3, 19n14–18; Subjectivity 98–99, 102–107, 108n2; Subjectivity, Active destruction of 99, 104–107; Body 98–99, 102–107; Forces 103–104, 109n18; Master/slave morality 104; Overcoming 98–99, 105, 107; Will to power 102, 104; Active destruction 99, 104–107

Noë, Alva 6, 51n10, 80–83

Objects 9, 11–12, 21–33, 41–42, 49–50, 80–82, 99 (object-directedness), 94n4, 121–128, 130, 132–137, 190, 234

Ontology 235–236

Orientation 25, 51n7, 94n4, 173, 189–190, 209–210, 215

Orr, Jill 111–12, 114, 118

Other/Otherness 79–80, 90, 97, 100, 163, 167, 173–174, 176–183, 214–216, 229, 236

Painting 22, 25, 27–31, 136; Painted 22, 27–31

Participation 13, 118, 126, 134, 136, 152, 156–163, 166–169, 170n5, 170n8

Perception 1–2, 4–6, 8–9, 10, 11, 14–16, 20–26, 28, 31, 35–49, 80, 81–83, 115–117, 121, 123, 132, 134–136, 169, 180, 206–216, 218–220, 226–228, 230–231, 233, 240n4, 241n11; Appearances 223, 226, 231; Aural 226; Embodied perception 5, 11, 20, 81, 115; Olfactory 226; Ordinary perception 21–22, 24–25; Relationality of perception 40–41; Sensory 226; Tactile 88, 95n10, 226; Visual 26, 82–83, 85–88, 92–93, 94n4; *See also*: Movement as object of perception; Synesthetic

Performance Studies 4–5, 7, 20, 33, 222

Performance Research 55

Performance creation 55

Performativity 6, 13–15, 147–148, 173, 178, (normative) 179, 182, 239–240; Race 173, 178, 182; Gender 186–202

Point of view 15, 38, 51n7, 57, 105, 106, 108n2, 121, 149, 183n5, 188, 204, 206, 208, 212–216, 232

Phantasy 22–31, 33n4, 33n5; Perceptual phantasy 27, 30; Fantasy 22–24, 30–31, 33n2, 33n3

Photography 22, 25, 37, 228; Photographic 25, 43; Chronophotography 45
Process philosophy 10, 15, 46, 55–56, 58, 72n1
Portanova, Stamatia 37–38, 45, 50n3
Possibility 121, 128, 177, 224, 240, 240n5
Postdramatic Theatre 124; *See also* Hans-Thies Lehmann
Post-phenomenology 14, 207–208; *See also* Ihde, Don

Race 1, 7, 13, 173–182, 183n4; Binary 13, 173–174, 177–179; Raced relationalities 174; Raced sociality 182; Racial epidermal schema 173, 178–179, 182–183; *See also* performativity (race)
Rainer, Yvonne 9, 35–50
Relationality 1, 5, 13, 16n2, 38, 41, 46, 50n2, 50n4, 60, 61, 64, 71, 152, 157, 159–160, 182
Representation 3, 14, 22, 25–26, 31–32, 33n1, 36, 56, 79, 113, 117, 141, 164, 227; Theatrical representation 22, 31–32
Responsibility 11, 118, 166
Reversibility 121–122, 132, 157, 236–238
Ridout, Nicholas 157, 163, 170n5
Ruprecht, Lucia 55, 72n2

Srinivasan, Priya 54, 58
Scenography 12, 121–123, 125, 134–137, 137n3
Sculpture 22, 29, 40–42, 46, 48, 51n5; Sculptural 24, 41, 46
Sensibility 225–228, 231–233, 235–240, 240n4, 241n15
Sensation 9, 37, 109n16, 204, 212, 233, 238, 240n4, 241n13
Sexuality 7, 175, 179
Skin 173, 177, 180–182; (Social) Skin 173, 177, 180–182
Sloterdijk, Peter 54–56
Spectator 9, 20–22, 29, 31, 35–50, 51n6, 58, 64, 81, 111–119, 125–126, 146–149, 166 (spectatorship), 209, 211, 233
Sobchack, Vivian 7
Social Turn 169n1; Socially turned performance 152, 157, 166, 169n1; *See also* Bishop, Claire

Solitude 13, 152, 157, 159, 164–169, 170n14; Tillich, Paul 166
Somatic 57, 64, 68–70, 89, 115, 180, 226
Space 5, 7, 11, 13, 24, 25 (imaged), 26, 28, 33n4, 37–38, 84–85, 90, 92–93, 95n9, 121, 123, 128, 135, 152–160, 163–166, 168, 179 (third), 182, 196, 206, 209–215, 223, 229–230, 233, 240
Stanislavsky, Konstantin 77, 80
States, Bert O. 4, 21, 26, 122–123, 241n7
Straus, Erwin 186–191, 196–197; On Walking 187–190, 192–195; On Posture 186–191, 196–197
Subjectivity 2, 5, 11, 78, 97–107, 108n2, 148, 158, 160, 178, 180, 206, 217–220, 232, 234–240, 241n17, [235–238, 240 (superjective/superjectal)]; Active destruction of 98–99, 104–107; Agency 11–12, 97, 102, 106, 108n2; Corporeal 98–107, 108n2, 108n7; Intersubjectivity 8, 165, 206, 217; Overcoming 98–99, 105, 107
Synesthesia 226

Taipale, Joona 2, 7, 42, 51n7
Technology 3, 5, 14, 35–38, 43–46, 155, 161, 166, 204, 206–219; Digital technology 35; Embodiment 3, 214–215, 218; Head-Swap 14, 204, 206, 210, 212, 216, 219–220; Technogenesis 46; *See also:* Heidegger; Martin; Hansen; Mark; Ihde; Don
Theatricality 9, 20–21, 30–31, 41–42, 51n6; Anti-theatricality 32, 41; Anti-theatrical prejudice 32, 41
Transcendental 2, 10, 20, 207, 231, 236, 238; Transcendental cogito 2
Thompson, Evan 75, 79, 88, 94n2
Time 12–13, 77, 140–149, 230 (hybrid), 241n15; Performance of 141, 143, 147, 149; Transition 141, 148–149; Doing time 12; Perceiving time 43\Time structures 48
Turkle, Sherry 167

Varela, Francisco 75, 79, 94n2,
Vision 82, 123, 204, 206, 209, 212, 215–220, 232(vision machine); Visual field 14, 82–83, 85–86, 94n4, 204, 215, 226, 240; Visuality 36, 115, 219; Seeing/seen 81–83, 86, 92, 93, 205–206, 211, 219, 232

Walker, Julia 21
Whitehead, Alfred North 230, 234, 236, 241n17
Whitley, Alexander 35, 46
Wright, Ben 59

Young, Iris Marion 7, 189; "Throwing Like a Girl" 7, 186

Zarrilli, Phillip 4, 10, 75–95
Zeami, Motokiyo 75–77, 80, 84, 89, 94n5
Zen (Buddhism) 77, 84, 86, 88, 94n5, 95n8, 95n9